MOON
COLLECTION

A Cookbook by The Landings Landlovers

To order additional copies of *Moon River Collection*, please contact:

Moon River Collection
50 Shellwind Drive
Savannah, GA 31411

All rights reserved.

Copyright© 2000

ISBN: 0-9704458-0-6

Library of Congress 00134341

Printed in the United States of America
STARR ★ TOOF
TOOF COOKBOOK DIVISION
670 South Cooper Street
Memphis, TN 38104

Introduction

The Moon River, its surrounding marshland and marine forests provide an idyllic scene truly romanticized by Savannah's own Johnny Mercer in his song. The hour of the day, phase of the moon, and season of the year give us different pictures of this local treasure.

These varied scenes have provided the theme for the Moon River Collection. Its purpose is to give us different pictures of the cuisine brought to the area by cooks who have come from many different parts of the country and the world, who enjoy the pleasures of great food and who wish to share their recipes.

This book will appeal to cooks of all talents and tastes. The recipes represent family favorites and chef's choices, and some showcase regional ethnic dishes. Whether your taste runs toward pasta or pot roast, you will find tasty dishes included in this collection. It is truly a potpourri of treasured fare.

Enjoy!

Preface

*M*oon River Collection is published by The Landings Landlovers of Skidaway Island, Georgia. The proceeds from the book will support our many on-island not for profit organizations. We are grateful for your support.

This cookbook is a collection of favorite recipes from members, family and friends of the Landlovers. They are not all original, but they are tried and true. Brand names have been used only when necessary. It is with regret that we were unable to publish all the wonderful recipes we received due to similarity, duplication and lack of space. Our heartfelt thanks to all contributors, for without you, there would be no *Moon River Collection*.

The Artist

*P*aige Word, our cover artist and illustrator, grew up in Virginia and was graduated from Roanoke College as an English major, with supplemental studies in Interior Design, emphasizing kitchen layout and cabinetry.

It was after moving to Savannah in 1995 that Paige began to display her artistic abilities by blending her love of painting with her architectural background. Her talents were quickly recognized as she won top awards in area art shows.

Paige is a member of the Savannah Art Association and other local groups where she continues to develop and display her artistic skills.

Table Of Contents

Letter From The Editor

"*Moon River Collection*" is the culmination of two years of planning and execution. We are grateful to The Landings Landlovers and its board for their support and caring throughout the project.

I extend my deepest gratitude to the committee, which brought this project to life – Jan Hietbrink, Anne Faxon, Jan Washenko, and Mary Lou Deeney. They have served unselfishly with energy, dedication, talent, and humor. They are the best!

A recipe is a part of our legacy. A wonderful meal shared with family or friends is not soon forgotten. Sharing a favorite recipe is sharing a part of ourselves. With this idea in mind, we present this cookbook for your enjoyment and the pleasure of sharing the recipes with family and friends for years to come.

Mary Cassady
Editor

Committee Members

Janet Hietbrink – Operations
Jan Washenko – Publicity
Anne Faxon – Distribution
Mary Lou Deeney – Marketing
Mary Cassady – Editor

The committee would like to express our appreciation to Mr. Greg McGinty of the Savannah Framing Company for his help.

Starters

WORD

"It's A Gim Me"

1	package frozen or 6-ounce can crab meat	1	tablespoon milk
8	ounce package cream cheese, softened	2	tablespoons onion, grated
		½	to 1 teaspoon horseradish

Preheat oven to 400 degrees.
Mix all ingredients and put in a bean pot and heat until bubbly. Serve with crackers. Can be made ahead and reheated.

Carol Bocard

Tortilla Pinwheels

2	8-ounce packages cream cheese, softened	½	cup finely diced red pepper
1	package Hidden Valley Ranch Original Dressing Mix	½	cup finely diced celery
		1	large can black olives, drained and minced
2	green onions, minced	12	6-inch flour tortillas

Mix all together and spread on tortillas. Roll tightly in jelly roll. Chill 2 hours. Cut ends off each roll and slice each roll into 1-inch pieces. Serve with salsa as dipping sauce.
Yield: approximately 3 dozen

Jane Heiser

Green Pepper & Onion Dip

1	egg, well beaten	1	8-ounce package cream cheese
1	tablespoon sugar		
1	tablespoon vinegar	1	medium onion, grated
		½	green pepper, grated

To the well-beaten egg, add the sugar and vinegar. Heat over low heat until it is slightly thick, stirring constantly. Mix with cream cheese until smooth. Add onion and green pepper.

Joan Pierce

8

Crab & Cheese Appetizers

1	5-ounce jar Olde English Cheese Spread	¼	teaspoon seasoning salt
1	stick butter or margarine, softened	¼	teaspoon garlic salt
1½	teaspoons lowfat mayonnaise	8	ounces crab meat
		6	English muffins, split

Preheat oven to 350 degrees.

Mix cheese, butter or margarine, mayonnaise, seasoning and garlic salts until well blended. Stir in crab. Spread on muffins. Freeze for 30 minutes (minimum). Cut muffin halves into 6 wedges each. Bake on greased cookie sheet for 10-12 minutes or until hot. Serve immediately.

Yield: 72 appetizers

Imitation crab can be substituted for the crab meat. Reduced fat cheese works well. Margarine can be reduced to 6 tablespoons to further cut fat. After appetizers have been assembled they may be frozen for several months.

Karen G. Hickman

Crab Meat Toast Cups

For toast cups cut very thin bread, white or whole wheat, with a round cookie cutter. Gently push rounds into mini-muffin tins that have been lightly buttered. Bake at 350 degrees for 8-10 minutes. Can be made ahead and frozen.

Filling:

1	can crab meat	8	ounces cream cheese
¾	cup mayonnaise	1	small onion, minced
¾	teaspoon Worcestershire sauce		Paprika

Mix all ingredients together. Fill shells; sprinkle with paprika. Heat in oven until hot.

Janet Hietbrink

Hummus

1	tablespoon sesame oil	½	cup sesame butter
1	small onion, chopped	¼	cup fresh lemon juice
1	clove garlic, minced	½	teaspoon turmeric
1	can garbanzo beans, drained	¼	teaspoon salt
2	tablespoons sesame seeds, toasted lightly		

Sauté onions and garlic in sesame oil until just tender. Purée beans in food processor. Add onions, garlic and remaining ingredients and blend until desired consistency. More sesame oil may be added if mixture is too thick. Garnish with parsley and additional toasted sesame seeds if desired. Serve with toasted pita triangles.

Serves 8.

Charles D'Ablaing
Chef, The Landings Club

Holiday Brie en Croûte

½	package (17.3-ounce size) frozen puff pastry sheets (1 sheet)	½	cup apricot preserves or seedless raspberry jam
⅓	cup dried cranberries	¼	cup sliced almonds, toasted
1	egg	1	Brie cheese round (about 1 pound)
1	tablespoon water		Water crackers

Preheat oven to 400 degrees.

Thaw pastry sheet at room temperature 30 minutes. Soak dried cranberries in hot water for 1 minute and drain. Set aside. Mix egg and water and set aside.

Unfold pastry on lightly floured surface. Roll into 14-inch square. Cut off corners to make a circle. Spread preserves to within 1-inch of pastry edge. Sprinkle cranberries and almonds over preserves. Top with cheese round. Brush edges of circle with egg mixture. Fold two opposite sides over cheese. Trim remaining two sides to 2-inches from edge of cheese. Fold these two sides onto the round. Press edges to seal. Place seam-side down on baking sheet. Decorate top with pastry scraps if desired. Brush with egg mixture. Bake 20 minutes or until golden. Let stand 1 hour. Serve with crackers.

Serves 12.

Ann Robertson

Deviled Pecans

4	tablespoons butter	Salt
2	tablespoons steak sauce	Cayenne pepper
2	cups pecan halves	

Preheat oven to 400 degrees.
Melt butter with sauce. Stir in pecans. Season with salt and cayenne. Bake 20 minutes. Drain and serve hot.

Agi Sutton

Mushroom Turnovers

3	3-ounce packages cream cheese, room temperature	½	cup butter, room temperature
		1½	cups flour

Mix the cream cheese and the butter thoroughly. Add the flour and work with the fingers or pastry blender until smooth. Chill well for at least thirty minutes.

Filling:

3	tablespoons butter	½	teaspoon salt
1	large onion, finely chopped		Freshly ground pepper to taste
½	pound mushrooms, finely chopped	2	tablespoons flour
¼	teaspoon thyme	½	cup sweet or sour cream

Preheat oven to 400 degrees.
Heat the butter in a skillet, add the onion and brown lightly. Add the mushrooms and cook, stirring often, about three minutes. Add the thyme, salt and pepper and sprinkle with the flour. Stir in the cream and cook gently until thickened.

Take the chilled dough and roll it out to ⅛-inch thickness on a lightly floured surface and cut into rounds with a 3-inch biscuit cutter. Place a teaspoon of mushroom filling on each round and fold the dough over the filling. Press the edges together with a fork. Lightly brush the turnovers with an egg yolk and water mixture, to give them a nice color. Prick top crusts to allow for the escape of steam. Place the turnovers on an ungreased baking sheet and bake until lightly browned, approximately ten minutes. Watch carefully.

Jackie Linder

11

Mushroom Palmiers

1	pound fresh mushrooms	½	teaspoon hot pepper sauce
1½	medium onions, peeled and quartered		Salt and freshly ground black pepper
5	tablespoons butter	1½	(17¼-ounce) boxes (3 sheets)
2	tablespoons flour		frozen puff pastry, thawed
1	teaspoon fresh lemon juice	2	eggs
1½	teaspoons dried thyme or 2 tablespoons finely chopped fresh thyme	4	teaspoons water

Preheat oven to 400 degrees.

In food processor finely chop mushrooms. Transfer to plate and set aside. Add onion to food processor and finely chop. In large skillet melt butter over medium heat. Add mushrooms and onion and cook until juice evaporates, stirring occasionally, about 8 minutes. Add flour, lemon juice, thyme and hot pepper sauce. Season with salt and pepper to taste. Reduce heat to low and cook about 2 minutes. Set aside to cool.

Place 1 unfolded pastry sheet on flat surface. Spread evenly with ⅓ of the mushroom mixture. Roll up from both long edges into center, pressing 2 rolls together. Repeat with remaining 2 pastry sheets. Wrap tightly in plastic wrap and freeze 1 hour. (May be prepared to this point and frozen. Let thaw partially before proceeding.) Slice into ¼-inch thick slices, using serrated knife. Place slices cut side down on ungreased baking sheet, 1-inch apart. In small bowl combine eggs and water and whisk to blend. Brush over tops of Palmiers and bake 18-20 minutes.

Yield: 4 to 5 dozen. Freezes well.

Ann Robertson

Mini Pizzas

10	ounces extra sharp cheddar cheese, grated	1	small onion, grated
1	4-ounce jar pimiento, drained, chopped fine	¾	teaspoon oregano
		½	cup mayonnaise
		1	loaf party rye bread

Preheat oven to 300 degrees.

Mix first 5 ingredients together. Spread mixture on each slice of rye bread but do not cover to the edge. Place on a cookie sheet. Bake 15-20 minutes until cheese is melted.

Jody Moran

Caviar Mousse

1	envelope plain gelatin	1	teaspoon Worcestershire
¼	cup cold water		sauce
2	ounces black caviar	1	teaspoon onion, minced
4	hard-cooked eggs, sieved		Salt and freshly ground pepper,
½	cup mayonnaise		to taste

Dissolve gelatin in cold water. Mix thoroughly with remaining ingredients and pour into a mold. Chill at least 4 hours. Unmold and serve with crackers or toast points.
Serves 6 to 8.

Agi Sutton

Pizza Hors D'oeuvres

1	13-ounce can black olives, chopped fine	1	cup shredded cheddar cheese
1	3-ounce can green olives, chopped fine	1	cup mayonnaise
		6-8	English muffins, split

Preheat oven to 350 degrees.
Mix first four ingredients together and spread on English muffins. Cut each muffin half in 4 equal pieces. Bake for 12 minutes.
Can be frozen before baking. Thaw and bake as above.

Mary Cassady

Herring Apple Spread

1	tablespoon Dijon mustard	1	eating apple, finely chopped
½	cup sour cream	1	medium red onion, chopped
1	8-ounce jar herring party snacks, drained and cut into ¼-inch cubes	1	tablespoon fresh dill

Stir mustard into sour cream. Combine with all other ingredients. Refrigerate several hours before serving. Serve on Waverly Wafers.
Yield: 3 cups

Dot Rookard

13

Layered Party Dip

1	can refried beans	¼	cup hot flavored salsa
¼	chopped onion		(raspberry preferred)
1	8-ounce package cream cheese	½	cup grated cheddar cheese

Preheat oven to 350 degrees.

In a medium casserole or ovenproof serving dish, spread the refried beans in an even layer of about ½-inch. Sprinkle onion over beans. Layer cream cheese evenly over top of beans and onions. Brush salsa over cream cheese. Sprinkle cheddar uniformly over the mix and bake for 20 minutes or until cheese is melted. Serve hot with crackers or chips of your choice.

Serves 10.

Gerald Fields

Hot Clam Dip

1	8-ounce package cream cheese	½	cup sour cream
1	teaspoon Worcestershire sauce	½	teaspoon onion salt
		1	6-ounce can clams, drained
2	tablespoons mayonnaise	8	ounces sharp cheddar cheese, shredded

Preheat oven to 350 degrees.

Mix all ingredients together except cheddar cheese. Put in greased 1-quart casserole dish or 8-inch square glass casserole dish. Top with cheddar cheese. Bake 20 minutes. Serve with crackers or chips. Good hot or cold.

Serves 12.

Ronnie Stimson

𝒯o invite a person into your house is to take charge of his happiness for as long as he is under your roof.

Brillat-Savarin

Toasted Cheese Rollups

1	cup Monterey Jack cheese, grated	¼	teaspoon seasoned salt
¼	cup mayonnaise	12	slices sandwich bread
¼	cup ripe olives, chopped	¼	cup butter or margarine, melted
1	teaspoon onion, minced		

Preheat oven to 450 degrees.

Combine all ingredients except bread and butter. Cut crusts from bread slices and roll very thin. Spread 1 tablespoon cheese mixture on each slice and roll up jelly roll fashion. (May be frozen at this point if desired.) Cut each roll into 3 pieces. Arrange seam side down on baking sheet. Brush with melted butter or margarine. Bake 5-7 minutes or until toasted. Serve hot.

Yield: 36

If frozen before baking, partially thaw and bake a little longer.

Anna M. Nichols

Blue Cheese Stuffed Mushrooms

3	pounds small mushrooms, stems removed and saved	6	ounces cream cheese, softened
9	tablespoons oil or margarine, divided	6	slices bacon, cooked and crumbled
3	minced shallots	2	teaspoons brandy
8	ounces crumbled blue cheese	1	teaspoon thyme

Preheat oven to 375 degrees.

Chop mushroom stems and sauté with shallots in 3 tablespoons of oil or margarine until liquid evaporates, about 3 minutes. Scrape into medium bowl and add all ingredients except mushroom caps. Cover and refrigerate.

Heat remaining oil or melt margarine. Remove pan from heat and add mushroom caps, stirring until well-coated. Put stem end up on baking sheet and fill each with 2 teaspoons of cheese mixture. Bake 10 minutes.

Yield: 72 servings

Stuffed mushroom caps can be made ahead and refrigerated. Bake just before serving.

Phyllis Albertson

15

Artichoke Dip

2	14-ounce cans artichokes, drained and roughly chopped	¾	cup grated cheddar cheese, divided
1	8-ounce package frozen chopped spinach, thawed and drained well	3	tablespoons fresh lemon juice
6	cloves garlic, finely minced	1	cup mayonnaise
¼	cup grated Parmesan cheese	1	cup sour cream
			Salt and freshly ground black pepper, to taste

Preheat oven to 350 degrees.

Combine artichokes, spinach, garlic, Parmesan, ½ cup cheddar cheese, lemon juice, mayonnaise, sour cream, salt and pepper in a nonmetal mixing bowl. Place in a 9-inch deep-dish pie pan or other similar nonreactive casserole or baking dish and bake 10 minutes or until hot through. Place ¼ cup grated cheddar on top and return to oven for 5 minutes or until cheese melts. Let cool for a few minutes before serving. Serve with French bread, crackers, chips or tortilla chips.

Yield: 4 cups

Chris Aiken

Sea Scallops Seviche

1	cup sea scallops (about 8 ounces)	2	tablespoons chopped green pepper
	Juice of 4 limes	3	tablespoons olive oil
2	tablespoons chopped onion		Salt and freshly ground pepper, to taste
1	tablespoon chopped parsley		
2	tablespoons chopped fresh cilantro		

Cut the raw scallops into quarters and cover with the lime juice. Marinate 1 hour or more in refrigerator. Drain. Combine onion, parsley, cilantro, green pepper and scallops. Add olive oil, mix well and season with salt and pepper. Serve as first course over bed of shredded lettuce.

Serves 4. Easily doubled.

Jerri Mayer

16

Hot Cheese Pockets

2	8-ounce packages cream cheese, room temperature	8	ounces Parmesan cheese, finely grated
5	eggs, beaten	1	pound package phyllo pastry
		2	cups butter, melted

Preheat oven to 375 degrees.

Mix together the cream cheese, eggs and Parmesan cheese. Place one sheet of phyllo pastry on work surface and brush with melted butter. Repeat until there are four sheets. (While working, keep remaining phyllo covered with a damp tea towel.) Cut the four sheets into 3-inch squares. Put 1 teaspoon of the cheese filling on each square and fold into a pocket; seal the edges with melted butter. Repeat with the remaining phyllo pastry. Bake for 15 minutes on an ungreased cookie sheet. Serve hot.

Yield: approximately 100 pockets

As these pockets take a while to prepare, it is best to freeze them. They can be defrosted and baked as directed or baked frozen for 20-25 minutes until golden.

Willie Phillips

Cheese & Bacon Appetizers

12	slices bacon, crisply fried and crumbled	2	teaspoons Worcestershire sauce
½	pound sharp cheddar cheese, grated	1	4.25-ounce can chopped olives
1	small onion, finely chopped	1	teaspoon curry powder
1	small package almonds, chopped		Salt and pepper, to taste
1	cup mayonnaise	1	loaf sandwich bread, crusts removed

Mix all ingredients except bread. Spread mixture on bread slices. Cut each slice into 4 to 6 pieces. Lay on cookie sheet and freeze. Store in plastic bag in freezer. When ready to use, bake at 400 degrees for 10 minutes.

Yield: 80 to 120

Almonds, olives or curry are optional depending on taste or allergies.

Marcia Suelflow

17

Spinach Squares

1	cup milk	1	package frozen chopped
½	cup margarine, melted		spinach, cooked and well
1	cup flour		drained
1	teaspoon salt	1	pound Monterey Jack
1	teaspoon baking powder		cheese, cut in 1-inch cubes

Preheat oven to 425 degrees.

Combine all ingredients but cheese. Spread on greased jelly-roll pan. Top with cheese. Bake until cheese is melted and slightly brown, 15-20 minutes. Cool slightly and cut into squares. Can be frozen and reheated in the microwave.

Dot Husak

Mexican Fudge

2	cups cheddar cheese, shredded	½	cup salsa
2	cups Monterey Jack cheese, shredded	½	cup green taco or green enchilada sauce
		3	eggs

Preheat oven to 350 degrees.

In medium bowl combine the cheeses and set aside. In small bowl combine the sauces and 3 eggs until thoroughly blended. In 9x9x2-inch pan, place half the cheese, pour the salsa mixture over cheese. Top with remaining cheese. Bake 30 minutes. Remove from oven and let stand 3 to 5 minutes. Cut into 1-inch squares. Place each square on a corn or nacho chip. Best served warm.

Yield: 81 squares

Carol Bocard

It's a lovely thing – everyone sitting down together, sharing food. So take a moment, before you dig in, to smile at your friends.

Alice May Brock
American cook and restaurateur

Crab Dip

2   8-ounce packages cream   2   teaspoons lemon juice
    cheese, softened   ½   teaspoon seasoned salt
1   6-ounce can crab meat,   ½   teaspoon MSG
    undrained   2   shakes hot pepper sauce

Preheat oven to 350 degrees.

Combine all ingredients and bake in casserole dish for 20 minutes. Serve warm with wheat thins.

Serves 10.

Gerry Baumgardner

Taco Tartlets

1   cup sour cream   ¾   cup corn chips, crushed
2   teaspoons taco sauce or salsa

1   pound ground sirloin   2   tablespoons ice water
2   tablespoons dry taco
    seasoning mix

1   cup shredded sharp cheddar
    cheese, (4 ounces)

Preheat oven to 425 degrees.

Prepare filling mixture by combining sour cream, taco sauce or salsa and crushed corn chips in a bowl. In another bowl mix ground sirloin, taco seasoning mix and ice water with hands. Press into bottom and sides of 1½-inch mini-muffin tins, forming a shell in each cup. Place a spoonful of filling mixture into each shell mounding slightly. Sprinkle the cheddar cheese over the tops. Bake 7-8 minutes. With the tip of a knife remove tartlets from pan. Serve immediately or refrigerate for up to 2 days and reheat for 10 minutes in 375 degree oven.

Yield: approximately 30 tartlets

These tartlets freeze well. If frozen, thaw and then reheat in a 375 degree oven for 10 minutes or until hot.

For a main dish pie, substitute a 9-inch pie plate for muffin tins. Bake in a preheated 375 degree oven for 45-60 minutes. Makes 6 main dish servings.

Jan Washenko

Ham-Green Onion Cheddar Cake

Crust:

¼ cup fine bread crumbs

¼ cup sharp cheddar cheese, finely grated

Butter 9-inch springform pan. Mix bread crumbs and cheddar cheese in medium bowl. Coat pan with crumb and cheese mixture and refrigerate.

Filling:

6 ounces ham, thinly sliced

3 8-ounce packages cream cheese

¾ pound sharp cheddar cheese, grated

1 cup cottage cheese

¼ cup diced green onion

¾ cup chopped green onion

4 eggs

3 tablespoons finely chopped jalapeño peppers

2 tablespoons milk

1 clove garlic, minced

Parsley

Preheat oven to 350 degrees.

Dice half of ham and reserve remaining slices. Mix diced ham with remaining ingredients in large bowl until smooth. Pour half of filling into pan. Top with reserved ham slices and cover with remaining filling. Set pan on baking sheet and bake 1 hour and 15 minutes. Turn oven off and cool cake 1 hour with oven door ajar. Remove from oven and cool. To serve, release cake from pan and place on serving platter. Sprinkle top of cake with green onions. Garnish with parsley around bottom edge of cake. Serve with crackers.

Virginia baked ham is recommended and recipe works equally well with fat free cream cheese.

Diane Munroe

Shrimp Crab Meat Dip

1 8-ounce package cream cheese, room temperature

1 8-ounce can crab meat, drained

1 8-ounce package frozen salad shrimp, thawed, rinsed and drained

⅛ teaspoon garlic salt

Juice from ½ lemon

Stir all ingredients together. Do not use blender or food processor.

Garrett Jackson

Mediterranean Mushrooms

1   4-ounce can artichoke
    hearts, drained and finely
    chopped
½   cup fine dry bread crumbs
½   cup finely shredded
    Parmigiano-Reggiano cheese
½   cup finely chopped
    prosciutto or Canadian
    bacon, (2 ounces)
2   cloves garlic, minced
1   tablespoon olive oil
1   tablespoon lemon juice

1½ teaspoons snipped fresh
    tarragon or ½ teaspoon
    dried tarragon, crushed
1   beaten egg
¼   teaspoon pepper
24 medium mushroom caps,
    1½-inch diameter
2   tablespoons finely shredded
    Parmigiano-Reggiano cheese
Snipped fresh tarragon or
    oregano, optional

Preheat oven to 425 degrees.

Stir together artichoke hearts, bread crumbs, the ½ cup cheese, prosciutto or bacon, garlic, olive oil, lemon juice, tarragon, egg and pepper. Arrange mushroom caps in a 15x10x1-inch baking pan. Spoon the artichoke mixture into the mushroom caps, mounding slightly. Top each with some of the remaining 2 tablespoons of cheese. Bake for 10 minutes or until heated through. Sprinkle with snipped fresh tarragon or oregano if desired. Serve warm.

Yield: 24

Dorothy Pero

Miniature Meat Turnovers

1   package dry mushroom soup
    mix
2   tablespoons chopped onion
1   cup bean sprouts, drained

½   cup chopped water chestnuts
½   pound ground beef
2   packages refrigerated
    crescent roll dough

Preheat oven to 350 degrees.

Combine first 5 ingredients and brown. Cut dough triangles in half. Put 1 teaspoon of mixture on each piece of dough, fold and seal edges. Bake for 10 minutes or until browned. Serve with hot mustard or sweet and sour sauce.

Serves 12 to 16.

Sarabel E. Sterner

21

Mini Quiche

3	eggs	4	ounces sharp cheddar
3	tablespoons sour cream		cheese, grated
1	pound small curd cottage	½	cup Bisquick
	cheese	4	tablespoons butter, melted
			Salt and pepper, to taste

Preheat oven to 375 degrees.

Lightly beat eggs. Add remaining ingredients. Combine until just blended. Fill mini-muffin tins ¾ full. Bake 25-30 minutes.

Yield: 4 dozen

Freezes well. To reheat, thaw first and bake for 10 minutes at 375 degrees.

Meredith Heaslip

Shrimp Dip

½	pound cooked, fresh shrimp	1	teaspoon Worcestershire
8	ounces cream cheese		sauce
2	tablespoons mayonnaise		Dash garlic powder
1	tablespoon milk		

Mash shrimp with a fork and combine with other ingredients using a hand mixer. Refrigerate until 30 minutes before serving time. Serve with crackers, chips or raw vegetables.

Marcia Johnson

Yummy Vegetable Dip

1	cup sour cream	1	teaspoon Worcestershire
2	teaspoons dry Italian salad		sauce
	dressing mix	2	tablespoons parsley, minced
½	teaspoon salt	2	tablespoons onion, minced
¼	teaspoon curry powder	3	teaspoons lemon juice

Mix all ingredients together and chill well to blend flavors. Serve with vegetables of your choice.

Carole Michna

Salsa

4	cups diced fresh Roma tomatoes	2	large garlic cloves, crushed
1	cup diced Vidalia onions	1	teaspoon granulated sugar
2	fresh jalapeño peppers, seeded and diced (Be sure to wear rubber gloves when cutting peppers.)	1	teaspoon salt
		2	tablespoons vinegar
		2	tablespoons fresh lime juice
			Stripped zest of one fresh lime
		½	cup chopped fresh cilantro

Combine all ingredients and allow flavors to blend about 10 minutes before serving. Serve over chili or with nacho chips.
Yield: about 5½ cups

Joy Borden

Clam Chutney Spread

1	8-ounce package cream cheese, softened	⅓	of an onion, minced
1	can minced clams, well-drained	1	generous teaspoon Worcestershire sauce

Mango chutney
Bacon bits

Chopped chives

Cream the cheese and add clams, onion and Worcestershire sauce. Spread onto a round 8-inch dish and chill for several hours. Spread with mango chutney; sprinkle with bacon bits and chopped chives. Serve with crackers.

Ann Robertson

he gentle art of gastronomy is a friendly one. It hurdles the language barrier, makes friends among civilized people, and warms the heart.

Samuel Chamberlain
American artist, author and gourmet

23

Lowfat Party Mix

8	cups Wheat Chex	5	tablespoons Butter Buds
8	cups Rice Chex		Sprinkles
8	cups Corn Chex	1½	tablespoons seasoned salt
1	16-ounce jar dry roasted	6	tablespoons Worcestershire
	peanuts		sauce
8	tablespoons Country Crock		
	Churn Style Spread		

In a very large plastic bowl, mix all dry ingredients. In a 2-cup glass measuring cup, melt spread in microwave. There will be a rather watery looking substance on the bottom. Mix the Butter Buds, seasoned salt and Worcestershire sauce with spread. Drizzle over all of the dry ingredients; mix carefully making sure that all ingredients are well-coated. Turn out into baking tins. Bake for 45 minutes then let stay in unheated oven another 30 minutes to cool. Store in airtight containers. Keeps for several weeks.

Yield: 25 cups

Marcia Wilk

Sun-Dried Tomato Dip

½	pound sun-dried tomatoes	1½	teaspoons dried oregano
10	cloves garlic, peeled and	1½	teaspoons dried thyme
	smashed	½	cup olive oil

Put tomatoes in a large pan, cover with water, and bring to a boil over medium heat then reduce to a simmer. Cook, covered, for 22 minutes. Drain and return the tomatoes to the pan. Add the garlic, oregano, thyme and oil. Cook over low heat, covered, for 20 minutes. Purée; then store in the refrigerator, tightly covered, for up to a month. Serve at room temperature with bread or crackers.

Yield: 3 cups

Donna Pfeifer

The real American pattern of feeding is the snack. It lasts from early morning to bedtime.

John and Karen Hess
American food critic, American cook

Hot Spinach Salsa

1   8-ounce package cream
    cheese, softened
1   16-ounce jar salsa, medium
    seasoning
1   package frozen chopped
    spinach, defrosted and
    drained

1   small can green chiles,
    chopped and drained
1   small can sliced ripe olives,
    drained
1   package (2 cups) shredded
    taco mix cheese, divided

Preheat oven to 350 degrees.

Mix first five ingredients plus ½ of taco cheese. Spread in baking dish and top with remaining taco cheese. Bake 30 minutes. Serve with favorite chips or curls.

Joy Koletar

Hors D'Oeuvre Cheesecake

½   cup bread crumbs
½   cup half-and-half
24 ounces cream cheese,
    softened
1¼ teaspoons dry mustard
1¼ teaspoons salt
¼   teaspoon red pepper

4   eggs
8   ounces cooked smoked ham,
    finely chopped
2   cups shredded Swiss cheese
Parsley
Sliced olives

Preheat oven to 325 degrees.

Sprinkle bread crumbs over bottom and sides of greased 9-inch springform pan. Combine half-and-half, cream cheese, seasonings and eggs in mixer bowl. Beat at medium speed for 5 minutes or until smooth. Stir in ham and Swiss cheese. Spoon into prepared pan. Bake for 1 hour or until set. Cool completely. Refrigerate, covered, for up to 48 hours. Let stand at room temperature for 2 hours. Place on serving plate; remove side of pan. Garnish with parsley and olives.

Serves 20.

Dot Rookard

Stuffed Celery

Several ribs of celery
1 chicken liver, cooked and
chopped well
Mayonnaise

1 hard-cooked egg, chopped
1 teaspoon grated onion
Green or black olives for garnish

Clean celery and cut into bite-size pieces. Combine all ingredients, adding enough mayonnaise to give good consistency. Stuff celery pieces. Garnish with sliced olives. Filling may be made a day ahead and celery stuffed day of serving. Be sure to refrigerate until serving.

Bobbie Stabe

Crab & Tomato Quesadillas

1½ cups (packed) grated
Monterey Jack Cheese,
(about 6 ounces)
2 ounces cream cheese, room
temperature

¼ cup chopped fresh cilantro
2 tablespoons orange juice
2 teaspoons grated orange peel
1 teaspoon grated lemon peel

8 ounces crab meat, drained
1 cup seeded and chopped
plum tomatoes
½ cup chopped green onions

1 tablespoon seeded and
minced jalapeño chile
8 7- to 8-inch flour tortillas

5 tablespoons (about)
vegetable oil

Mix first 6 ingredients in medium bowl to blend. Season cheese mixture to taste with salt and pepper. (Can be made 1 day ahead. Cover and chill. Bring to room temperature before continuing.)

Mix crab meat, tomatoes, green onions and chile in large bowl. Spread cheese mixture over half of each tortilla. Spoon crab meat mixture atop cheese mixture, dividing equally. Sprinkle with salt and pepper. Fold tortillas in half. Press gently to seal.

Heat 1½ tablespoons oil in each of 2 heavy large skillets over medium heat. Working in batches, cook quesadillas in skillets until cheese melts and tortillas are golden brown, adding more oil as needed, about 3 minutes per side. Cut quesadillas into wedges and serve.

Jan Hazel

Southwest Bean Appetizer

1	15-ounce can black-eyed peas, drained and rinsed	6	green onions with tops, chopped
1	15-ounce can black beans, drained and rinsed	2	jalapeño peppers, seeded, deveined and chopped
1	15-ounce can great northern beans, drained and rinsed	3	tomatoes, seeded, chopped
1	box frozen shoe peg corn, thawed	½	red bell pepper, seeded, chopped
1	small can sliced black olives	½	green bell pepper, seeded, chopped
¼	cup chopped fresh cilantro	3	tablespoons lime juice
¼	cup salsa	¼	cup Italian salad dressing
		¼	cup crumbled feta cheese

Mix all ingredients in a low serving dish. Sprinkle crumbled feta cheese on top. Serve with Fritos or tortilla chips.

The flavors of this marinated dip are best when prepared several hours in advance or night before and refrigerated. Cheese should be added at serving time to retain color and freshness.

Suzy Goldman

Mushroom Walnut Paté

1	pound fresh mushrooms, diced	1	teaspoon salt
½	cup sliced green onion	1	8-ounce package cream cheese, softened
¼	teaspoon dried thyme	1	cup finely chopped toasted walnuts
¼	cup butter		
⅓	cup dry sherry		Dash red pepper sauce

Sauté mushrooms, onions and thyme in butter until onions are tender. Add sherry and salt and continue cooking until liquid is almost evaporated. Remove from heat and cool. Combine mushroom mixture with cream cheese and blend thoroughly. Stir in walnuts and red pepper sauce. Chill several hours. Serve with crackers.

Yield: 3 to 4 cups

A combination of button mushrooms and portobello mushrooms can be used.

Jan Hazel

Rosemary Walnuts

2½ tablespoons unsalted butter
2   teaspoons dried rosemary,
    crumbled

1   teaspoon salt
½   teaspoon cayenne pepper
2   cups walnut halves

Preheat oven to 350 degrees.

Melt butter in large baking pan. Combine with rosemary, salt and cayenne. Toss with walnuts. Spread in one layer and bake for 10 minutes. Serve warm.

Betty J. Miller

Dilly Shrimp Spread

½   pound shrimp, cooked,
    peeled
¼   cup mayonnaise
8   ounces cream cheese,
    softened
2   tablespoons finely minced
    onion

1   teaspoon monosodium
    glutamate (MSG)
Salt, to taste
½   teaspoon dried dill weed
½   teaspoon red pepper sauce

Finely chop half of the shrimp (can use food processor) and chop the other half in small pieces; set aside. Beat mayonnaise and cream cheese until smooth. Add onion, MSG, salt, dill weed and red pepper sauce. Mix well. Stir in reserved shrimp and serve with crackers.

Pat Palmer

Cheese Ball

2   3-ounce packages cream
    cheese, softened
1   8-ounce can crushed
    pineapple

¼   cup chopped green bell
    pepper
1   teaspoon dehydrated onion
1   teaspoon seasoned salt
Chopped nuts

Mix all ingredients except nuts. Form into ball and roll in chopped nuts. Cool to firm before serving with crackers of your choice.

Gerald Fields

Romaine Leaves With Garlic Cheese Dip

2	ounces blue cheese, crumbled	½	teaspoon Worcestershire sauce
1	cup mayonnaise	1	medium clove garlic, finely chopped
1	teaspoon finely chopped onion		Chopped parsley
			Hearts of romaine lettuce

In a small bowl, combine blue cheese, mayonnaise, onion, Worcestershire sauce and garlic. Cover and chill at least 6 hours to allow flavors to blend. To serve, stand well washed smaller romaine leaves in a bowl. Put dip in a separate bowl and sprinkle with chopped parsley. Let guests use leaves for dipping.
Yield: 1¼ cups

Marcia DaPont

Asparagus Canapés

1	can Mary Washington-style asparagus	8	ounces cream cheese
1	regular loaf white bread	1	tablespoon mayonnaise
8	ounces Roquefort cheese	1	egg, beaten
			Butter, melted

Preheat oven to 350 degrees.
Cut all crusts off the bread. Roll bread out flat. Spread with the mixture of cheeses, mayonnaise and egg. Top with one stalk of asparagus per slice of bread. Roll up and cut into three pieces. Dip each piece in melted butter. Place on ungreased cookie sheet. These may be made ahead or frozen before baking. Bake for about 15 minutes or until well-browned.

Joan Pierce

C heese – milk's leap toward immortality.

Clifton Fadiman
American author and critic

29

Sausage & Spinach Pinwheels

1	pound seasoned bulk sausage	1	10-ounce package frozen, chopped spinach, drained and squeezed dry
1	medium onion, chopped		
¾	teaspoon red pepper sauce	3	eggs, divided, beaten
½	teaspoon salt	½	pound Gruyère cheese, grated (about 2 cups)
½	teaspoon mace	2	sheets frozen puff pastry dough

Preheat oven to 375 degrees.

In large skillet brown sausage over medium heat. Add onion and cook five minutes. Stir in pepper sauce, salt and mace and cook 2 minutes. Combine sausage mixture, spinach, two eggs and cheese.

Thaw puff pastry dough sheets 20 minutes at room temperature; gently unfold. Roll out each sheet on a floured surface to a rectangle 18x8-inches. Spread half the sausage mixture over each rectangle leaving a 1-inch border on the long sides. Roll up jelly roll fashion. Press to seal tightly and brush with remaining beaten egg. Make cuts along top of each roll every 1-inch. Place on ungreased cookie sheet and bake for 30 minutes or until golden. Let stand 15 minutes before cutting. Can be frozen.

Yield: 36 slices

Mary Lou Deeney

Curry Cheese Appetizers

1½	cups cheddar cheese, shredded	½	cup green onions, thinly sliced
1	cup ripe (black) olives, sliced	½	teaspoon curry powder
½	cup mayonnaise		Party rye or pumpernickel bread

Mix first 5 ingredients and chill in refrigerator for 24 hours. Spread mixture on party bread slices and broil 3 inches from top of broiler until bubbly. Mixture will keep in refrigerator for up to two weeks.

Barbara Sewell

Tomato & Goat Cheese

3	teaspoons olive oil	1	cup goat cheese
3	cloves garlic, chopped	½	cup chopped fresh basil
4	large tomatoes, diced		Grated Parmesan cheese
¼	teaspoon salt		

Preheat oven to 325 degrees.
In skillet, "sweat" garlic in olive oil. Do not brown. Add tomatoes and salt. Add goat cheese to tomatoes. Add basil and fold all together. Remove from heat and place mixture in baking dish. Top with Parmesan cheese. Bake until bubbly. Serve with crackers.

Lynda Ibach

Bacon & Crackers

Preheat oven to 250 degrees.
Cut bacon strips into thirds. Wrap each piece around a Waverly or saltine cracker. Secure with a toothpick. Place on a rack which has been placed in a jelly-roll pan. Bake until bacon is crisp and brown, about 45 minutes to 1 hour. Best served hot.

Anna M. Nichols

Baked Cheese & Pepper Jelly

8	ounces cream cheese, softened	1	jar pepper jelly, mild or hot, divided
2	cloves garlic, minced	6	ounces sharp white cheddar cheese, shredded
1	egg		

Preheat oven to 350 degrees.
Beat together cream cheese, garlic, egg and ½ jar of pepper jelly. Fold in shredded cheese. Grease a 6- or 7-inch springform pan. Pour ingredients into pan and bake for 35 minutes. (Put foil under springform pan in oven.) Let cool completely before removing from pan. Heat remaining jelly in microwave and pour over top. Serve with crackers.

Ginger Heussler

Rosemary Pecans

2	tablespoons butter, melted	¼	teaspoon ground red pepper
1½	teaspoons rosemary	2	cups pecan halves
1½	teaspoons salt		

Preheat oven to 350 degrees.

Mix all ingredients together and spread on cookie sheet. Bake 10-15 minutes. Stir. Spread on paper towels to cool. Store in covered container.

June Turnbull

Asparagus Appetizer

Boil 2 pounds asparagus spears in small amount of water in skillet 2-3 minutes. Run cold water over spears immediately. Drain well and chill. Spears should be crispy.

Mix together:

| 6 | tablespoons mayonnaise | 1 | tablespoon mustard |
| 2 | tablespoons honey | | |

Serve in chilled dish and use as dipping sauce for asparagus.

Barbara Coakley

Party Sandwiches

1	bunch green onions including tops, chopped	8	ounces cheddar cheese, shredded
1	pound bacon, cooked crisp and chopped		Miracle Whip salad dressing
			Cocktail rye bread

Preheat oven to 400 degrees.

Mix all ingredients with just enough salad dressing to hold mixture together. Spread on cocktail rye and bake until cheese melts, 3-5 minutes.

Roberta Fields

Sun-Dried Tomato Spread

8 ounces cream cheese, softened	4 green onions, chopped
¼ cup oil-packed sun-dried tomatoes, drained and chopped	¼ cup chopped pecans
	Hot pepper sauce, to taste
	Worcestershire sauce, to taste

Beat the cream cheese with a mixer until smooth. Add the tomatoes, green onions, pecans and seasonings; mix well. Serve with sliced French baguettes or plain crackers.

¼ cup drained, seeded and diced, oil-packed roasted red peppers can be substituted for the tomatoes. Walnuts can be used in place of pecans.

Chris Savage

Caponata

1 eggplant, ¼-inch diced	1 tablespoon brown sugar, packed
½ yellow bell pepper, ¼-inch diced	2 tablespoons fresh lemon juice
½ red bell pepper, ¼-inch diced	1 teaspoon salt
1 onion, chopped	¼ cup raisins
1 clove garlic, minced	2 tablespoons drained capers
¼ cup water	2 tablespoons chopped parsley

Sauté first 9 ingredients 15-30 minutes. Add raisins and capers. Cool to room temperature. Add parsley when serving. Can be made two days ahead. Serve on crostini or toasted baguette slices.

Betsy Contino

I saw him even now going the way of all flesh, that is to say towards the kitchen.

John Webster
English dramatist

33

Nancy's Layered Party Dip

2 16-ounce cans nonfat refried beans

1 teaspoon, or to taste, Pickapeppa sauce

Combine well.

1 large avocado, peeled, seeded and mashed

½ cup salsa
2 tablespoons lemon juice

Combine and set aside.

1 cup lowfat sour cream
1 cup reduced fat mayonnaise

1 ¼-ounce envelope taco seasoning mix

Mix in small bowl and set aside.

6-8 ounces Jack or cheddar cheese

Chopped fresh tomatoes
Sliced black olives

Spread bean mixture in 2-quart or 7x11-inch dish. Layer with avocado mixture and then top with sour cream mixture. Sprinkle Jack or cheddar cheese, tomatoes and olives over sour cream layer. Serve immediately or refrigerate, covered, overnight. Serve with bite-size tortilla chips or Fritos.

1 small can of chopped, green chiles, drained, may be substituted for the taco seasoning mix.

Nancy Craig

Cheese Ball

2 8-ounce packages cream cheese, softened
1 small can crushed pineapple, drained well
1 small green bell pepper, chopped fine

4 green onions with tops, chopped fine
1 teaspoon seasoned salt
1 cup chopped pecans

Mix first five ingredients well and shape into a ball. Refrigerate overnight. Before serving, roll in pecans. Serve with crackers.

Holly Lantz

Chicken Balls

1	teaspoon red wine	2	tablespoons finely chopped almonds
½	cup finely chopped cooked chicken	2	tablespoons finely chopped chutney
½	teaspoon curry powder	1	cup finely chopped coconut
1½	teaspoons mayonnaise		

Mix all ingredients except coconut. Form into small balls. Roll the balls in coconut. Place on a wax paper covered cookie sheet and chill at least 1 hour. Can be kept in refrigerator, covered, for 1-2 days. Serves 12.

Karen Blado

Cowboy Caviar

1	15-ounce can black beans, drained	¼	teaspoon crushed red pepper
1	4-ounce can chopped ripe (black) olives	¼	teaspoon ground cumin, optional
1	small onion, finely chopped	⅛	teaspoon pepper
1	clove garlic, finely chopped	1	8-ounce package cream cheese, softened
2	tablespoons vegetable oil	2	hard-cooked eggs, chopped
2	tablespoons lime juice	1	green onion, with top, sliced or chopped
¼	teaspoon salt		

Mix together all ingredients except cream cheese, eggs and green onion. Refrigerate at least 2 hours or overnight. Spread cream cheese on plate, spoon bean mixture evenly over cheese, arrange eggs on beans in ring around edge of plate, sprinkle with green onion. Serve with any crackers or chips.

Maureen Miller

W/*hat you eat standing up doesn't count.*

Beth Barnes
American social worker

Mushroom Cheese Mold

2	8-ounce packages cream cheese	¼	cup finely chopped onion
½	pound cheddar cheese, shredded	2	tablespoons finely diced pimiento
1	clove garlic, crushed	2	tablespoons chopped parsley
1½	teaspoons brown mustard		Sliced mushrooms, optional for garnish
	Salt, to taste		Parsley, optional for garnish
1	4-ounce can mushroom stems and pieces, chopped		

Combine cheeses, garlic, mustard and salt in a bowl. Add chopped mushrooms, onion, pimiento and chopped parsley. Mix well. Turn mixture into a buttered 3-cup mold. Refrigerate until firm. Unmold onto serving platter. Garnish with sliced mushrooms and parsley. Serve with crackers.

Gerry Baumgardner

Dried Beef Pecan Dip

2	teaspoons margarine	½	cup finely chopped green bell pepper
½	cup chopped pecans		
1	8-ounce package cream cheese	2	tablespoons dehydrated onion flakes
1	tablespoon milk	½	teaspoon garlic salt
2½	ounces dried beef, chopped	¼	teaspoon pepper
		1	cup sour cream

Preheat oven to 350 degrees.

Melt margarine and sauté pecans. Mix cream cheese and milk together. Add remaining ingredients, except pecans, and mix together. Put in shallow baking dish, sprinkle pecans on top. Bake 20 minutes. Serve with crackers.

Serves 8.

Marolyn Overton

Fiesta Pinwheels

16 ounces cream cheese,
softened
2 teaspoons chili powder
4 tablespoons minced onion
2 tablespoons fresh coriander,
chopped

1 8-ounce can mild green
chiles, drained and chopped
1 8-ounce can black olives,
drained and sliced
Salt and pepper, to taste
10 10-inch wheat tortillas

Stir cream cheese and chili powder until smooth. Stir remaining ingredients into cream cheese mixture. Spread ⅓ cup on each tortilla and roll up jelly roll style. Wrap in plastic, seam sides down. Chill up to 4 hours; remove plastic wrap. Trim ends and cut into 1¼-inch pieces. Serve at room temperature with salsa.

Yield: approximately 80 pinwheels

Phyllis Albertson

Smoked Salmon & Goat Cheese Toasts

8 ounces soft, fresh goat
cheese
1½ tablespoons fresh tarragon,
chopped
1½ teaspoons fennel seeds, finely
crushed
2 teaspoons grated lemon peel

½ teaspoon coarsely ground
pepper
2½ tablespoons olive oil
30 thin slices of French bread
baguette
12 ounces thinly sliced smoked
salmon

Preheat oven to 350 degrees.

Mix first 5 ingredients in a small bowl to blend. Set aside. Brush oil over both sides of bread. Arrange bread in single layer on large baking sheet. Bake until bread is just crisp, about 5 minutes per side. Spread cheese mixture over toasts. Top with salmon, trimming to fit.

Yield: 30 toasts

Cheese mixture and toasts may be made 2 days ahead and then assembled before serving.

Mary Lou Deeney

Orange Muffins With Smoked Turkey

1	cup sugar	1	cup raisins
½	cup (1 stick) unsalted butter		Zest and juice of 2 oranges
2	eggs	½	cup sugar
1	teaspoon baking soda	½-1	pound thinly sliced smoked
1	cup buttermilk		turkey breast
2	cups sifted all-purpose flour		Cranberry-Horseradish Sauce
½	teaspoon salt		

Preheat oven to 400 degrees.

Grease small muffin tins with butter or cooking spray.

With electric mixer, cream the sugar and butter until smooth. Add the eggs and beat until fluffy. Add the baking soda to the buttermilk. Sift the flour and salt together and add to the sugar-butter mixture alternately with the buttermilk. Stir until well-mixed. Mince the raisins and orange zest in a food processor. Add to the batter and combine. Spoon the batter into the prepared muffin tins and bake until golden brown and firm to the touch, about 12 minutes. Remove the tins to a baking rack and set close together. Brush tops of muffins with orange juice and sprinkle with ½ cup sugar while still warm. After 5 minutes, turn out from pans. Let cool completely before cutting each muffin in half.

Cut the turkey into small pieces and put a small amount on each muffin bottom. Top the turkey with the Cranberry-Horseradish Sauce, cover with muffin top and serve.

Yield: 30 small muffins

Variations: Orange muffins with slivers of smoked ham and mustard; country ham and cranberry relish. Very good served plain for brunch.

Cranberry-Horseradish Sauce is available from the Byrd Cookie Company.

Arlene Gilligan

here is an emanation from the heart in genuine hospitality which can not be described but is immediately felt, and puts the stranger at once at his ease.

Washington Irving

Cucumber Sandwich

1	loaf party bread, dark or rye	1	cucumber, peeled and thinly
1	package regular Italian		sliced
	dressing mix		Dill weed
1	8-ounce package regular		
	cream cheese		

Mash cream cheese and dry dressing mix together and refrigerate overnight. Spread over party bread slices. Add a cucumber slice to each piece of bread and sprinkle with dill weed.

Betty Mitchell

Freebird Smoked Salmon Dip

1	8-ounce package cream	½	teaspoon salt
	cheese, softened	½	teaspoon pepper
Red pepper sauce		½	teaspoon garlic powder
½	cup sour cream	1	tablespoon snipped parsley
¼	cup butter or margarine,	1	teaspoon grated onion
	softened	¼	teaspoon dill weed
2	teaspoons horseradish	8	ounces smoked salmon
1	tablespoon lemon juice		

Combine first six ingredients and mix together until well-blended. Add remaining ingredients, except salmon, mixing well. Stir in flaked salmon. Cover and chill until ready to serve.

Canned salmon can also be used but you will need to add liquid smoke flavoring to taste.

Joyce Glenn

S mall cheer and great welcome makes a merry feast.

William Shakespeare

39

Asparagus-Blue Cheese Rolls

12	slices soft white bread, crusts removed	12	asparagus spears, ⅜ to ½-inch in diameter, cooked and well-drained on paper towels
⅓	cup blue cheese, room temperature		
	Mayonnaise, to taste	⅓-½	cup melted butter

Preheat oven to 375 degrees.
Using a rolling pin, gently flatten each slice of bread to about half the original thickness. In a small bowl, mix blue cheese with enough mayonnaise to make it spreadable. Spread each slice of bread with 1 teaspoon of cheese mixture. Place 1 asparagus spear on one end of bread and roll up. (Length of asparagus may be longer than bread slice.) Melt butter in small skillet. Dip each roll in melted butter, coating well. Place seam side down on cookie sheet. Bake for 10-12 minutes or until crisp and brown. Cut each roll in 4 pieces.
Yield: 48 pieces

Evelyn Saum

Boursin At Home

2	large, fresh cloves garlic	½	teaspoon salt
2	8-ounce packages cream cheese, room temperature	½	teaspoon thyme
		½	teaspoon basil
1	8-ounce package whipped sweet butter, room temperature	½	teaspoon oregano
		½	teaspoon dill
⅓	teaspoon fresh ground pepper	½	teaspoon marjoram

Drop garlic into food processor fitted with chopping blade and mince. Add rest of ingredients and process until blended, soft and creamy. Refrigerate overnight.

Robbie Forester

Shrimp Mold

1	8-ounce package cream cheese	½	cup chopped onions
1	can tomato soup, undiluted	½	cup chopped celery
1	envelope unflavored gelatin	2	cans deveined shrimp
¼	cup cold water	1	cup mayonnaise

Combine cream cheese and tomato soup in pan. Heat until melted and well-mixed. Combine gelatin with cold water. Add to heated mixture and blend well. Place in refrigerator for 20 minutes, no more. Remove from refrigerator and add remaining ingredients. Refrigerate at least 2-5 hours until molded. Can be made a day ahead.

Crab can be used in place of shrimp.

Sandy Andrews

Salmon Mousse

1	3-ounce package lemon flavored gelatin	⅔	cup finely chopped onion
1	cup hot water	⅔	cup diced celery
1	10-ounce can condensed tomato soup	½	cup mayonnaise
4	ounces cream cheese	4	ounces canned salmon or tuna

Dissolve gelatin in hot water. Stir in remaining ingredients using a mixer. Do not use a blender. Mix until smooth, pour into 5 cup mold and chill overnight in refrigerator. Unmold and serve with crackers, party rye or pumpernickel bread.

Serves 16.

Priscilla Stahl

*W*e may live without friends, we may live without books. But civilized man cannot live without cooks.

Edward Robert Bulwer-Lytton
English diplomat and poet

41

Peppered Shrimp

9	scallions, sliced, reserve green and white parts separately	⅓	cup tomato sauce
		¾	teaspoon red pepper flakes
		1½	tablespoons peanut oil
1½	tablespoons chopped fresh ginger	1½	pounds medium shrimp, shelled and deveined
1½	tablespoons soy sauce		Salt and pepper
1½	tablespoons horseradish		

Combine the white part of the scallions with the ginger, soy sauce, horse-radish, tomato sauce and red pepper flakes. Sauté lightly. In the oil over moderately high heat, cook the shrimp, stirring until pink, about 3 minutes. Add sauce mixture and heat together a few minutes longer. Season with salt and pepper to taste. Cover and keep at room temperature. If preparing ahead of time, refrigerate covered. Can reheat quickly before serving if necessary. Garnish with sliced scallion tops and place toothpicks on the side.

Betsy Contino

Garlic Lover's Spread

2	large cloves garlic	1	teaspoon dill weed or mixed herbs
1	8-ounce package cream cheese or Neufchâtel cheese		Freshly ground pepper
3	tablespoons reduced fat mayonnaise		

Place garlic in food processor with metal blade. Process until finely minced. Add remaining ingredients and process about one minute, pausing to scrape down sides of bowl at least once. Remove to bowl or storage container and refrigerate overnight or several hours. Serve with crackers or as a dip for vegetable crudités. Freezes well.

Serves 6 to 8.

Phyllis L. Tildes

C ookbooks are fairy tales for grown-ups.

The Times, London

Roquefort Endive

3	ounces Roquefort cheese, room temperature	25-30	walnut or pecan halves
		25-30	Belgian endive leaves
3	ounces cream cheese, room temperature		

In a bowl, mash the two cheeses until well-mixed or use blender. Place a small mound of cheese mixture on the thick end of each endive leaf. Top the cheese with a walnut or pecan half. Transfer to a platter and serve at room temperature.

Yield: 25 to 30 pieces

Evelyn Saum

Cucumber Canapés

2	8-ounce packages cream cheese, softened	1	large cucumber, sliced
		1	loaf party rye bread
3	tablespoons mayonnaise		Dill weed
1	package Hidden Valley Original Dressing		

Mix cream cheese with mayonnaise and package of dressing. Let sit in refrigerator for 2-3 days. Spread on party rye slices. Put a slice of cucumber on top and sprinkle with dill weed.

Donna Meterko

Baked Pita Chips

Split each of six 6-inch whole wheat pita rounds into 2 rounds. Cut each into 8 wedges to make 96 triangles. Arrange in a single layer on two baking sheets. Coat with butter flavored cooking spray. Bake at 350 degrees for 15 minutes.

Before baking, pitas can be sprinkled with garlic powder or salt.

Recommend serving with hummus or salsa. Keeps well if stored in plastic bag.

Linda Torpie

43

Venetian Crowns

2	6-ounce jars marinated artichoke hearts, drained	10	slices pepperoni sausage, finely chopped
1	egg, beaten	2	tablespoons fine bread crumbs
¼	cup Parmesan or Romano cheese, grated	10	stuffed olives, sliced
½	cup ricotta cheese		

Preheat oven to 325 degrees.

Grease a 13x9-inch baking dish. Arrange artichokes in dish. In a small bowl, combine egg and cheeses. Add pepperoni to egg mixture. Spoon onto centers of artichoke hearts and sprinkle with bread crumbs. Bake 20 minutes or until cheese has melted. Top with olive slices. Serve hot.

Yield: 20

A little chopped dill may be added to egg mixture. Fresh bread crumbs are best.

Anna M. Nichols

Sweet & Sour Meatballs

¾	pound extra lean ground beef	¾	cup ketchup
¾	pound ground turkey	⅓	cup white vinegar
1	small onion, minced	¼	cup low-sodium Worcestershire sauce
¼	cup egg substitute	3	tablespoons sugar
½	cup Italian seasoned bread crumbs	2	teaspoons dry mustard

Combine first 5 ingredients; shape mixture into 1-inch balls. Brown meatballs, in batches, in a large nonstick skillet over medium-high heat. Remove meatballs from skillet and wipe skillet clean. Stir together ketchup and next 4 ingredients in skillet; bring to a boil. Add meatballs, reduce heat and simmer 5 minutes or until meatballs are no longer pink.

Yield: 3½ dozen

Meatballs may be thoroughly cooked without sauce and frozen. To serve, thaw and reheat with sauce.

Mary Ann Schmitt

Chili Dip

4	garlic cloves, minced	1	8-ounce package cream
1	medium onion, chopped		cheese
2	tablespoons butter	1	small can chopped olives
1	15-ounce can chili (no beans)	1	8-ounce jar mild salsa
			Corn chips

Sauté garlic and onion in butter. Stir in all remaining ingredients except chips. Heat and serve with chips.

Phyllis Albertson

Spicy Black Bean & Corn Salsa

16	ounces cooked black beans	⅓	cup fresh or bottled lime
16	ounces fresh, frozen or		juice
	canned corn kernels	3	tablespoons vegetable oil
½	cup chopped fresh cilantro	1	tablespoon ground cumin
¼	cup chopped green onions		Salt and pepper
¼	cup chopped red onion	½	cup ripe tomatoes, chopped
			and drained

In large bowl, combine beans, corn, cilantro, green onion, red onion, lime juice, oil and cumin. Season with salt and pepper to taste. Cover and chill at least 2 hours or as long as overnight. Just before serving, stir in tomatoes. Serve with white corn chips or corn chip scoops.

Ann Robertson

Marinated Shrimp & Artichoke Hearts

24	medium shrimp, cooked	¼	cup white vinegar
2	onions, sliced into rings	2	tablespoons Dijon mustard
2	cans artichoke hearts,	2	tablespoons parsley, minced
	quartered	2	tablespoons chives, minced
¾	cup olive oil		

Layer first 3 ingredients. Mix remaining ingredients and pour over shrimp and artichokes. Marinate at least 12 hours. Lasts about a week.

Bobbie Weber

45

Portobello Mushrooms
Stuffed With Eggplant & Gorgonzola

6	5- to 6-inch diameter portobello mushrooms, stemmed	2	garlic cloves, minced
¼	cup olive oil	¼	cup dry red wine
4	Japanese eggplants (unpeeled), finely chopped	6	ounces crumbled Gorgonzola cheese
6	tablespoons chopped, drained, oil-packed, sun-dried tomatoes	2	tablespoons chopped fresh basil, divided
		¼	cup freshly grated Parmesan cheese

Preheat oven to 375 degrees.

Arrange mushrooms, rounded side down, on large baking sheet. Heat oil in heavy medium skillet over medium heat. Add eggplant, sun-dried tomatoes and garlic. Sauté until eggplant is soft, about 8 minutes. Stir in red wine and simmer until liquid evaporates, about 2 minutes. Remove skillet from heat; stir in Gorgonzola cheese and 1 tablespoon basil. Season with salt and pepper.

Spoon mixture evenly into mushroom caps. Sprinkle with Parmesan cheese. Cover mushrooms with aluminum foil. Bake mushrooms for 15 minutes. Remove foil and continue baking until cheese melts, filling bubbles and mushrooms are tender when pierced with sharp knife, about 10 minutes. Sprinkle mushrooms with remaining 1 tablespoon basil and serve warm.

Serves 6.

Chris Aiken

Scoopa-Doop

2	cans green chiles, roasted and peeled, not "hot"	2	eggs
12	ounces sharp cheddar cheese, grated	2	tablespoons milk

Preheat oven to 325 degrees.

Butter glass pie plate well. Drain and cut up chiles and line bottom of dish. Sprinkle the cheese over chiles. Beat egg and milk together and pour over chiles. Bake, uncovered, 45 minutes. Serve over crackers using a long-handled spoon. Can be made ahead.

Agi Sutton

Cucumber Sandwiches

8-10	ounces cream cheese	1	teaspoon chopped fresh dill
2	tablespoons mayonnaise	⅛	teaspoon salt
1	tablespoon chopped scallions		Dash pepper
			Dash garlic powder
1½	tablespoons chopped black olives	1	cucumber, thinly sliced
		1	loaf white sandwich bread

Combine all ingredients except cucumber and bread. Spread mixture on bread slices. Top half of bread with cucumber slices. Cover with remaining bread. Cut off crusts and cut into quarters. Wrap sandwiches in damp paper towels and then plastic wrap. Refrigerate until ready to use.

Yield: 36

Marcia Suelflow

Montrachet Torte

12	sheets 14x18-inch phyllo dough	1	cup onions, very thinly sliced and sautéed
6	tablespoons butter, melted	8-10	Italian plum tomatoes, cut in
10	tablespoons Parmesan cheese, grated and divided		¼-inch slices
		½	cup fresh basil, chopped
1	cup mozzarella cheese, grated	½	teaspoon dried oregano
		¼	teaspoon dried thyme
4	ounces Montrachet cheese, crumbled		Salt and pepper, to taste

Preheat oven to 375 degrees.

Lay sheet of phyllo on lightly buttered baking sheet. Brush lightly with butter. Sprinkle with 1 tablespoon Parmesan cheese. Repeat procedure with 5 more sheets of phyllo, stacking one on top of another.

Sprinkle last sheet of phyllo with all of mozzarella and Montrachet cheeses. Spread sautéed onion slices over cheese followed by tomato slices, basil, oregano, thyme, salt and pepper.

Layer 6 more sheets of phyllo, lightly brushing each sheet with melted butter. Sprinkle remaining Parmesan cheese over top sheet of phyllo. Bake 30-35 minutes. Slice into squares and serve warm on plates.

Serves 12.

Joyce Huber

Vidalia Onion Appetizer

4	large Vidalia onions	4	tablespoons margarine or
4	teaspoons instant beef		butter
	bouillon or 4 beef bouillon		
	cubes		

Slice onions in half. Mix the bouillon with the melted margarine or butter. Drizzle over each onion half. Place in microwave with rotating turntable or be sure to rotate onions in a regular microwave. Plan to cook each ½ onion for 1½ minutes at high power. Serve immediately on individual plates. Serves 8.

Marcia Wilk

Island Meatballs With Curry Dip

½	pound ground beef	1	cup bread crumbs
½	pound ground pork	2	cloves garlic, finely chopped
½	pound ground turkey	½	cup chopped parsley
½	cup chopped onions		Salt and pepper, to taste
2	eggs		Curry Dip

Preheat oven to 350 degrees.
Combine all ingredients except Curry Dip. Mix well. Shape into meatballs, about 1-inch in diameter. Bake meatballs on a baking sheet, uncovered, for 20 minutes or microwave for 10 minutes on high. Meatballs may be made ahead and frozen. Reheat before serving.
Yield: approximately 60 meatballs

CURRY DIP

1	cup plain yogurt	3	tablespoons chopped fresh
1	teaspoon curry powder		mint

Combine all ingredients; mix well. Chill. Serve as a dipping sauce for Island Meatballs. Makes 1 cup.

Anonymous

Beverages

WORD

Poinsettia Punch

2   750-milliliter bottles white
    Zinfandel wine
2   750-milliliter bottles
    champagne

2   ounces crème de cassis
2   limes, cut into thin slices

Fill punch bowl with ice or ice ring. Pour Zinfandel over ice. Add champagne and then crème de cassis. Float lime slices in punch bowl for garnish.
Yield: 16 servings

Jan Washenko

Hot Florida Tea

1   cup pink grapefruit juice
2½ cups apricot nectar
1   cup water
2   tablespoons sugar

2   sticks cinnamon
4   lemon slices, ½-inch thick
12 whole cloves
2   teaspoons instant tea

In large saucepan combine grapefruit juice, apricot nectar, water, sugar, and cinnamon sticks. Stud lemon slices with cloves; add to saucepan. Bring to a boil. Simmer covered 10 minutes. Stir in tea. Serve piping hot.
Serves 8.

Bobbye Hildebrand

Wassail

2   quarts apple juice or cider
1   pint cranberry juice
¾   cup sugar
2   sticks cinnamon

1   teaspoon whole or ground
    allspice
1   small orange, studded with
    whole cloves
1   cup rum (optional)

Put all ingredients in crockpot. Cover and cook on High for 1 hour, then on low for 4-8 hours. Serve warm from crockpot.
Yield: approximately 12 cups

Mary Cassady

Peachy Dessert Drink

2	ripe fresh peaches or 1 cup canned, sliced peaches, drained	3	generous scoops vanilla or butter pecan ice cream (1½ cups)
1	tablespoon sugar (only if using fresh peaches)	3	tablespoons light rum or peach liqueur
2	cups crushed ice		

Peel the fresh peaches by submerging them in boiling water for 30 seconds or until skin puckers. Rinse with cold water and slip off skins. Cut peaches into slices, discarding the pits. In a blender or food processor, combine the peach slices, sugar, crushed ice, ice cream and rum. Process until well-blended and as smooth as possible. Divide between two stemmed glasses and serve. Garnish with a peach slice and whipped cream.
Serves 2.

Carol Bocard

Cranberry-Rum Punch

¾	cup brown sugar	¾	teaspoon ground cloves
4	cups water, divided	2	cans jellied cranberry sauce, crushed with fork
¼	teaspoon salt		
¼	teaspoon nutmeg	1	quart pineapple juice
½	teaspoon cinnamon	1	pint rum (optional)
½	teaspoon allspice		

Mix brown sugar, 1 cup water, salt, spices and cranberry sauce in saucepan. Stir until smooth and heat to boiling. Add remaining water and pineapple juice. Stir and heat to boiling. Add rum and serve hot.
Serves 12.

Mary Cassady

*L**ove and scandal are the best sweeteners of tea.*

Henry Fielding
English novelist

51

Picnic Tea Punch

8	cups water, divided	½	cup frozen orange juice
4	tea bags or 1 family-size		concentrate, thawed
	tea bag	½	cup frozen lemonade
1	stick cinnamon		concentrate, thawed
½-¾	cup sugar	8	lemon slices
		8	sprigs fresh mint

Boil 4 cups water. Remove from heat and add tea bags and cinnamon stick. Let steep 5 minutes. Remove tea bags. Add sugar. Stir in orange juice and lemonade concentrates. Add remaining 4 cups of water. Chill 4 hours or overnight. Remove cinnamon stick. Add ice cubes, lemon slices and mint to each of 8 glasses. Pour tea mixture into glasses.
Serves 8.

Nancy Canadé

Margarita Wine Punch

3	6-ounce cans frozen limeade concentrate, thawed	Ice ring
		Margarita salt
1	12-ounce can frozen	Lemon or lime wedges
	lemonade concentrate,	Green food coloring
	thawed	(optional)
3	750-milliliter bottles cold, dry white wine	

Make an ice ring using limeade, lemonade or a mixture of all punch ingredients. Lemon or lime wedges may be frozen in the ring.

Shortly before serving, mix all ingredients together in punch bowl. If desired, tint with green food coloring. Add ice ring. Place a bowl of margarita salt and a bowl of lemon and lime wedges near the punch bowl so guests, if they like, can run glass rims in the salt and add fruit wedges before ladling punch.

Yield: 3 quarts

Jan Washenko

Strawberry Smoothie

1	8-ounce container vanilla yogurt	1	banana, sliced (can be frozen)
1	10-ounce package frozen strawberries	¼	cup orange juice
		1	tablespoon honey

Blend all ingredients in a blender until smooth. Serve immediately.
Yield: 3¼ cups

Anne Faxon

Orange Juliennes

⅓	cup frozen orange juice concentrate	¼	cup sugar
½	cup milk	½	teaspoon vanilla
½	cup water	5-6	ice cubes

Combine all ingredients and blend 30 seconds. Serve immediately.
Yield: 3 cups

Gail Andrus

Cranberry Tea

2½	quarts water	4	3-inch cinnamon sticks
1	32-ounce jar cranberry juice cocktail	1	tablespoon whole cloves
¼	cup lemon juice	3	family-size tea bags
2	cups sugar	1	cup orange juice
			Fresh mint sprigs for garnish

Bring first 6 ingredients to a boil in a large Dutch oven; reduce heat and simmer 10 minutes. Remove from heat and add tea bags; cover and steep 5 minutes. Using a slotted spoon, remove and discard tea bags, cinnamon, and cloves; stir in orange juice. Chill; serve over ice with lemon wedges.

Garnish, if desired.

Yield: about 4 quarts

This tea would also be good served warm in the wintertime.

Mary Cassady

Virginia Ice Tea

2	quarts sweetened instant tea	1	cup lemonade
1	cup orange juice	2	cups ginger ale
1	cup pineapple juice		

Mix all together, adding ginger ale just before serving.

Joan Pierce

Irish Cream Liquor

8	ounces rye whiskey	2	tablespoons heavy cream
1	8-ounce can sweetened	1	tablespoon chocolate syrup
	condensed milk	1	teaspoon vanilla
4	eggs		

Combine all ingredients and blend well.

Mary Giacchini

Barbara's Famous Margaritas

| ¾ | cup gold tequila | ⅓ | cup triple sec |
| ¾ | cup sweet and sour mixer | | |

Pour above ingredients into ice-filled blender and blend to desired consistency. Garnish rim of each glass with ½ slice of fresh lime and salt, if desired. Serves 4.

Marcia DaPont

Golden Pheasants

6	jiggers gin	1	egg
6	jiggers lemon juice	1	jigger of creme soda
1	cup confectioners' sugar		

Blend first four ingredients. For each drink, use 1 jigger of gin mixture and 1 jigger of creme soda. Serve over crushed ice.

Gail Andrus

Kahlúa

4	cups water	1	vanilla bean cut into
1	2-ounce jar instant coffee		4 pieces
3-3½	cups sugar	32	ounces 100 proof vodka

Boil water, add coffee and sugar, stir well until dissolved. Add vanilla bean and simmer 15 minutes. Remove from heat; remove vanilla bean and add vodka. Pour into dark bottles. Store in dark place. Shake bottles once a day for 14 days.

Mary Giacchini

Southern Sweet Tea

6	cups water	1-1¾ cups sugar
4	family-size tea bags	

Bring water to a boil in a saucepan; add tea bags. Boil 1 minute and remove from heat. Cover and steep 10 minutes. Remove tea bags, squeezing gently. Add sugar stirring until dissolved. Pour into a 1-gallon pitcher and add enough water to fill pitcher. Serve over ice.

Yield: 1 gallon

Anne Faxon

Brandy Slush

7	cups water	1	12-ounce can frozen orange
1	cup sugar		juice
2	tea bags	2	cups apricot brandy
1	12-ounce can frozen		7-Up or Sprite
	lemonade		

Boil water and sugar. Cool. Steep tea bags in a cup of hot water. Combine sugar water and tea with lemonade, orange juice and apricot brandy. Place in a plastic container in freezer. Half fill glass with slush and pour 7-Up or Sprite over. Will stay in slush form in freezer for a long time. Can also be made with cherry vodka in place of apricot brandy.

Donna Meterko

55

Frozen Fruit Slush

2	cups sugar	1	12-ounce can frozen
9	cups water		lemonade concentrate
1	12-ounce can frozen orange	2	cups gin
	juice concentrate		7-Up or Squirt

Bring sugar and water to a boil. Simmer 15 minutes and cool. Add juices and gin to sugar water mixture and freeze. When ready to serve, fill glass half full with slush. Add 7-Up or Squirt to fill glass.

Yield: 2½ quarts of slush

Jan Washenko

Springtime Punch

1	46-ounce can pineapple juice	3	bananas, mashed
1	12-ounce can frozen orange	2	cups sugar
	juice concentrate	4	cups water
1	12-ounce can frozen	2	liters Sprite
	lemonade concentrate	2	liters 7-Up

Mix first 6 ingredients and freeze. When ready to serve, stir mixture in punch bowl until mushy. Add Sprite and 7-Up. Serve.

Serves 25.

Jan Washenko

San Francisco Irish Coffee

1	cup freshly brewed coffee	½	pint of real whipping cream,
3	sugar cubes		whipped
1	jigger (3 tablespoons) of		
	Irish whiskey		

Pour coffee into large mug. Add sugar and stir to dissolve. Add whiskey and stir. Top with fresh whipped cream and enjoy!

Serves 1.

Marcia DaPont

Breakfast & Brunch

WORD

Fresh Strawberry Puff Pancake

¼	cup butter	¼	teaspoon salt
3	eggs	3	cups fresh strawberries,
1½	cups milk		washed and halved
½	cup sugar, separated	1	pint light sour cream
¾	cup flour		Brown sugar

Preheat oven to 425 degrees.

Put butter in a 9-inch round cake pan or pie plate. Place dish in oven until butter melts and bubbles, about 8 minutes.

Beat together in medium bowl the eggs, milk, 6 tablespoons of the sugar, flour and salt until smooth.

Remove hot dish from the oven and pour egg mixture in all at once. Return to oven and bake for 30 minutes or until edges are puffed and browned.

Sprinkle strawberries with remaining 2 tablespoons of sugar and stir. When pancake is done, remove from oven and immediately spoon strawberries into the center. Cut in wedges and pass sour cream and brown sugar to each guest.

Serves 4 for brunch or 6 for dessert.

Marcia DaPont

Almond-Apricot Streusel

¾	cup butter	2	cups flour
1	cup sugar	1½	cups flaked coconut
½	teaspoon salt	½	16-ounce jar apricot
½	teaspoon vanilla		preserves
1	egg	½	cup sliced almonds

Preheat oven to 350 degrees.

Cream butter and sugar until light. Add salt, vanilla and egg, creaming well. Stir in flour, blending well. Add coconut. Spread ¾ of the batter in a greased 7x11-inch glass baking dish. Spread preserves on top. To remaining batter, stir in almonds and crumble mixture on top of preserves. Bake for 40-45 minutes, until golden. Cut into bars and serve while warm or at room temperature. Store in refrigerator. Freezes well.

Yield: 12 to 18 small servings

Sally Robyn

Victorian French Toast

1	cup brown sugar, packed	5	eggs
⅓	cup butter	1½	cups milk
2	tablespoons light corn syrup	1	teaspoon cinnamon
6	slices French bread, 1-inch		Confectioners' sugar
	thick slices		Assorted fresh fruit

In a small saucepan combine the brown sugar, butter and corn syrup. Cook over medium heat, stirring constantly, until the butter melts. Pour the brown sugar mixture into an ungreased 9x13-inch baking dish. Be sure to cover the bottom of the dish. Arrange the bread slices in a single layer over the top of the brown sugar mixture. Depending on the shape and size of the French bread loaf you may need more than 6 slices – be sure to cover the bottom of the baking dish. Beat the eggs, milk and cinnamon. Pour the batter over the bread, saturating all the slices. Cover and refrigerate for at least 2 hours or overnight.

Preheat oven to 350 degrees.

Uncover baking dish and bake for 30 to 35 minutes or until the center is set and top is lightly browned. Let stand 10 minutes before serving. Top with confectioners' sugar. Serve with fruit.

Egg substitutes and skim milk also work well in this recipe.

Joyce Englerth

Stuffed French Toast

8	eggs	1	loaf bread, cubed (cinnamon
⅓	cup honey		raisin is good)
1⅓	cups milk	1	8-ounce package cream
			cheese, cubed

Mix eggs, honey and milk; set aside. In a greased 9x13-inch pan layer half the bread cubes, then the cheese and top with remaining bread cubes. Pour the egg mixture evenly over the bread. Cover and refrigerate overnight. Preheat oven to 350 degrees and bake for 35 to 40 minutes. Serve with syrup.

Serves 6 to 8.

Pat Cook

Baked French Toast

¾	cup packed brown sugar	1¼	cups milk, half-and-half, or
6	tablespoons margarine		fat free evaporated milk
3	tablespoons light corn syrup	1	tablespoon vanilla
8	slices sourdough French	¼	teaspoon salt
	bread, cut 1¾-inch thick	3	tablespoons sugar, optional
3	large eggs, slightly beaten	1	teaspoon cinnamon, optional
		2	tablespoons butter, melted

Combine first 3 ingredients in a small pan. Cook over medium heat until bubbles form, stirring frequently. Pour mixture evenly into lightly buttered 11x7-inch dish. Arrange bread over syrup and then turn over so slices are covered with syrup. Combine eggs, milk, vanilla and salt. Gently pour mixture over bread. Cover and chill overnight. When ready to cook, preheat oven to 350 degrees. Mix sugar and cinnamon together and sprinkle over bread; drizzle with melted butter and bake 45-55 minutes.

Serves 4 generously.

Nancy Craig

Apple Cinnamon Baked French Toast

1	large loaf French bread	3	teaspoons cinnamon
8	large eggs	1	teaspoon nutmeg
1	cup sugar, divided	6	medium cooking apples,
3½	cups milk		peeled, cored and sliced
1	tablespoon vanilla	½	stick butter

Slice bread into 1½-inch slices. Spray a 9x13-inch glass baking dish with cooking spray. Place bread slices tightly together in dish. In separate bowl beat together eggs, ½ cup sugar, milk and vanilla with a whisk for 30 seconds. Pour ½ of egg mixture over bread. Combine remaining ½ cup sugar with cinnamon and nutmeg and mix with apples. Put this mixture on top of bread. Pour balance of egg and milk mixture over apples. Dot with butter. Cover and refrigerate overnight. When ready to bake set oven at 350 degrees and cook, uncovered, for 1 hour.

Joann Borton

Peachy French Toast

4	English muffins, split	6	tablespoons butter or
3	large eggs		margarine, divided 2/2/2
¾	cup milk	1	16-ounce can sliced peaches
¼	cup almond liqueur, divided		in heavy syrup, undrained
½	teaspoon salt	1	10-ounce jar apricot
½	teaspoon vanilla extract		preserves
	Dash of ground nutmeg		Sifted confectioners' sugar

Arrange muffin halves in a single layer in a lightly greased 13x9-inch baking dish. Whisk together eggs, milk, 2 tablespoons liqueur, salt, vanilla and nutmeg; pour over muffins. Cover and chill 8 hours.

Melt 2 tablespoons butter in a large nonstick skillet; add half of muffins, and cook over medium heat 2-3 minutes on each side or until lightly browned. Remove from skillet and keep warm. Repeat procedure with remaining muffins and 2 tablespoons butter. Melt remaining 2 tablespoons butter in skillet; add peaches, and cook over low heat 2-3 minutes, stirring occasionally, or until thoroughly heated. Stir in preserves and remaining 2 tablespoons liqueur; cook, stirring often, until hot and bubbly. Pour mixture over muffins, and sprinkle with confectioners' sugar.

Serves 4.

Joy Borden

Apple Baked French Toast

1	12-ounce package frozen	3	eggs
	scalloped apples, thawed	1	cup milk
⅓	cup dark brown sugar	½	teaspoon vanilla
2	tablespoons butter, melted	6-7	slices day old French bread

Preheat oven to 350 degrees.

Combine apples, brown sugar and butter in 9x13-inch baking dish. Whisk eggs, milk and vanilla until well-blended. Dip bread into egg mixture. Place bread on top of apples. Bake 35-40 minutes or until center is firm.

Gerry Baumgardner

My Mother's Famous French Toast

1	loaf unsliced white bread	4	tablespoons Grand Marnier
6	eggs	1½	teaspoons salt
2¼	cups milk	2	tablespoons sugar

Slice bread in 1-inch slices. Beat remaining ingredients and pour in 9x13-inch baking dish. Dip each slice of bread in egg mixture and turn over, allowing bread to soak overnight (or two). Melt butter in a frying pan and sauté each bread slice. Sprinkle with confectioners' sugar. Cut in triangles or serve whole.

Serves 4 to 8.

Gail Andrus

Grand Marnier French Toast

6	eggs	1	teaspoon ground cinnamon
¼	cup Grand Marnier	4	tablespoons unsalted butter
2	tablespoons maple syrup	1	1-pound loaf challah bread,
2	tablespoons heavy cream		cut into 12 thick slices
Finely grated orange peel from		Confectioners' sugar	
	1 orange	Orange slices for garnish	

In large bowl beat eggs, Grand Marnier, maple syrup, heavy cream, orange peel and cinnamon with wire whisk until smooth. Melt 1 tablespoon butter in large skillet over medium heat. Dip four slices of challah bread into egg mixture until well saturated. Sauté in butter, turning once, until golden brown, approximately 5 minutes. Transfer to warm oven. Whisk egg mixture again and repeat with remaining bread slices adding more butter to skillet as needed. Sprinkle tops generously with dusting of confectioners' sugar and garnish with orange slices. Serve sausage patties as an accompaniment if desired.

Arlene Gilligan

I have always been a discriminating but light eater, and never sit down to breakfast. Being also by habit a late riser, I await the joys of "brunch."

William Styron, *Sophie's Choice*

French Toast Casserole

½   cup butter, melted
1   cup brown sugar
Large loaf French bread, cut into
    1-inch slices
½   cup chopped pecans

6   eggs
1½ cups milk
1   teaspoon vanilla
½   teaspoon cinnamon

Mix butter and brown sugar together. Spread in bottom of 9x13-inch baking dish. Place bread slices on top. Sprinkle chopped nuts evenly over bread. Mix together remaining ingredients and pour over bread. Cover and refrigerate overnight. When ready to bake, preheat oven to 350 degrees and cook, uncovered, for 45-50 minutes or until bubbly.

Serves 6 to 8.

Sandra Williams

Egg Casserole "Breakfast"

7   eggs
2¼ cups milk
¼   cup butter, melted
8   slices bread, crusts removed
    and torn into pieces

1   pound bacon, smoked
    sausage or ground sausage,
    optional
12 ounces sharp cheddar
    cheese, grated

Beat eggs and milk together. Add melted butter. Set aside. Grease a 9x13-inch or 9x15-inch baking dish. Put bread pieces in bottom of dish, add meat if using, then cheese. Pour egg and milk mixture over all. Let stand overnight or at least 3 hours. When ready to bake, preheat oven to 325-350 degrees and cook for 45-60 minutes. Let sit a few minutes before serving and then cut into squares.

Serves 12 generously. Freezes well.

If you choose to add meat to this dish, do not add the melted butter to the eggs and milk. Meat should be cooked and drained of grease.

Sue Winship

There is no such thing as a pretty good omelet.

French Proverb

63

Spicy Egg Casserole

6	eggs	6	ounces mild cheddar cheese,
½	cup flour		grated
1	teaspoon baking powder	1	pound sausage, cooked,
1	cup milk		crumbled and drained
1	3-ounce package cream	⅛	teaspoon salt
	cheese	1	12-ounce can sliced
1	8-ounce carton small curd		mushrooms, drained
	cottage cheese	1	bunch green onions, chopped
10	ounces Monterey Jack	6	tablespoons butter
	cheese, grated		Paprika

Preheat oven to 350 degrees.

Beat eggs well. Add flour, baking powder and milk. Cut cream cheese into small cubes. Add cream cheese, cottage cheese, Monterey Jack cheese and cheddar cheese to egg mixture. Add sausage, salt, mushrooms and onions. Pour into buttered 9x13-inch casserole dish. Dot with butter and sprinkle with paprika. Cover and refrigerate overnight. Bring to room temperature and bake for 45 minutes.

Serves 8.

Note: Can be partially baked for 30 minutes and then frozen. Reheat thawed dish for about 20 minutes.

Kathy Siler

Sausage Brunch Casserole (Pizza)

1	pound sausage	4	eggs, beaten
1	8-ounce can crescent rolls	¾	cup milk
2	cups shredded mozzarella	¼	teaspoon salt, optional
	cheese (8 ounces)	⅛	teaspoon pepper

Preheat oven to 425 degrees. Butter a 9x13-inch baking dish.

Brown, crumble and drain the sausage. Line dish with the crescent rolls firmly pressing the perforations to seal. Spread the sausage on top and cover with cheese. Combine eggs, milk and seasonings; beat well and pour over sausage and cheese. Bake 15-20 minutes or until set. Let stand 5 minutes then cut into squares and serve immediately.

Serves 6 to 8.

Joy Borden

Breakfast Casserole

10	slices thin white bread, crusts removed; cut slices into cubes	2	cups grated extra sharp cheddar cheese

Mix together:

6	extra large eggs	½	teaspoon pepper
2	cups milk	½	stick melted butter
½	teaspoon salt		

Butter a round or rectangular casserole dish. Layer half of bread cubes and half of grated cheese in dish. Repeat layers. Pour egg and milk mixture evenly over bread and cheese. Cover and refrigerate overnight. To bake, preheat oven to 325 degrees and cook, uncovered, 50-60 minutes. Let sit 15 minutes before serving.

Serves 6 to 8.

Sandra Williams

Tangy Apple Sausage Quiche

	Pie shell, unbaked	½	teaspoon crushed red pepper flakes
12	ounces sausage		
1	tablespoon minced onion	1	cup shredded cheddar cheese
¾	cup peeled, cored and shredded tart apple		
		3	eggs
1	tablespoon lemon juice	1½	cups half-and-half
1	tablespoon sugar		Salt and pepper, to taste
			Minced parsley

Preheat oven to 375 degrees.

Brown sausage and onions and pour off grease. Add shredded apple, lemon juice, sugar and pepper flakes. Cook, stirring until apples are tender and liquid evaporates. Cool. Spoon cooled sausage and apple mixture into pie shell. Top with cheese. Whisk together eggs, half-and-half, salt and pepper and pour over mixture in pie shell. Bake 55-60 minutes. Garnish with parsley.

Joann Borton

Sausage Apple Ring

2	pounds bulk sausage	½	cup milk
1½	cups cracker crumbs	¼	cup minced onion
2	eggs, slightly beaten	1	cup finely chopped apples

Scrambled eggs

Paprika, parsley and fresh fruit
for garnish

Preheat oven to 350 degrees.

Combine first 6 ingredients and mix thoroughly. Press lightly into 6-cup ring mold. Turn out into shallow baking pan. Bake for 1 hour. Drain fat from pan. Fill center with scrambled eggs. Sprinkle with paprika. Garnish.

Serves 8.

This sausage ring may be partially baked for 30 minutes the day before using. Finish baking the next morning. It can also be frozen.

Marby Varley

Cheese Blintz Soufflé

Batter:

2	sticks butter	3	teaspoons baking powder
½	cup sugar	½	cup milk
2	eggs, beaten		Pinch salt
1	cup flour	1	teaspoon vanilla

Filling:

1	pound cream cheese	1	cup sugar
1	pound small curd cottage cheese		Pinch salt
2	eggs, beaten		Juice of 1 lemon

Preheat oven to 300 degrees.

Mix batter ingredients. Mix filling ingredients in separate bowl. Pour ½ batter in 9x13-inch baking dish. Pour filling over. Add remaining batter. Bake 45 minutes. Serve with stewed fruit.

Serves 8 to 10.

Robbie Forester

Cheese Omelet

4	slices white bread, buttered and broken into small pieces	4	eggs, slightly beaten
1	teaspoon dry mustard	2	cups milk
½	pound cheddar or colby cheese, grated	1	3-ounce package dried beef, chopped

Mix all ingredients together and place in covered bowl. Refrigerate overnight. At breakfast time, pour mixture into buttered 8x8-inch baking dish. Preheat oven to 350 degrees and bake 45 minutes or until eggs are set. Double recipe for 9x13-inch baking dish. Warms well in microwave.
Serves 4.

Phyllis Huffer

German Pancake Omelet

3	eggs	½	cup butter, melted (keep warm)
½	cup light cream		
¼	teaspoon salt		Sugar and cinnamon, blended
2	tablespoons butter	1	6½-ounce jar applesauce, heated
2	tablespoons vegetable oil		

Preheat oven to 400 degrees.
Beat together eggs, cream and salt. Heat a 10-inch ovenproof skillet (preferably iron) until very hot. Add 2 tablespoons butter and the oil. Tilt pan to coat all surfaces, including sides. Pour in egg mixture and tilt pan until bottom and sides of pan are covered. Cook 3 minutes over medium heat, then put immediately into heated oven. Bake until pancake puffs very high and is lightly browned, about 5 minutes. Remove from oven and transfer pancake to a warm plate. Pour some of the melted butter over pancake, then sprinkle with sugar-cinnamon mixture. Spoon on applesauce and roll up. Pour on remaining butter and sprinkle with additional sugar-cinnamon mixture. Serve immediately.
Serves 1 to 2.

Pat Dickinson

67

Curried Eggs In Shrimp Sauce

12	eggs, hard-cooked	¼	teaspoon dry mustard
⅓	cup mayonnaise	½	cup soft bread crumbs
½	teaspoon salt	1	tablespoon butter
¼	teaspoon curry powder		Parsley
½	teaspoon paprika		

Preheat oven to 350 degrees.

Cut eggs in half lengthwise. Remove yolks and mash. Mix with mayonnaise and seasonings and refill eggs. Arrange in 10x6x1½-inch baking dish in single layer. Pour Shrimp Sauce over eggs. Mix bread crumbs with 1 tablespoon of melted butter and sprinkle around edge of pan. Bake 15-20 minutes. Garnish with parsley.

Serves 12.

SHRIMP SAUCE

2	tablespoons butter	1	soup can milk
2	tablespoons flour	½	cup sharp cheddar cheese,
1	can frozen shrimp soup		shredded

Melt 2 tablespoons butter. Blend in flour. Stir in soup and milk and cook, stirring until sauce thickens. Add grated cheese. Stir until melted.

Polly Webb

Granola

4-5	cups rolled oats	1	handful sunflower seeds
2	handfuls coconut	1	tablespoon vegetable oil
2	handfuls wheat germ	½	cup honey
1	handful sesame seeds		

Raisins	Nuts
Dates	

Preheat oven to 325 degrees.

Mix first seven ingredients together and spread on jelly-roll pan. Bake for 25 minutes stirring every 5 minutes. Add raisins, dates and nuts.

Sue Barnett

Soups & Sandwiches

WORD

French Quarter Soup

1	16-ounce package bean mix	2	medium onions, chopped
1	pound ham, chopped	2	cloves garlic, crushed
2	teaspoons salt	¼	teaspoon red pepper
3	ribs celery, chopped	Salt and pepper, to taste	
2	bay leaves	2	chicken breasts
½	teaspoon dried thyme	1	pound smoked sausage,
1	teaspoon parsley, chopped		sliced thin (precook and
1	16-ounce can tomatoes		drain)
1	10-ounce can Rotel tomatoes		

Wash and soak dried beans overnight. Drain beans and add ham, salt and water to cover beans. Add celery, bay leaves, thyme and parsley. Simmer 2½ to 3 hours, adding water as needed. Add all tomatoes, onions, garlic and red pepper. Salt and pepper to taste. Cook uncovered 1½ hours. In separate pot, boil chicken breasts, in water to cover, until tender. Remove from broth, (save broth), debone and shred. Add chicken, sausage and broth to soup. Continue to simmer until thick.

Serves 6 to 8.

Mary Lee Winnert

Deviled Chicken Soup

2	cans chicken broth	1	small can baby green lima
1	can tomato soup		beans
1	can tomato sauce	2	tablespoons prepared
2	cups water		mustard
1	large green bell pepper, chopped	1	teaspoon Worcestershire sauce
1	large onion, sliced	1½	teaspoons chili oil
3	ribs celery, chopped	½	teaspoon garlic powder
1	large can yellow corn	To taste: paprika, hot pepper	
2	pounds chicken, cooked and diced		sauce, salt
1	tablespoon tapioca (to thicken)	Dash sugar	

Combine all ingredients in a large stock pot. Cover and simmer for two hours.

Karen Sellick

70

Crab Meat Bisque

1	can green pea soup	1	bay leaf
1	can celery soup	1	quart half-and-half
2	cans tomato soup	1	pound crab meat, flaked
1	can chicken broth	⅔	cup bourbon
1	carrot, minced		Fresh chopped parsley for
1	clove garlic, minced		garnish

Combine soups, broth, carrot, garlic and bay leaf. Add half-and-half and stir. Simmer 10 minutes. Remove bay leaf, add crab meat and bourbon. Garnish with parsley.

Serves 8.

Can prepare day before serving and reheat.

Lynda Ibach

Tomato Soup

8	ounces cream cheese	1	large onion, diced
28	ounces stewed tomatoes	3	cloves garlic, diced
6	cans tomato soup	½	stick butter
1	pint half-and-half	2	tablespoons dried basil
1	46-ounce can V-8 juice		Salt and pepper, to taste

Process cheese and stewed tomatoes in blender. Combine tomato soup and half-and-half. Add the blender mixture to V-8 juice. Sauté onions and garlic in butter. Add to soup with seasonings. Cook on low on stove or in a 250 degree oven until flavors blend, at least three hours. Stir occasionally. Serve with grated mozzarella cheese and croutons.

This makes a fairly large amount of delicious, creamy soup. I use a medium size roaster and cook in oven. This eliminates scorching.

June Turnbull

It's a comforting sort of thing to have, said Christopher Robin.

A. A. Milne
House at Pooh Corner

71

Soup Vert Au Pistou

⅔ cup dried flageolet beans (or small navy beans)
3 tablespoons extra virgin olive oil
1 medium onion, sliced
3 medium leeks, trimmed and sliced
1 bulb of fennel, diced
1 large potato, peeled and finely diced
A few sprigs of fresh thyme
2 bay leaves
8 ounces fresh spinach, washed and shredded

12 ounces broccoli, divided into florets
2 medium zucchini, diced
1 cup green beans, cut in short lengths
⅔ cup peas
½ cup dried vermicelli, broken in short lengths
1-2 (or more) chicken or vegetable bouillon cubes
Freshly grated Parmesan or Gruyère cheese

Soak beans in cold water overnight. The next day, drain beans and transfer to a saucepan. Cover with cold water and bring to a boil, cover and simmer 45-60 minutes, until beans are almost tender. Heat oil in a large pan, add onion, leeks and fennel. Cook gently for 10 minutes or until soft. Add the cooked beans and all of the other ingredients and enough water to cover, if necessary. Simmer 30 minutes until beans begin to disintegrate and all vegetables are done. Adjust seasoning to taste. Best made a day or two ahead. Serve with cheese and a small dollop of pistou.

PISTOU

1 cup packed fresh basil
4 garlic cloves, peeled
2 ripe tomatoes, skinned and seeded

½ cup Parmesan cheese, freshly grated
⅔ cup extra virgin olive oil
Salt and pepper, to taste

Put all ingredients in blender or food processor and combine thoroughly.

Margaret McCulloch

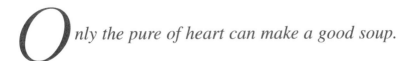

O nly the pure of heart can make a good soup.

Ludwig van Beethoven

Italian Cheese Chowder

1	16-ounce can stewed tomatoes, undrained	1½	teaspoons salt
1	15.5-ounce can garbanzo beans, drained	2	teaspoons instant minced garlic
½	pound zucchini, sliced	1	teaspoon dried basil, crumbled
2	onions, chopped	¼	teaspoon freshly ground pepper
1½	cups dry white wine		
¼	cup butter	1	bay leaf
1	cup grated Monterey Jack cheese	1	cup grated Romano cheese
		1	cup whipping cream

Preheat oven to 400 degrees.

Combine first 11 ingredients in 4-quart baking dish. Cover tightly and bake 1 hour, stirring once or twice. Remove bay leaf. Blend in remaining ingredients. Cover and bake until cheese melts, about 10 minutes. Serve immediately. Serves 6 to 8.

1 pound of ground round or bulk sausage, browned and drained, may be added with cheese and cream for a heartier soup.

Janet Hietbrink

Fresh Tomato Wine Soup

½	cup butter	⅛	teaspoon basil
2	cups fresh ripe tomatoes, peeled and diced		Pepper to taste
		¼	teaspoon baking powder
2	tablespoons flour	1	cup cream or half-and-half
1	teaspoon salt	½	cup dry white wine
⅛	teaspoon nutmeg		

In ½ cup butter, simmer tomatoes for 5 minutes. Process in blender or strain to purée. Put tomato purée back in pan. Blend in flour, salt, nutmeg, basil and pepper. Stir constantly. Bring to a boil. Reduce heat. Simmer 2 minutes, stirring. Stir in baking powder and cream or half-and-half. Cook over low heat until slightly thickened. Add white wine. Heat just to simmering. Serves 4.

Gail Andrus

Nadine's Strawberry Soup

1	pint strawberries	1	cup heavy sweet cream,
1½	cups chicken broth		lightly whipped

Wash strawberries. Slice three berries and reserve for garnish. Stem, then crush or process remainder in blender. Beat in chicken broth and cream. Pour into serving bowl and garnish with berries. If desired, top with sparkling white wine and stir lightly.

Serves 4 to 6.

Yogurt may be substituted for heavy cream.

Gail Andrus

Quick Summer Soup

1	46-ounce can V-8 juice	1	teaspoon Worcestershire
½	cup sour cream		sauce
1-2	teaspoons grated onion		Salt and pepper, to taste
			Chopped chives

Mix all ingredients, except chives, in blender. Chill. Serve with dollop of sour cream topped with chives.

Yield: approximately six 1-cup servings

Ann Quinn

Clam Chowder

4-5	strips bacon	2	cups raw potatoes, cubed
2	7½-ounce cans minced clams	1	can cream of celery soup
1	onion, minced		Milk

Cook bacon, crumble and set aside. Save 3-4 tablespoons bacon grease and sauté onions in grease until soft. Add potatoes and juice from clams. Cover and cook until potatoes are done but still firm, 5-15 minutes. Add clams and soup; stir so mixture is well-blended. Add milk until soup is thickness you prefer. Top each serving with sprinkle of bacon.

Margaret McCulloch

Wild Mushroom Soup

5	ounces portobello mushrooms	2	tablespoons brandy
8	ounces button mushrooms	1	teaspoon thyme
5	ounces shiitake mushrooms	2	bay leaves
2	tablespoons butter	½	cup finely chopped parsley
4	shallots, chopped	1	gallon chicken stock
3	cloves garlic, chopped		Salt and pepper, to taste
		½	cup heavy cream

Thinly slice all mushrooms but leave shiitakes whole. Put butter in soup pot on high heat. Add shallots and garlic and sauté until they start to caramelize. Add mushrooms and brandy. Cook until almost all liquid rendered from the mushrooms has been reduced. Add thyme, bay leaves and parsley. Cook for 2 more minutes. Add stock and cook for 30 minutes on medium heat. Remove from heat and add salt, pepper and heavy cream. Stir well to blend.

Charles D'Ablaing
Chef, The Landings Club

Sausage Soup

½	pound bulk sausage, hot	1	cup chopped celery
½	pound bulk sausage, mild	1	cup chopped carrots
49	ounces chicken broth	1	cup chopped onions
2	14-ounce cans diced tomatoes, undrained	½	head cabbage, sliced
		2	eggs, beaten

Brown sausage and drain. Add all other ingredients except eggs. Cook ½ hour. Drizzle beaten eggs into the soup. Cook ½ hour more. Freezes well. Serves 8.

Bulk sausage works best. If you use link sausage, remove the casings before browning.

Julie Washenko

I live on good soup, not on fine words.

Moliere

75

Corn & Crab Gazpacho

3   pounds large tomatoes, peeled, seeded, coarsely chopped or 3 14½-ounce cans of diced tomatoes, drained

1   medium green bell pepper, coarsely chopped

1   small cucumber, peeled, seeded, chopped

1   small red onion, coarsely chopped

4   garlic cloves, 2 coarsely chopped, 2 whole and peeled

¼   cup olive oil, divided

1   teaspoon rice wine vinegar or ½ teaspoon white wine vinegar

Large pinch of cayenne pepper

Large pinch of cumin

Large pinch of salt and pepper

1   cup fresh or frozen corn

½   pound fresh crab meat or chopped, boiled shrimp

1   baguette, cut in 12 thin, diagonal slices

1   tablespoon minced fresh basil

In a large bowl combine tomatoes, green pepper, cucumber, red onion, chopped garlic, 3 tablespoons olive oil, vinegar, cayenne and cumin. In batches, process mixture in food processor. Keep chunky. Put in large bowl; season with salt and pepper. Cover and refrigerate 1 to 8 hours.

Cook corn in ¼ cup water on high heat for 3 minutes. Drain and cool. Stir corn and crab or shrimp into gazpacho. Preheat broiler. Arrange baguette slices on baking sheet. Toast until golden. Rub toasts with whole garlic, drizzle with remaining 1 tablespoon of olive oil and sprinkle with basil. Keep warm. Ladle gazpacho into chilled soup bowls and serve with baguette toasts on the side.

Serves 6.

Phyllis Albertson

It breathes reassurance, it offers consolation; after a weary day it promotes sociability – There is nothing like a bowl of hot soup, its wisp of aromatic steam teasing the nostrils into quivering anticipation.

The Soup Book
Louis P. DeGouy

Spicy Tropical Gazpacho

2	cups tomato juice	½	cup chopped green bell
2	cups pineapple juice		pepper
1	cup peeled, chopped mango	½	cup chopped red bell pepper
1	cup peeled, chopped papaya	4	tablespoons minced fresh
1	cup chopped fresh pineapple		cilantro
1	cup peeled, seeded, chopped	½	teaspoon salt
	cucumber	2	teaspoons hot sauce

Combine all the ingredients in a food processor or blender. Pulse 4 times or until combined. Cover and chill.
Serves 8.

Diane Munroe

Tortilla Soup

1	green bell pepper, coarsely chopped	1	yellow bell pepper, coarsely chopped
1	red bell pepper, coarsely chopped	1	white onion, chopped
		2	cloves garlic, chopped
			Olive oil
2	(or more) 14½-ounce cans chicken broth		Chopped cilantro to taste
1	can Rotel tomatoes	2-3	uncooked chicken breasts, cut into bite-size pieces
1	small can corn		

Taco chips	Avocado
Cheddar cheese, shredded	Sour cream
Salsa	

Sauté peppers, onion and garlic in olive oil until tender. Add chicken broth, tomatoes, corn, cilantro and chicken pieces. Simmer until hot and chicken is done. Crumble taco chips in each bowl. Pour hot soup over chips; top with shredded cheddar cheese. Serve with salsa, avocado and sour cream on the side.

In place of taco chips, you can sauté your own tortillas, cut in strips, until crisp or use those commercially available. Do not use baked fat free as they become too soft.

Margaret McCulloch

Southwest Chicken Soup

2	tablespoons olive oil	2	garlic cloves, minced
8	ounces skinned and boned chicken breasts cut into ½-inch cubes	1	teaspoon ground cumin
		½	teaspoon salt
		½	teaspoon chili powder
¼	cup onion, diced	⅛	teaspoon ground red pepper

1	14½-ounce can chicken broth	1	15-ounce can black beans, drained and rinsed
1	15¼-ounce can whole kernel corn, undrained	1	14½-ounce can Mexican style stewed tomatoes

3	6-inch corn tortillas, stacked and halved and cut into ½-inch thick strips	2	tablespoons chopped cilantro
		6	tablespoons plain lowfat yogurt

Heat oven to 450 degrees.

Heat oil in heavy Dutch oven. Add chicken cubes to oil and cook 3-4 minutes, stirring until opaque. Stir in next 6 ingredients and cook 1 minute. Stir in broth and next 3 ingredients. Increase heat to high and bring to a boil. Reduce heat, cover and simmer 15 minutes.

While soup is simmering, spread tortilla strips in a single layer on a cookie sheet. Bake 5 minutes until crisp and lightly browned, stirring once. Reserve.

Stir cilantro into soup and ladle into bowls. Top servings with tortilla strips and a tablespoon of yogurt. May be thinned by adding more chicken broth.

Serves 6.

Priss Wentworth

Virginia Peanut Soup

1	can cream of chicken soup	½	cup crunchy peanut butter
1½	cans milk		

Add ingredients together. Stir over medium heat until well-blended.

Serves 4.

Marie Jones

Orzo Soup

1	onion, chopped	½	pound sweet Italian sausage
1	garlic clove, crushed	½	pound hot Italian sausage
1	16-ounce can crushed	¾	cup orzo
	tomatoes	¼	cup mozzarella cheese,
2	14½-ounce cans chicken		shredded
	broth		

Sauté the onion and garlic until translucent. Add to crushed tomatoes and chicken broth in a pot. Remove sausage from casing and either cook it in the microwave or cook it in a skillet until all pink is gone. Drain and add to tomatoes and chicken broth. Add orzo to the pot and bring to a boil. If soup is too thick, add more broth; if too thin, add more orzo. Shred mozzarella on top and serve piping hot.

Serves 4.

If there are leftovers, add V-8 or tomato juice and heat.

Joan Keever

Tomato Basil Bisque

4	16-ounce cans diced tomatoes	¼	cup dry sherry
3	tablespoons fresh garlic,	½	cup brown sugar
	finely chopped	2	cups heavy whipping cream
3	tablespoons fresh basil,	4	tablespoons butter
	chopped fine		Parsley
2	teaspoons dry oregano		Parmesan cheese

Place the first 5 ingredients in a heavy-bottomed pan. Bring to a boil and reduce heat. Stir in the remaining ingredients. Serve topped with chopped parsley and Parmesan cheese.

Serves 6 to 8.

Carol Bocard

*S**oup is cuisine's kindest course.**

Savannah Black Bean Soup

2	pounds black beans	1½	tablespoons black pepper
¾	cup olive oil	1	pinch cayenne pepper
2½	cups onions, diced small	¼	cup chopped parsley
2	tablespoons grated garlic	¼	cup diced red bell pepper
1	ham bone with ham	¼	cup sherry
1	teaspoon ground cumin seed	1	tablespoon lemon juice
1	gallon chicken stock		Chopped green onion for garnish
1	tablespoon oregano		Grated mild cheddar cheese for
3	bay leaves		garnish
1	tablespoon salt		

Use 8-quart pot. Soak beans overnight in enough water to cover. (Twice as much water as beans.) Drain beans. Sauté diced onions and garlic in olive oil. Add drained beans, the seasonings, the ham bone and chicken stock. Simmer until beans are tender. Constantly skim top of soup to remove oil. The process should take approximately 3 hours. During the last 30 minutes stir in red bell peppers, sherry, parsley and lemon juice. Remove ham bone. Cut ham from bone into small pieces and place back in pot. Garnish with chopped green onion and cheese when serving.

Elayne Blecker

Sausage Bean Soup

¾	pound bulk Italian sausage	1	14½-ounce can diced tomatoes, undrained
½	cup chopped onion		
1	garlic clove, finely chopped	1	14½-ounce can beef broth
1	15½-ounce can butter beans, rinsed and drained	1	tablespoon fresh basil, finely chopped, or 1 teaspoon dried basil
1	15-ounce can black beans, rinsed and drained		
		2	tablespoons Parmesan cheese

In a large saucepan cook sausage, onion and garlic until the sausage is browned; drain. Add beans, tomatoes, broth and basil. Cover and simmer for 10 minutes. Sprinkle each serving with Parmesan cheese. Freezes well. Serves 4 to 6.

Barbara B. Barker

Pumpkin Soup With Curry, Mushrooms & Raisins

½   cup chopped celery   2   tablespoons butter
½   cup chopped onion

Sauté gently until crisp tender in skillet. Place in a large saucepan or skillet.

1½ cups mushrooms, chopped   ½   cup long grain rice

Sauté mushrooms until just tender, approximately 4 minutes. Set aside. Cook rice according to package directions.

2   cups (16-ounce can)   ¼   teaspoon nutmeg
     pumpkin purée   1½ teaspoons curry powder, or
3   cups water   to taste
3   chicken bouillon cubes   1   cup raisins
Dash pepper   2   cups milk
½   teaspoon cinnamon

Mix pumpkin with water then add bouillon cubes, pepper, cinnamon, nutmeg, curry powder and raisins. Heat until bouillon cubes are dissolved. Add sautéed vegetables and rice. Simmer until flavors blend, about 15 minutes. (Flavor will improve if cooked up to this point the day before serving and refrigerated.) When ready to serve, add milk. Heat.
Serves 10.

Gail Andrus

Vidalia Onion Vichyssoise

3   leeks, white part only,   2   cups chicken broth
     cleaned and sliced   1¼ cups half-and-half
1   large Vidalia onion, chopped   1   cup heavy cream
2   tablespoons butter   Salt, to taste
2   baking potatoes, peeled and   Chives for garnish
     sliced

Cook onions and leeks in butter until soft. Add potatoes and broth and simmer 30 minutes. Purée soup. Add half-and-half and refrigerate. Add heavy cream just before serving and combine. Serve chilled and garnish with chives.

Mary Cassady

Far East Pea Soup

1	cup fresh or frozen peas	3	cups chicken broth
1	small onion, diced	1	cup light cream
1	small carrot, sliced		Salt and pepper, to taste
1	rib celery, diced	2	tablespoons thinly sliced
1	potato, peeled and diced		scallions for garnish
1	teaspoon curry powder		

Simmer vegetables, curry and broth for 15 minutes or until vegetables are tender. Cool. When cool, purée in batches in blender. Return to saucepan and add cream and seasonings. Heat and serve. Sprinkle with scallions. Serves 6.

Jean Hepper

Pumpkin Mushroom Soup

1-2	cups onion, finely chopped	2	10½-ounce cans chicken broth
¼	cup butter		
¼	cup flour	1	soup can water
½	teaspoon salt	1	28-ounce can prepared pumpkin
½	teaspoon pepper		
½	teaspoon ginger	2	cups half-and-half
½	teaspoon nutmeg	½	pound fresh mushrooms, sliced

In Dutch oven sauté onions in butter until transparent. Stir in dry ingredients and add broth, water and pumpkin. Simmer for 10-15 minutes. Add the half-and-half and mushrooms. Bring to a boil and simmer for 10 minutes.

Yield: 3 quarts

Serving suggestion: Serve in individual soup bowls garnished with sour cream topped with fresh, chopped parsley or croutons.

Evelyne Miller

C howder breathes reassurance. It steams consolation.

Clementine Paddleford
American food editor

Hearty Winter Soup

3	tablespoons butter	1	14-ounce can Italian tomatoes with basil
4	medium onions, chopped		
1	clove garlic, chopped	2	bags frozen cut green beans
2	pounds ground beef	2	bags frozen baby carrots
5	cans beef bouillon	4	cups potatoes, peeled and diced
2	cups red wine		
2	28-ounce cans Italian tomatoes with basil		Salt and pepper, to taste

Sauté onions and garlic in butter. Brown meat. Add bouillon, wine and tomatoes. Mix well. Add remaining ingredients and simmer for 2 hours. Freezes well. Serves 16.

Gail Vergoz

Pasta & Fagioli Soup

2	tablespoons olive oil	3	14-ounce or 19-ounce cans kidney beans, drained, divided 2/1
3	bacon strips, chopped		
1	cup sliced carrots		
1	cup onion, chopped	1½	cups small shell pasta, uncooked
½	cup chopped celery		
½	teaspoon minced garlic		Salt and pepper, to taste
6	cups chicken or vegetable stock		

Heat olive oil in saucepan. Add bacon, carrots, onion, celery and garlic. Sauté until onion is tender. Add stock; cover and bring to a boil; simmer 10 minutes. Purée 2 cans of beans. When vegetables in stock are tender, run them through the blender and add to remaining stock and bean purée. Add whole beans and pasta; bring to boil and cook, stirring occasionally, until pasta is al dente. Season with salt and pepper.

Marjorie Mouat

O f all the items on the menu, soup is that which exacts the most delicate perfection and the strictest attention.

Auguste Escoffier

83

Barbara's Broccoli Cheese Soup

2	tablespoons margarine or butter	1	teaspoon salt and pepper, or to taste
¾	cup chopped onion	2	10-ounce packages frozen, chopped broccoli
6	cups water		
6	chicken bouillon cubes or 6 teaspoons of granules	⅛	teaspoon garlic powder
		6	cups milk
8	ounces fine noodles, crushed	1	pound Velveeta cheese

Sauté onion in butter in soup pan until soft. Add water and bouillon. Bring to boil and stir until bouillon is dissolved. Add noodles, salt and pepper. Boil uncovered 5 minutes, stirring occasionally. Stir in broccoli (can be used unthawed) and garlic powder and cook 4 minutes after broccoli is thawed. Add milk and cheese and stir constantly until cheese melts. Do not let soup boil after milk and cheese are added.

Yield: 5 quarts

Mary Cassady

My Mother's Vegetable Soup

2	pounds soup bones	1	small head cabbage, cut in half, then in wedges
2	onions, chopped		
2-3	leeks	1	15-ounce can lima beans
2	28-ounce cans tomatoes	1	15-ounce can whole kernel corn
2	pounds chuck		
1	pound carrots	1	15-ounce can peas
½	pound turnips	1	15-ounce can okra
1	pound potatoes	2	large packages frozen mixed vegetables
1	package parsnips		

In a 16-quart, or larger, stock pot boil soup bones in lots of salted water with onions and leeks for 2 hours. Add canned tomatoes, then add meat and simmer until it is very tender and begins to fall apart. Remove meat, cut in pieces and return to soup before serving. Add carrots, turnips, potatoes and parsnips; cook until tender. Add cabbage, lima beans, corn, peas, okra, and frozen mixed vegetables; cook until heated through. You may need to add water near the end.

Gail Andrus

Tomato Carrot Soup

3 pounds ripe red tomatoes, skinned and seeded, or 6 cups canned tomatoes, drained and seeded	6 cups chicken broth
	½ cup orange juice
	1 lemon
	2 tablespoons sugar
1 orange	Juice from 1 orange
4 tablespoons butter	1 bay leaf
1 cup onions, finely chopped	Salt, to taste
1¾ cups carrots, thinly sliced	Freshly ground pepper, to taste
4 tablespoons flour, whole wheat preferred	½ cup scallions, finely chopped

Chop tomatoes coarsely. Peel the orange and julienne the peel. Set aside. Heat butter in a soup pot. Add onions and carrots. Cook, stirring to prevent scorching, until onions are golden. Do not brown. Add flour to coat pieces. Add tomatoes, stirring. Bring to boil and add the broth. Return to boiling. Peel the lemon in one long strip. Add the lemon peel to the tomato mixture. (Save the peeled lemon for another dish.) Add sugar, orange juice and bay leaf. Salt and pepper to taste. Simmer for 40 minutes, remove and discard lemon peel and bay leaf. Ladle soup into the container of a food processor or blender and blend thoroughly. Do this in 2 or 3 batches. Return soup to a clean kettle. Bring to a boil. Stir in orange strips and scallions just before serving. Can be served hot or cold. Freezes well.

Yield: approximately 4 quarts or 16 servings

Pam Campbell

Diced Zucchini Soup

4 medium zucchini, sliced	White pepper to taste
1 14.5-ounce can chicken broth	1 cup half-and-half
	1 tablespoon fresh dill or 1 teaspoon dried
¼ to ½ cup chopped onions	
½ teaspoon garlic salt	

Simmer zucchini in broth until tender; sauté onions until tender. In food processor process broth, zucchini and onions until smooth. Return to saucepan and stir in seasonings and half-and-half. Stir until heated. Garnish with fresh dill.

Serves 4.

Marby Varley

Aztec Five-Step Soup

3	tablespoons olive oil	2	teaspoons basil
3	medium onions, chopped	2	teaspoons oregano
10	cloves garlic, chopped	2	teaspoons ground cumin
2	28-ounce cans crushed tomatoes	2	teaspoons black pepper

Heat oil and sauté onions and garlic until translucent and soft, 8-10 minutes. Add tomatoes and seasonings, partially cover and cook over low heat 10-12 minutes. Cool, blend until smooth in a food processor or blender. Set aside.

4	quarts water	2	6-ounce cans tomato paste
2	chickens, cut up	5	bay leaves
2	sprigs fresh or dried epazote (Mexican herb)		

Bring water to boil; add chicken, bay leaves and epazote. (Water should cover chicken by an inch or more.) Skim off foam and fat that surface in first 5 minutes. Add reserved purée from first step and tomato paste and cook, partially covered with liquid, at rolling simmer for 20 minutes. Transfer chicken to platter, reserving liquid. When chicken is cool enough to handle, remove skin and bones and shred.

1	cup red bell pepper, thinly sliced and cut in 1-inch long pieces	2	large carrots, sliced thin
		2	cups celery, sliced thin
1	cup green bell pepper, thinly sliced and cut in 1-inch long pieces	2	cups diced zucchini

Add peppers, carrots and celery to reserved broth and cook over low heat 5 minutes. Add zucchini and cook 5 minutes more. Remove vegetables from broth. Salt broth to taste.

3	medium potatoes, peeled and parboiled

Dice potatoes and sauté in olive oil until brown.

	Tortilla strips (can use commercial unsalted ones, broken in small pieces)	1	pound fresh spinach, coarsely shredded
		2	avocados, cubed
		1½	pounds Jack cheese, shredded

Place a scoop of vegetable mixture and a heaping tablespoonful of potatoes in a large soup bowl. Next, add tortilla strips, spinach, chicken, avocado and cheese. Pour piping hot broth over everything and serve immediately. Serve with thick, hot flour tortillas.

Serves 12 to 16.

Margaret McCulloch

Green Velvet Soup

2	cups leeks	1½	quarts chicken stock
¼	cup butter		Salt and white pepper to taste
2	cups potatoes, peeled and cut into small cubes	1-2	cups light cream
			Snipped chives
2	cups asparagus, cut in ½-inch pieces		

Halve leeks lengthwise; wash carefully and slice thin. In large heavy pan lightly sauté leeks in butter. Dry potato cubes and toss with leeks. Sauté again for about 3 minutes. Add asparagus, stock, salt and pepper. Bring to a boil; lower heat and simmer gently for 30-40 minutes until all vegetables are very soft. Put contents in food processor or blender and purée. Add cream and adjust for seasoning. Garnish with chives. Good hot or cold.

Serves 8.

Pam Campbell

Western Chili Soup

1	pound ground beef	1	15-ounce can kidney beans, undrained
1	cup chopped onion		
1-2	teaspoons garlic powder	3	cups cooked elbow macaroni, rinsed and drained
1	can condensed beef broth		
3	cans condensed tomato soup		
2	soup cans water	2	tablespoons chili powder

Brown meat and onion in a large kettle. Add remaining ingredients and simmer for 30 minutes, stirring occasionally.

Serves 8.

Ginger Heussler

Low Country Gumbo

2	tablespoons olive oil	1	teaspoon minced fresh
½	cup chopped onions		oregano
¼	cup chopped celery	1	teaspoon fresh thyme leaves
¼	cup chopped bell pepper	1	cup sliced okra
1	tablespoon salt	½	teaspoon cayenne pepper
4	turns fresh ground pepper	½	teaspoon red pepper flakes
2	tablespoons minced garlic	½	pound shrimp, peeled and
1	tablespoon minced shallots		deveined (31-35 count)
½	pound chicken, diced	½	pound lump crab meat,
½	pound Andouille sausage,		picked over for shells
	sliced	1	teaspoon filé powder
2	quarts chicken stock	½	cup Italian plum tomatoes
6	bay leaves	4	cups long grain rice, cooked
1	teaspoon minced fresh basil		

Heat oil in a large pot over high heat. Add onions, celery, bell pepper and cook for 1 minute. Add salt, pepper, garlic and shallots and sauté stirring occasionally for about 4 minutes. Add chicken and sausage and cook for 5 minutes. Stir in stock and add bay leaves, basil, oregano and thyme. Bring to a boil. Cook over high heat and stir occasionally for about 8 minutes. Fold in okra, cayenne pepper and red pepper flakes and simmer for 15 minutes. Skim impurities from top of gumbo. Fold in shrimp, crab meat and tomatoes; reduce heat. Sprinkle filé over top to incorporate it thoroughly. To serve, ladle gumbo over ¼ cup of rice in each bowl.

Oscar Mejia
Executive Chef
The Landings Club

Iowa Corn Chowder

5	slices bacon	1	16-ounce package frozen
1	medium onion, sliced into		corn
	rings	1	can cream of mushroom
2½	cups milk		soup
		1	cup diced and cooked potato

Cook bacon until crisp, reserving fat. Cook onion rings in bacon fat until tender. Add milk, corn, mushroom soup and potato. Bring to a boil and simmer 1½ to 2 hours. Garnish with crumbled bacon when serving.

Serves 6 to 8.

88

Judy Hanna

Corned Beef Sandwich

1	can corned beef	¼	cup grated onion
½	cup ketchup	2	tablespoons Worcestershire
1	cup grated American cheese		sauce
	or Cheez Whiz	12	sandwich buns

Preheat oven to 350 degrees.

Mix ingredients and spread on buns. Wrap each in foil and heat for 15 minutes. Can be frozen, thawed and then heated.

Mary Cassady

Grilled Portobello Mushroom Burger

6	large portobello mushroom	¼	cup mayonnaise
	caps	6	sourdough buns or rolls,
½	cup roasted garlic marinade		split
6	1-ounce slices part skim milk		
	mozzarella cheese		

Preheat grill to 350-400 degrees.

Combine mushroom caps and marinade in a heavy duty plastic bag, turning to coat. Seal and let stand 20 minutes. Grill mushrooms, covered, 2 minutes on each side. Top with cheese slice and grill 2 minutes. Spread mayonnaise on cut sides of buns. Grill buns, cut side down, 1 minute or until toasted. Place mushrooms on buns and serve immediately.

Serves 6.

Broiling "burgers" is not recommended. Roasted garlic marinade can be found in the Asian food section of the grocery store.

Priss Wentworth

oo few people understand a really good sandwich.

James Beard

Super Bowl Day Sandwiches

Mix together:

½	pound butter, softened	½	tablespoon poppy seed
1	large onion, chopped	1	teaspoon Worcestershire
3	tablespoons mustard		sauce

3	pounds shaved ham	14	sandwich buns
2	pounds grated Swiss cheese		

Preheat oven to 300 degrees.

Spread buns with butter mixture and top with ham and cheese. Wrap each bun in foil and bake for 30 minutes.

Suzie Busch

Cholesterol Free Egg Salad

1	8-ounce carton egg substitute, thawed	¼	cup finely chopped celery
		¼	cup finely chopped green bell pepper
4	eggs, hard-cooked		
⅓	cup lowfat/cholesterol free mayonnaise	2	tablespoons finely chopped onion (optional)
1	tablespoon Dijon mustard		Salt and pepper, to taste

Pour egg substitute into 8-inch nonstick skillet. Cover tightly and cook over very low heat until egg becomes firm to the touch, about 10 minutes. Don't overcook. Remove from heat and allow to cool, then remove the resulting egg "pancake" and cut into small cubes. Remove and discard the yolks from the hard-cooked eggs and cut the remaining egg whites into small cubes. In a bowl, combine the chopped egg substitute and egg whites with all of the other ingredients. Cover and refrigerate until serving time. Use as a sandwich filling or as a snack or hors d'oeuvre on fat free crackers.

Yield: 4 to 6 sandwiches

Bob Ferrari

A crust eaten in peace is better than a banquet partaken in anxiety.

Aesop (c. 620-560 B.C.)
Greek fabulist

90

Oven Grilled Reubens

2	cups sauerkraut, drained	12	slices rye bread
¾	teaspoon caraway seeds	6	slices Swiss cheese
1¾	cups Thousand Island dressing	24	slices corned beef

Preheat oven to 475 degrees.

Stir together sauerkraut and caraway seeds. Spread dressing evenly on one side of each bread slice. Layer six slices evenly with cheese, sauerkraut mixture and corned beef. Top each layered slice with remaining slices to make six sandwiches.

Coat a baking sheet with vegetable cooking spray and arrange sandwiches on baking sheet. Coat bottom of a second baking sheet with cooking spray and place, coated side down, on top of sandwiches. Bake 15-20 minutes or until golden and cheese is slightly melted.

Serves 6.

Check sandwiches after about 13 minutes and if bottom side is getting quite crispy, turn sandwiches over. Oven-baked sandwiches are much hotter and all ready at the same time.

Suzie Moore

Pizzaburgers

½	pound ground beef	¾	cup spaghetti sauce
¼	pound bologna, minced	¾	cup grated cheese
⅛	teaspoon salt		Parsley, chopped
⅛	teaspoon sage		Sandwich buns
⅜	teaspoon oregano		

Preheat oven to 425 degrees.

Brown beef. Add bologna, salt, sage and oregano. Add spaghetti sauce and grated cheese. Place mixture on each half of bun and garnish with parsley and additional cheese. Bake 12-15 minutes.

Filling can be prepared ahead and frozen.

Judy Pelok

Tailgate Sandwich Crowns

6	red bell peppers	¼	cup balsamic vinegar
½	cup olive oil	2	small garlic cloves, minced
2	1½-pound round rye or pumpernickel loaves	¼	pound spinach leaves, trimmed
Honey mustard or Dijon mustard		12	provolone cheese slices
12	hard salami slices	12	thin red onion rings
		12	thin slices cooked turkey

Char peppers over gas flame or in broiler until blackened on all sides. Wrap in paper bag and let stand 10 minutes to steam. Peel and seed peppers. Rinse if necessary; pat dry. Cut into ¼-inch wide strips. Combine oil, vinegar and garlic in medium bowl. Add peppers and turn to coat. Marinate at least 1 hour at room temperature. (Can be prepared 1 day ahead, covered and refrigerated.) Drain peppers.

Using serrated knife, cut off tops of loaves and reserve. Remove insides of loaves and tops, leaving ½-inch shells. Spread inside of loaves and tops with thin layer of mustard. Place ½ of salami and spinach in each loaf. Add ¼ of peppers to each. Top with cheese and onion rings, then remaining peppers. Cover with turkey. Replace tops. Wrap each loaf in plastic and foil. Refrigerate overnight. Cut in wedges to serve.

Serves 12.

Gayle Burkhardt

Giacchini Zucchini

2	slices lowfat bread, toasted	Sliced mushrooms	
4	ounces cider vinegar	Sliced tomatoes	
Sliced onions		½	green bell pepper, sliced
Sliced zucchini		4	ounces cheese of your choice

Soak onions and zucchini in vinegar which has been sweetened with sugar substitute. Drain and layer each piece of toast with vegetables, top with cheese and place under broiler for 3-4 minutes.

Serves 2.

Mary Giacchini

Breads

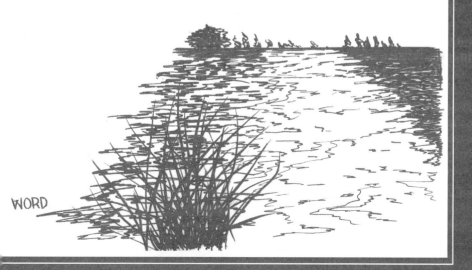

WORD

Banana Bran Muffins

1½ cups natural bran
1 cup all-purpose flour
1 teaspoon baking powder
1 teaspoon baking soda
¼ teaspoon salt
⅓ cup corn oil or vegetable oil

⅓ cup brown sugar
1 egg
2 medium size ripe bananas
¾ cup buttermilk, unflavored yogurt or sour cream
½ cup raisins

Preheat oven to 400 degrees.

Butter muffin pan or line with fluted baking cups.

Fit metal blade in food processor. Add bran, flour, baking powder, baking soda and salt. Process 3 seconds, remove from bowl and reserve.

Place oil, brown sugar and egg in bowl, blend 2 seconds, break bananas in pieces, add to mixture. Process till puréed, add buttermilk, yogurt or sour cream and blend.

Add flour mixture to banana mixture and blend 3 or 4 pulses. Add raisins. Dry ingredients should be just blended together with liquid, do not overprocess. Spoon mixture into prepared muffin cups and bake 20 minutes.

Yield: 12 muffins

Coconut, nuts, dry cranberries and wheat germ can be added. Egg substitute may also be used in place of the egg. Freeze well.

Louise M. Hamel

Pumpkin Bread

3 cups sugar
1 cup corn oil
5 eggs, beaten well
1 pound can pumpkin
3 cups flour
1 teaspoon baking powder

2 teaspoons baking soda
2 teaspoons salt
½ teaspoon ground cloves
1 teaspoon cinnamon
1 teaspoon nutmeg
⅔ teaspoon water

Preheat oven to 350 degrees.

Mix ingredients in order listed and put batter in greased and floured loaf pans. Will make 2 loaves using 9x5x3-inch pans or 3 loaves in smaller pans. Bake for 1 hour.

Mary Cassady

Toffee Coffee Cake

½	cup butter or margarine, softened	1	teaspoon baking soda
1	cup brown sugar, lightly packed	1	teaspoon vanilla
½	cup sugar	3-4	chocolate covered English toffee candy bars (1.4-ounce each), chopped
2	cups flour	¼	cup chopped pecans or walnuts
1	cup buttermilk		
1	egg		

Preheat oven to 350 degrees.
In a mixing bowl blend butter, sugars and flour; set aside ½ cup. To the remaining butter mixture, add buttermilk, egg, baking soda and vanilla; mix well. Pour into a greased and floured 13x9x2-inch baking pan. Combine chopped candy bars and pecans with reserved butter mixture; sprinkle over coffee cake. Bake for 30-35 minutes or until a toothpick inserted near the center comes out clean. Cool on a wire rack.
Serves 12 to 16.

Gwen Leathley

Cinnamon Pecan Coffee Cake

¾	cup margarine, softened	1½	teaspoons baking powder
1½	cups sugar	1½	teaspoons baking soda
3	eggs	¼	teaspoon salt
1½	teaspoons vanilla	1½	cups sour cream
3	cups all-purpose flour		

Filling:

½	cup brown sugar, packed	1½	teaspoons cinnamon
½	cup chopped pecans		

Mix together.
Preheat oven to 350 degrees. Grease tube pan.
Cream margarine and sugar thoroughly. Beat in eggs and vanilla. Stir flour, baking powder, baking soda and salt together. Mix into the creamed mixture alternating with sour cream. Spread ⅓ of the batter in prepared tube pan then sprinkle on ⅓ of the filling and repeat twice. Bake 1¼ hours. Cool about 10 minutes in pan before removing. Save a little of the filling to spread on top of cake.

Joan McKenzie

Old-Fashioned Orange Scones

2	cups all-purpose flour	½	cup dried currants
¼	cup sugar	1	teaspoon grated orange peel
1	tablespoon baking powder	1	egg
½	teaspoon salt	1	egg, separated
¼	cup (½ stick) chilled unsalted butter, cut into pieces	¾	cup whipping cream
			Sugar

Preheat oven to 400 degrees.
Combine first 4 ingredients in processor. Add butter and cut in using on/off turns until mixture resembles coarse meal. Transfer to large bowl. Mix in currants and orange peel. Beat 1 egg with yolk in small bowl. Whisk in cream. Add to flour-butter mixture and stir until dough pulls away from sides of bowl. Transfer dough out on lightly floured surface and knead gently until smooth. Roll dough out to thickness of 1 inch. Cut into 3-inch rounds using cookie cutter. Transfer rounds to large baking sheet, spacing 1 inch apart. Brush tops with egg white. Sprinkle lightly with sugar. Bake scones on ungreased baking pan until puffy and light brown, about 18 minutes.
Yield: 9

Mary Lou Deeney

Sour Cream Muffins

2	sticks melted butter	2	cups self-rising flour
1	cup sour cream		

Preheat oven to 400 degrees.
Fold sour cream into melted butter. Add flour. Drop by teaspoon into 2 ungreased mini-muffin tins. Bake for 15 minutes.
Yield: 24 muffins
Can be frozen after baking. Defrost and reheat on cookie sheet at 325 degrees.

Ginger Heussler

Condiments are like old friends, highly thought of, but often taken for granted.

Marilyn Kayton

Sour Cream Coffee Cake

2	cups sugar	2	cups all-purpose flour
2	sticks butter or margarine, softened	1	teaspoon baking powder
			Pinch salt
2	eggs	⅓	cup brown sugar
1	8-ounce carton sour cream	2	teaspoons cinnamon
1	teaspoon vanilla	¼	cup pecans, chopped

Preheat oven to 350 degrees.

Cream sugar, butter or margarine and eggs. Add sour cream and vanilla. Add flour, baking powder and salt. In separate bowl, mix together brown sugar, cinnamon and pecans. Put half of batter in greased Bundt pan, crumble half of brown sugar mixture over and cover with remaining batter. Sprinkle rest of brown sugar mixture on top. Bake for 60 minutes. Cool before turning out of pan. Freezes well. Serves 16.

Thelma Miller

Kathy's Cranberry Bread

2	cups sifted all-purpose flour	1	egg, beaten
1	cup sugar	1	teaspoon grated orange peel
1½	teaspoons baking powder	¾	cup orange juice
1	teaspoon salt	1½	cups fresh or frozen cranberries
½	teaspoon baking soda		
¼	cup butter or margarine		

Preheat oven to 350 degrees.

Sift flour, sugar, baking powder, salt and baking soda into a large bowl. Cut in butter until mixture is crumbly. Add egg, orange peel and orange juice all at once. Stir just until mixture is evenly moist. Fold in cranberries. Spoon bread into a greased 9x5x3-inch loaf pan. Bake for 1 hour and 10 minutes or until a toothpick comes out clean. Remove from pan and cool.

Mary Cassady

I do like a little bit of butter to my bread.

A. A. Milne

Whole Wheat Banana Bread

2	tablespoons butter or margarine, melted	1	cup all-purpose flour
1	cup sugar, white or brown or combination	½	teaspoon salt
		1	teaspoon baking soda
2	tablespoons applesauce	⅓	cup hot water
2	eggs, slightly beaten	1	cup whole wheat flour
3	medium sized bananas	½	cup chopped nuts, optional

Preheat oven to 325 degrees.

Melt butter; stir in sugar and applesauce. Mix in eggs and bananas, blend until smooth. Add white flour, salt and baking soda. Alternately add hot water and whole wheat flour, ending with flour. Stir in nuts. Save a few for sprinkling on top. Turn into 9x5-inch loaf pans. Bake 1 hour and 10 minutes. Cool well before storing in plastic bags. Store in refrigerator. Freezes well.

If you prefer not to use applesauce, increase the amount of butter to 4 tablespoons.

Linda Torpie

Sour Cream Coffee Cake

¾	cup margarine	½	teaspoon vanilla
1½	cups sugar	¼	teaspoon salt
2	eggs	1	teaspoon baking powder
1	cup sour cream	2	cups flour

In separate bowl, mix well for topping:

2	tablespoons margarine	½	cup nuts
4	tablespoons brown sugar	½	teaspoon cinnamon

Preheat oven to 350 degrees. Grease Bundt pan.

Mix margarine and sugar together and beat well. Add eggs, sour cream and vanilla. Add dry ingredients and blend well. Pour ½ of batter into pan. Sprinkle with ½ of topping and repeat with batter and topping. Bake 45 minutes.

Robin Pulaski

Banana Or Zucchini Bread

2	cups sugar	1	teaspoon baking soda
3	cups sifted flour	3	teaspoons cinnamon
1	teaspoon salt	½	teaspoon baking powder
3	lightly beaten eggs	2	cups mashed bananas or
1	cup vegetable oil		grated, peeled zucchini
3	teaspoons vanilla		

Preheat oven to 350 degrees.

Combine dry ingredients and set aside. Mix together the eggs, oil, vanilla, bananas or zucchini and add to the dry ingredients. Pour batter equally into 2 greased 5x9x3-inch baking pans. Bake for 1 hour.

Shredded coconut and/or sliced almonds can be sprinkled on top of each loaf before baking.

Sue Barnett

Blueberry-Nut Bread

1	cup whole wheat flour	1	egg, beaten
1	cup all-purpose flour	1	tablespoon grated orange
1	cup sugar		rind
1½	teaspoons baking powder	¼	cup orange juice
½	teaspoon baking soda	¾	cup boiling water
¼	teaspoon salt	1	cup fresh blueberries
2	tablespoons butter or	¼	cup pecans
	margarine, melted		

Preheat oven to 350 degrees.

In a large bowl, combine the flours, sugar, baking powder, baking soda and salt. Add the butter or margarine and the beaten egg to the flour mixture, stirring the ingredients to combine. In a small bowl or measuring cup combine the orange rind, orange juice and water. Add the juice mixture to the flour mixture stirring the ingredients until they are just combined. Stir in the blueberries and nuts and transfer the batter to a greased 9x5-inch loaf pan. Bake for 50-60 minutes or until a tester inserted into the center of the bread comes out clean.

Joyce Glenn

Saranne's Morning Muffins

½ cup sugar
¼ cup brown sugar

¼ cup applesauce
¼ cup oil

2 eggs

1 teaspoon vanilla

1 cup flour
2 teaspoons baking soda
¼ teaspoon salt

1 tablespoon cinnamon
Pinch of nutmeg
Pinch of cloves

¾ cup grated carrots
¾ cup grated zucchini
½ cup walnuts

⅓ cup raisins
½ cup coconut

Preheat oven to 350 degrees.
Beat together first four ingredients. Add eggs and vanilla. Blend in dry ingredients. Carefully add carrots, zucchini, walnuts, raisins and coconut. Fill well-greased muffin pans and bake 20 minutes.
Yield: 16 muffins

Sue Barnett

Orange Nut Bread

1 large orange
Boiling water
1 cup raisins or dates
1 teaspoon baking soda
1 cup sugar
2 tablespoons butter

1 teaspoon vanilla
1 egg, beaten
2 cups flour
1 teaspoon baking powder
¼ teaspoon salt
½ cup chopped nuts

Preheat oven to 350 degrees.
Squeeze juice from orange; combine with boiling water to equal one cup. Add raisins or dates, baking soda, sugar, butter and vanilla. Cool. Add beaten egg. Add sifted dry ingredients. Beat thoroughly and add nuts. Bake in a 9-inch greased loaf pan for about 50 minutes. Cover with foil for the last 10 minutes to insure doneness. Partially cool in the pan. May be frozen.

Joan Pierce

Strawberry Bread With Spread

3	cups flour	2	10-ounce packages frozen
1	teaspoon baking soda		strawberries, thawed and
1	teaspoon cinnamon		sliced, reserve juice
2	cups sugar	1¼	cups vegetable oil
1	teaspoon salt	4	eggs, well-beaten
		1	cup chopped pecans

Preheat oven to 350 degrees.
Reserve ½ cup strawberry juice for Spread. Mix all dry ingredients together. Make a hole in the center of mixture. Pour strawberries, oil and eggs into the hole. Mix by hand until all ingredients are thoroughly combined. Stir in the chopped pecans. Pour into two greased and floured 9x5x3-inch pans. Bake for 40-60 minutes.

SPREAD

½	cup strawberry juice	1	8-ounce package cream cheese, softened

Place juice and cream cheese in blender. Process until spreading consistency. Spread on cooled bread.

Pat Dickinson

Hush Puppies

2	cups cornmeal	2	tablespoons bacon fat
2	teaspoons baking powder	1	egg
1	teaspoon salt	⅔	cup milk
1	whole onion, minced	6	cups peanut oil

Mix cornmeal, baking powder and salt. Sauté onion in bacon fat until just limp; cool slightly. Beat egg until light, stir in milk and onion. Stir into dry ingredients to form a stiff batter. Heat oil in deep fryer to 350 degrees. Shape batter into 3-inch long crescents. Fry in single layer batches in hot oil until golden brown. Serve hot with fried fish.
Serves 6.

Charles D'Ablaing
Chef, The Landings Club

Ever Ready Bran Muffins

1	15-ounce box of bran cereal with raisins	1	teaspoon salt
		1	cup vegetable oil
2½	cups sugar	1	quart buttermilk
3	cups whole wheat flour	4	eggs, beaten
5	teaspoons baking soda		

Preheat oven to 400 degrees.

Mix cereal, sugar, flour, soda and salt together. Add salad oil, buttermilk and eggs. Store covered batter in refrigerator. Mixture will keep 6 or 7 weeks. To bake, fill greased muffin pans and cook for 20 minutes.

Grated carrots, chopped walnuts or additional raisins may be added.

Julie Barrett

Date Nut Loaf

1	cup chopped dates	2	eggs, well-beaten
1	teaspoon baking soda	2	cups flour
1	cup boiling water	1	teaspoon baking powder
½	cup vegetable shortening	½	cup chopped nuts
1	cup brown sugar	1	teaspoon rum flavoring

Preheat oven to 325 degrees.

Combine dates, baking soda, and boiling water. Allow to cool, and then drain, reserving liquid. Cream shortening and sugar with eggs. Beat well. Sift dry ingredients. Add alternately with liquid drained from date mixture. Beat well. Add dates, nuts and flavoring. Mix thoroughly. Bake for 45 minutes in greased loaf pan.

Serve with Lemon Sauce.

LEMON SAUCE

½	cup sugar	1½	teaspoons lemon juice
1	teaspoon cornstarch		Pinch of salt
1	cup boiling water		Dash nutmeg
3	tablespoons butter		

Combine sugar and cornstarch. Add boiling water. Stir constantly. Blend in other ingredients. Boil until slightly thickened.

Pat Dickinson

Boston Brown Bread

⅔	cup sifted all-purpose flour	⅓	cup yellow cornmeal (not
¼	teaspoon salt		stone-ground)
½	teaspoon baking powder	⅓	cup dark molasses
½	teaspoon baking soda	1	cup buttermilk
½	cup unsifted whole wheat	½	cup seedless raisins
	flour (not stone-ground)		

Sift all-purpose flour with salt, baking powder and soda into a mixing bowl. Add all remaining ingredients except raisins and beat with an electric mixer 30 seconds until well blended; stir in raisins. Spoon half mixture into a lightly greased 1-pint glass measuring cup. Cover with vented plastic food wrap and microwave on MEDIUM (50%) power 5½ to 6 minutes, rotating measuring cup 180 degrees at half the baking time, until toothpick inserted in center of bread comes out clean. (Do not use a turntable; it will make loaf "mushroom" in the middle.) Uncover and let stand 5 minutes to complete cooking. Invert and ease loaf onto platter. Cool 5 minutes. Meanwhile, microwave remaining batter in the same way. Slice loaves ½ inch thick and serve slightly warm. This bread will firm up after a day or so and can be cut more easily and thinly. Makes 2 small loaves. Spread with Lemon Cheese Curd.

Lemon Cheese (Curd)

⅔	cup fresh lemon juice	1	cup unsalted butter (no
3	tablespoons lemon rind,		substitute)
	finely grated	4	eggs
2	cups sugar		

Mix lemon juice, lemon rind and sugar in a 2-quart casserole. Add butter; cover with wax paper and microwave on HIGH (100% power) for 4½-5 minutes, whisking after 2 minutes until sugar dissolves and butter melts; whisk again. Beat eggs until frothy; blend in about ½ cup hot lemon mixture; stir back into casserole and whisk well. Cover with wax paper and microwave on MEDIUM (50% power) 4½-5 minutes, whisking every 2 minutes until thick as mayonnaise.

Note: Do not boil or it will curdle. If edges begin to bubble at any time, reduce power to MEDIUM-LOW (30% power) immediately. When lemon curd is done, whisk well, ladle into hot, sterilized, half-pint preserving jars. Cover, cool to room temperature and store in refrigerator.

Elaine Stahl

Cranberry-Orange Scones

2	cups all-purpose flour	½	cup unsalted butter, cut up
1	tablespoon baking powder	⅔	cup buttermilk
½	teaspoon baking soda	1	cup dried cranberries
¼	teaspoon salt	1	tablespoon milk
2	tablespoons sugar	1	tablespoon sugar
1	tablespoon grated orange rind		

Preheat oven to 425 degrees.

Combine first 6 ingredients; cut in butter with a pastry blender until mixture is crumbly. Add buttermilk and dried cranberries, stirring just until moistened. Turn dough out onto a lightly floured surface; knead 5 or 6 times. Pat into an 8-inch circle. Cut into 8 wedges and place 1-inch apart on a lightly greased baking sheet. Brush with milk and sprinkle with sugar. Bake for 15 minutes or until scones are golden brown.

Serves 8.

Mary Lou Deeney

Best Biscuit Recipe

2	cups sifted all-purpose flour	2	teaspoons sugar
4	teaspoons baking powder	½	cup vegetable shortening
½	teaspoon salt	⅔	cup milk
½	teaspoon cream of tartar		

Preheat oven to 450 degrees.

Sift together flour, baking powder, salt, cream of tartar and sugar. Cut in shortening until mixture resembles coarse crumbs. Add milk all at once and stir only until dough follows fork around the bowl. Turn out on lightly floured surface and knead gently for 30 seconds. Pat or roll out to a ½-inch thickness and cut with a biscuit cutter or a glass. Bake on ungreased pan for 10 to 12 minutes.

Can be used for shortcake, serve while warm topped with berries and whipped cream.

Carole Michna

Morning Glory Muffins

2	cups flour	1	apple, peeled and grated
1	cup sugar	½	cup raisins
2	teaspoons baking soda	½	cup chopped pecans
2	teaspoons cinnamon	3	eggs, lightly beaten
½	teaspoon salt	1	cup vegetable oil
2	cups grated carrots	2	teaspoons vanilla

Preheat oven to 350 degrees.
Grease 18 muffin cups or use paper liners.
Sift first five ingredients into large bowl. Stir in carrots, apple, raisins and nuts. Mix in eggs, oil and vanilla. Fill muffin cups with batter and bake 20-25 minutes.

Ingrid VanderVliet

Aunt Vic Daddario's Biscuits

4	teaspoons baking powder	6	tablespoons shortening
4	tablespoons sugar	1	egg
2	cups flour	½-⅔	cup milk
Salt, optional		1	tablespoon vanilla

Preheat oven to 400 degrees.
Mix dry ingredients, cut in shortening. Combine egg with milk and vanilla and add to dry mixture. Drop by spoonfuls on greased cookie sheet. Bake about 12-15 minutes.
Use milk with discretion. If batter is too "wet," crunchy peaks do not form.

Mary Giacchini

*B*read deals with living things, with giving life, with growth, with the seed, the grain that nurtures. It is not coincidence that we say bread is the staff of life.

Lionel Poilane

Banana Bread

2	tablespoons margarine		Pinch of salt
⅔	cup granulated sugar	3	large ripe bananas, mashed
¾	cup packed dark brown sugar	⅓	cup milk mixed with 1 teaspoon lemon juice
2	eggs, lightly beaten	1	teaspoon vanilla
3	cups all-purpose flour	⅔	cup pitted dates, chopped
1	teaspoon baking powder	1	cup walnuts, roughly chopped
1	teaspoon baking soda		
½	teaspoon ground cinnamon		

Preheat oven to 300 degrees.

Grease two 7x3-inch loaf pans with additional 1 tablespoon of margarine.

Beat the 2 tablespoons of margarine with the white and brown sugars and eggs in a large bowl with an electric mixer until light and creamy. Sift the flour, baking powder, soda, cinnamon and salt together in a separate bowl. Gradually add the sifted flour mixture to the creamed mixture, beating thoroughly after each addition of flour. Stir in the bananas, milk, vanilla, dates and walnuts. Divide the mixture between the loaf pans and bake in the center of the oven for about 1 hour, or until a skewer inserted into the center of the loaves comes out clean. Remove from the oven, run a knife around the inside of the pans and invert the loaves onto a wire rack to cool. Serve spread with butter.

Makes 2 loaves.

Oscar Mejia
Executive Chef
The Landings Club

Cornmeal Pancakes

1	cup white cornmeal	½	cup milk
2	tablespoons vegetable shortening	2	beaten eggs
		1	teaspoon salt
Water		2	teaspoons baking powder

Mix cornmeal and shortening. Moisten with enough water to make mush. Add milk, eggs, salt and baking powder. Mix well. Fry in a little oil just as with regular pancakes, turning only once.

Yield: 8 to 9 pancakes

Nice to serve with fish or soup.

Joan McKenzie

106

Salads & Salad Dressings

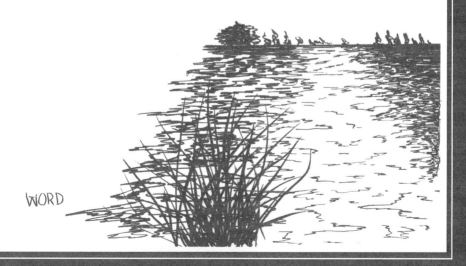

WORD

Bean Salad

1	16-ounce can kidney beans	½	cup chopped celery
1	16-ounce can pinto beans	¾	cup olive oil
1	16-ounce can yellow niblet corn	3	tablespoons vinegar
1	16-ounce can chickpeas	1	crushed clove of garlic
½	cup chopped scallions	½	teaspoon salt
1	small green bell pepper, chopped		Dash of pepper
		2	tablespoons Chianti or other red wine

Drain and rinse the beans, corn and chickpeas. In a large bowl, combine them with scallions, green pepper and celery. Mix the remaining ingredients well and pour over bean mixture. Toss well to coat. Cover and refrigerate for several hours or overnight.

Serves 10 to 12.

Chris Savage

Chinese Noodle Tuna Salad

2	6- or 7-ounce cans of white tuna, drained	1	cup celery, sliced or chopped
1	10-ounce package frozen peas, uncooked		
¾-1	cup mayonnaise	⅛	teaspoon garlic salt
½	teaspoon curry powder, or more to taste	1	tablespoon lemon juice
		1	3-ounce can Chinese noodles

Mix in a medium bowl, flaked tuna, frozen peas which have been broken apart, and celery. Cover and chill.

In another bowl combine mayonnaise, curry, garlic salt and lemon juice. Chill separately. Just before serving mix the tuna combination with mayonnaise dressing and add the Chinese noodles.

Ginger Heussler

It isn't so much what's on the table that matters, as what's on the chairs.

108   W. S. Gilbert

Tortellini Salad

1	16-ounce package cheese-filled tortellini, cooked	1	cup fresh pea pods, blanched (boil a minute, drain and put into ice water)
½	cup Parmesan cheese	½	teaspoon salt
	Cherry tomatoes, halved		Dash of pepper

Combine ingredients adding Mustard-Basil Vinaigrette Dressing when ready to serve.
Serves 6.

MUSTARD-BASIL VINAIGRETTE

½	cup olive oil	1	teaspoon dried dill weed, crumbled
3	tablespoons white wine vinegar	2	tablespoons finely chopped shallots or green onions
2½	tablespoons Dijon mustard	1	large clove garlic, minced
3	tablespoons or more finely chopped basil	½	teaspoon sugar

Mix all together and chill in refrigerator until ready to serve.

Sandy Trice

Strawberry Spinach Salad

½	cup sugar	1	tablespoon poppy seeds
2	tablespoons sesame seeds	½	teaspoon minced onion
¼	teaspoon Worcestershire sauce	½	cup vegetable oil
¼	teaspoon paprika	¼	cup cider vinegar or raspberry wine vinegar

Blend first six ingredients in blender. Slowly add oil and vinegar. Pour over spinach and strawberries.

2	bunches spinach	1	pint strawberries, sliced

Jan Hazel

109

Texas Spiced Beans

1	16-ounce can garbanzo beans	6	green onions, sliced
1	15-ounce can red kidney beans	¼	cup parsley, chopped
1	16-ounce can pinto beans	2	celery ribs, sliced
1	12-ounce can whole kernel corn, drained	1	4-ounce can chopped green chiles, drained

Drain beans and rinse with water. Drain again. Transfer to bowl and mix with corn, green onions, parsley, celery and green chiles. Pour Dressing over, toss, cover and refrigerate 6 hours.

DRESSING

¾	cup olive oil or vegetable oil	1	teaspoon chili sauce
¼	cup wine vinegar	1	teaspoon oregano
1	garlic clove, minced	¼	teaspoon cumin
½	tablespoon salt	⅛	teaspoon hot pepper sauce

Mary Ellen Fox

Orzo Salad

1	cup orzo	1	large tomato, chopped
1	cup feta cheese, diced	⅓	cup salad oil
3	tablespoons parsley, chopped	½	cup fresh lemon juice
3	tablespoons fresh dill, chopped	½	teaspoon salt
		¼	teaspoon pepper

Cook orzo according to package directions. Drain and rinse with cold water. Add feta, parsley, dill and tomato. In a covered jar combine oil, lemon juice, salt and pepper. Shake well. Pour this mixture over salad and toss. Refrigerate until chilled. Toss again before serving.

Serves 8.

Lynda Ibach

H e who flatters the cook never goes hungry.

Old Proverb

Herb & Roasted Pepper Salad

6	red, yellow and/or green sweet bell peppers	2	tablespoons snipped fresh basil or 1 teaspoon dried, crushed
½	cup sliced pitted ripe olives		
3	tablespoons olive oil	1	tablespoon snipped fresh oregano or 1 teaspoon dried, crushed
2	tablespoons balsamic vinegar		
2	tablespoons sliced green onions	¼	teaspoon pepper
			Lettuce leaves
2	tablespoons drained capers	¼	cup crumbled feta cheese
2	cloves garlic, minced		

Preheat oven to 425 degrees.

To roast peppers, quarter lengthwise. Remove stems and seeds. Cut small slits in ends so pieces lie flat. Place skin sides up, on a foil-lined baking sheet. Bake for 20-25 minutes or until skins are dark and bubbly. Place in a clean paper bag. Close the bag tightly; cool to room temperature. Remove skins; cut peppers into strips.

Combine pepper strips, olives, oil, vinegar, onion, capers, garlic, basil, oregano and pepper in a bowl; toss to coat. Cover and chill up to 24 hours. Serve on lettuce leaves. Top with feta.

Serves 8.

Dorothy Pero

Salad Of Pine Nuts & Avocados

Combine in bowl:

	Mixed greens	2	tablespoons pine nuts, toasted
1	avocado, peeled and cubed		
2	plum tomatoes, sliced	1	tablespoon cilantro, minced

Whisk together and pour over salad:

1	tablespoon white wine vinegar	1	teaspoon honey
		1	clove garlic, crushed
2	teaspoons Dijon mustard	3	tablespoons olive oil

Serves 4.

Mary Schoenwald

111

Three Green Salad With Warm Brie

Deer tongue lettuce
Buttercrunch lettuce
Oak leaf lettuce

8   wedges of Brie cheese, each
    about 4-inches long and
    1-inch wide at base
Lemon Olive Oil Dressing

Preheat oven to 350 degrees.

Tear lettuce into large bowl. Whisk dressing over greens and toss well. Divide among serving plates. Arrange Brie on baking sheet and bake until warmed but not runny, about 1 minute. Top each salad with wedge of cheese and serve immediately.

Serves 8.

Any variety of crisp, fresh lettuce may be substituted.

LEMON OLIVE OIL DRESSING

$\frac{2}{3}$ cup light olive oil
$\frac{1}{3}$ cup lemon juice

Salt and freshly ground
white pepper

Combine light olive oil, lemon juice, salt and pepper and whisk to blend well. Allow to stand at least 1 hour at room temperature.

Jerriann Kirkwood

Cashew Pea Salad

1   10-ounce package frozen
    peas, thawed and drained
6   strips of bacon, cooked crisp,
    drained and crumbled

1   cup coarsely chopped
    cashews
$\frac{1}{2}$ cup chopped celery
$\frac{1}{2}$ cup sour cream
$\frac{1}{2}$ teaspoon salt

Mix all ingredients together and chill thoroughly. Serve as stuffing for tomatoes or spooned over thick slices of tomato. Garnish with additional chopped cashews.

Yield: 4 cups

Donna Eamon

Cobb Salad With French Dressing

6	cups lettuce, shredded	6	slices bacon, cooked crisp
3	cups cooked chicken, shredded		and crumbled
2	medium tomatoes, seeded and chopped	1	medium avocado, cut into wedges
3	ounces blue cheese, crumbled	1	small Belgian endive (optional)

Place lettuce on six individual dishes. Evenly divide rest of ingredients and top with French Dressing.

FRENCH DRESSING

In a screw top jar combine:

⅓	cup red wine vinegar	½	teaspoon pepper
1	tablespoon lemon juice	½	teaspoon sugar
1	teaspoon Worcestershire sauce	½	teaspoon dry mustard
½	teaspoon salt	1	clove garlic, minced

Cover and shake well to mix.
Add ½ cup olive oil and shake well. Chill before serving.

Priss Wentworth

German Potato Salad

⅔	cup white vinegar, divided	¼	cup sugar
1	medium onion	1	tablespoon salt
⅓	cup canola oil	3	pounds small red potatoes

Place ⅓ cup vinegar and onion, cut in pieces, in food processor and process until onion is well grated. Pour into large bowl and add oil, ⅓ cup vinegar, sugar and salt. Boil potatoes in skins. Do not overcook. Cool, skin while still warm and slice thinly into the large bowl of dressing. Toss lightly. Keep at room temperature at least 2 hours before serving.
Serves 8.

Marie Scheuermann

113

Tomatoes Stuffed With Shrimp

6	large, ripe, round, meaty tomatoes	1½	tablespoons capers, the tinier the better
¾	pound small shrimp	1	teaspoon strong mustard, Dijon or German
1	tablespoon red wine vinegar		Parsley
Salt			
½	cup mayonnaise		

Cut off stem end of tomato and hollow out. Invert the tomatoes to drain for 20 minutes. Rinse the shrimp in cold water. Add vinegar and salt to 2 quarts of water and bring to a boil. Drop in the shrimp and cook for just 2 minutes after the water returns to a boil. Drain, peel and devein the shrimp and set aside to cool. Pick out six of the best looking, best shaped shrimp and set them aside. Chop the rest of the shrimp roughly. Put them in a bowl and mix the chopped shrimp with the mayonnaise, capers and mustard. Shake off the excess liquid from the tomatoes but don't squeeze them. Stuff to the top with the shrimp and mayonnaise mixture. Garnish each tomato with a shrimp and one or two parsley leaves. Serve at cool room temperature or slightly chilled.

Serves 6.

Alden Mead

Lemon Yogurt Salad

2	3-ounce packages lemon-flavored gelatin	½	cup cold water
1½	cups hot water	2	8-ounce cartons pineapple yogurt

Dissolve lemon gelatin in hot water; add cold water. Refrigerate until liquid starts to thicken, add yogurt and mix well. Return to refrigerator. When ready to serve, unmold and decorate to suit or sprinkle graham cracker crumbs on top.

Serves 8 to 12.

If pineapple yogurt is not available, use plain or vanilla plus one small can drained crushed pineapple.

Marie Jones

he greatest dishes are very simple dishes.

Escoffier

Mandarin Orange Tossed Salad

1	head leaf lettuce, torn	1	11-ounce can Mandarin
3	stalks celery, thinly sliced		orange sections, drained
4	green onions, sliced		Vinaigrette Dressing
			Caramelized Almonds

Combine first four ingredients in a salad bowl; cover and chill up to 3 hours. Just before serving, toss with Vinaigrette Dressing and sprinkle with Caramelized Almonds.

Serves 6 to 8.

VINAIGRETTE DRESSING

¼	cup vegetable oil	½	teaspoon salt
2	tablespoons sugar	¼	teaspoon pepper
1	tablespoon white vinegar	6	drops hot sauce

Combine all ingredients and chill. Stir well before serving.

Yield: ⅓ cup

CARAMELIZED ALMONDS

¼	cup slivered almonds	2	tablespoons sugar

Combine ingredients in a heavy saucepan. Cook over medium heat, stirring constantly, until golden. Pour onto waxed paper; cool. Break into pieces and store in an airtight container.

Yield: ¼ cup

Norma Shaw
Lois Flanagan

Georgia Pecan Turkey Salad

2½	cups cooked turkey, very finely minced	½	teaspoon celery salt
		⅔	cup mayonnaise
½	cup chopped pecans		Salt and freshly ground black
¼	cup sweet pickle relish		pepper

Mix turkey, pecans, relish and celery salt together. Fold in the mayonnaise. Season to taste with salt and pepper and serve.

Serves 4.

Elayne Blecker

115

Orzo Salad With Tomatoes, Basil & Feta

½	cup pine nuts	½	cup olive oil
3	cups orzo		Pepper, to taste
3	Roma tomatoes, peeled, seeded and diced	1¼	cups feta cheese, crumbled
¼	cup parsley, finely chopped	½	cup fresh basil, finely chopped
¼	cup fresh lemon juice		

Toast pine nuts under broiler for 2 minutes or until lightly browned. Remove. Bring a large pot of water to a boil. Add orzo and cook 6-8 minutes. Drain and rinse under cold water. Pour cooked orzo into a bowl. Add tomatoes and parsley to the orzo. In a small bowl, mix together lemon juice and olive oil. Add pepper for seasoning. Pour dressing over orzo and stir. Cover and refrigerate at least 30 minutes. When ready to serve, add feta cheese, basil and pine nuts to orzo and stir. Serves 10.

Mary Schoenwald

Rich Potato Salad

10	medium-size potatoes, unpeeled	5	tablespoons sour cream
7	hard-cooked eggs, chopped	8	tablespoons Miracle Whip
1	medium-size onion, chopped	3	tablespoons white or cider vinegar
2	ribs celery, chopped		Salt and pepper, to taste
12	pimiento stuffed green olives, chopped		Paprika for garnish

Boil potatoes in water until tender. Cool, peel and dice. Place potatoes, eggs, onion, celery and olives in a large bowl. Combine sour cream, Miracle Whip, vinegar, salt and pepper; pour over potato mixture and gently toss. Sprinkle with paprika. Serves 8.

Irene Washenko

According to the Spanish proverb, four persons are wanted to make a good salad: a spendthrift for oil, a miser for vinegar, a counsellor for salt, and a madman to stir it all up.

116   Abraham Hayward

Cabbage Salad

1	pound of packaged cabbage slaw mix	2	small packages sunflower kernels
2	packages beef flavored ramen noodles, broken in fine pieces	1	cup slivered almonds
		1	bunch chopped green onions

Mix all ingredients together and toss with dressing just before serving. *Angel hair cabbage slaw is recommended if available. Broccoli slaw would also be good.*

DRESSING

1	cup oil	1	package of seasoning from ramen noodles
½	cup sugar		
⅓	cup white vinegar		

Mix all ingredients together and heat, dissolving sugar. Let cool before using over salad.

Dottie Strickler

Garbage Bag Salad

2	heads cauliflower cut in bite-size pieces	2-3	ribs celery cut in bite-size pieces
2	boxes cherry tomatoes	2	cans button mushrooms, drained
1	bunch broccoli cut in bite-size pieces	1	8-ounce bottle Italian dressing
3-4	carrots, julienned		
8	scallions, chopped		

Put everything in a double plastic kitchen trash bag. Refrigerate and turn several times during 12 to 24 hours.
Easily increased for a party.

Mary Ellen Fox

Festive Romaine Salad

Romaine lettuce		1	pint fresh strawberries,
½	red onion, sliced and separated into rings		sliced

Combine all ingredients in large bowl and toss with Dressing.
Serves 6 to 8.

DRESSING

⅓	cup sugar	¼	cup milk
2	tablespoons poppy seeds	2	tablespoons vinegar
¾	cup mayonnaise		

Combine all dressing ingredients in small bowl; mix well.

Carol Foster

Asparagus Water Chestnut Salad

2	packages unflavored gelatin	1	cup green asparagus, chopped and drained
½	cup water		
¾	cup sugar	1	can water chestnuts, chopped
½	teaspoon salt		
1	cup water	1	cup chopped celery
½	cup white vinegar	1	teaspoon grated onion
¼	cup chopped pimientos		Juice of 1 lemon

Dissolve gelatin in ½ cup water. Set aside. Boil sugar, salt, water and vinegar together. Add softened gelatin. Chill until partially set. Add well-drained pimientos, asparagus and water chestnuts. Fold in celery, onion and lemon juice. Pour into mold and chill until firm. Serve with or without mayonnaise. Prepare a day before serving.
Serves 8 to 10.

Betty Childs

It took a Civil War, the circus and baseball to spark a national appetite for peanuts.

P. C. King, Jr., *The Chattahooche River*

Embassy Cauliflower Salad

2   heads cauliflower
1   bunch spring onions, sliced
Salt and pepper, to taste

½   cup blue cheese, crumbled
Bibb or Boston lettuce

DRESSING

1   cup sour cream
1   cup mayonnaise

1   package cheese garlic salad
    dressing mix

Slice cauliflower florets vertically. Add sliced onions, salt, pepper and cheese. Combine Dressing ingredients and mix with cauliflower. Place in center of bed of lettuce. Vegetables and Dressing can be made in advance and combined before serving.

Serves 8 to 10.

Robbie Forester

A Slightly Different Salad

2¾ cups corn kernels, cut from
     fresh ears or use frozen
     white corn
1   pint grape tomatoes

4   ribs celery, finely sliced
½   red onion, finely sliced
1   large package Italian mix
    salad greens

Toss all ingredients together, mixing well.

DRESSING

2   tablespoons balsamic vinegar
⅓   cup olive oil

1   cup crumbled blue cheese,
    reserve ¼ cup

Mix dressing ingredients together until thoroughly blended. Pour over salad ingredients and let stand 2 or 3 hours. Just before serving, sprinkle remaining ¼ cup blue cheese over salad and serve.

Serves 6 to 8.

Sandra Williams

Broccoli Salad

2   large bunches broccoli
1   cup mayonnaise
2   tablespoons raspberry
    vinegar
¼   cup sugar

¼   cup red onion, chopped
½   pound bacon, cooked and
    crumbled
1   cup shredded cheddar
    cheese

Wash broccoli and use only buds, discarding stems. Combine mayonnaise, vinegar and sugar, mixing well with wire whisk. Place broccoli, onion, bacon and cheese in separate bowl. Pour dressing over and mix well. Refrigerate. Stir several times during the day. Best made early in the day you plan to serve it.

Serves 6 to 8.

Barbara Hampton

Diner Health Salad

2   carrots, grated
3   cucumbers, cut lengthwise
    and sliced thin

1   green bell pepper, put strips
    through slicer
2   pounds shredded cabbage
1   red onion, grated

Mix together:

¾   cup white vinegar
½   cup oil
¼   cup water

¼   cup sugar
Salt and pepper, to taste

Mix dressing and pour over prepared vegetables. Refrigerate in covered bowl stirring several times while salad is marinating. Make at least one day before serving. Flavor improves the longer it marinates.

Serves 20 to 30.

Preparing the vegetables is easier if you use a food processor. Balsamic vinegar or red vinegar can be substituted for half of the white vinegar.

Beth Roth

he taste of an olive is older than meat, older than wine.

Laurence Durrell

Spinach-Pear Salad

3	cups fresh baby spinach or arugula, washed and dried	2	tablespoons blue cheese, crumbled
3	yellow pears, medium ripe, cored but not peeled, sliced lengthwise		

DRESSING

2	tablespoons balsamic vinegar	1	clove garlic, crushed
3	tablespoons olive oil	½	cup walnuts, toasted and chopped
3	tablespoons orange juice		
Salt, to taste			

Place spinach or arugula, pears and cheese in a salad bowl. Whisk together Dressing ingredients except walnuts. Dress salad and sprinkle warm walnuts over it and serve.

Serves 4.

Toast chopped walnuts for 5 minutes in 325 degree oven just before serving salad.

Nancy Canadé

Sauerkraut Salad

1	27-ounce can sauerkraut, undrained	2	cups chopped celery
1	cup chopped onion	1	jar chopped pimiento, drained
1	cup chopped green bell pepper		
2	cups sugar	¼	cup vegetable oil
½	cup cider vinegar	½	teaspoon marjoram
1	teaspoon salt		

Mix the last 5 ingredients and combine with vegetables. Refrigerate at least 4 hours, stirring occasionally.

Katie Wood

121

Spinach Bacon Salad

10	ounces fresh spinach	3	hard-cooked eggs, sliced
4	fresh mushrooms, sliced		¼-inch thick
6	slices bacon, fried crisp and crumbled		

Rinse spinach in cold water, removing any damaged leaves; tear into bite-size pieces. Combine mushrooms and bacon with spinach. Add Dressing and toss. Garnish with egg slices.

Serves 6.

DRESSING

2	teaspoons grated onion	2	teaspoons Dijon mustard
1	teaspoon salt	2	tablespoons wine vinegar
½	teaspoon pepper, freshly ground	8	tablespoons olive oil
		½	teaspoon lemon juice

Combine onion, salt, pepper and mustard in mixing bowl. Add vinegar and then beat in olive oil, one tablespoon at a time, until smooth; stir in lemon juice.

Helen Lantz

Strawberry & Spinach Salad

Fresh spinach	Fresh dill
Strawberries	Sesame seeds
Red onion	

All ingredient amounts are at the discretion of the cook. (A generous amount of dill is recommended.) Combine, adding sesame seeds just before serving.

DRESSING

1	cup oil	½	cup red wine vinegar
1	clove garlic, minced	2	teaspoons salt
3	tablespoons sugar		

Combine dressing ingredients in food processor and mix well. Will keep in the refrigerator for a couple of weeks.

Pat Palmer

Marco Polo Salad

½	pound spaghetti	½	cup grated Parmesan
¼-⅓	cup olive oil		cheese
2-3	cloves fresh garlic, crushed	¼	pound Jarlsberg cheese,
1	teaspoon oregano		julienned
1	teaspoon basil	¼	cup chopped walnuts
½	teaspoon salt	½-1	green bell pepper, julienned
½	teaspoon pepper		or sliced
½	teaspoon garlic powder	½-1	red bell pepper, julienned
⅓	cup fresh parsley, chopped		or sliced
½	cup black olives, drained	3	tablespoons white vinegar
	and sliced		

Cook spaghetti and drain. Warm olive oil with garlic. Pour oil over spaghetti and mix carefully. Set aside to cool or chill. In a separate bowl mix together all the spices, peppers, parsley, olives, cheeses, walnuts and vinegar. Mix with spaghetti until well-blended. Chill before serving.
Serves 4.

Arlene Gilligan

Spinach Salad

1	package fresh spinach	½	large red onion, cut in slices
1	cup sliced mushrooms	8	slices bacon, fried crisp and
1	can mandarin oranges,		crumbled
	drained	3	hard-cooked eggs (optional)

Wash spinach and dry well. Tear into bite-size pieces. Mix first four ingredients. Garnish with bacon and egg.

DRESSING

1	cup vegetable oil	¼	cup cider vinegar
¾	cup sugar	1	tablespoon Worcestershire
⅓	cup ketchup		sauce

Dressing may be made in blender. Keeps well in refrigerator.

Melissa Parrish

Rice Salad

¾	cup water	¾	cup canned sliced
¾	cup Italian dressing		mushrooms, drained
1½	cups minute rice	6	tablespoons scallions
1	pound green peas, canned or	6	tablespoons sliced green
	frozen – cook, drain and cool		olives
	if frozen	1	cup mayonnaise, or less
¾	cup cucumber, peeled,		
	seeded and diced		

Boil water and Italian dressing; add rice and cook. Add prepared vegetables. Fold in enough mayonnaise to bind salad together.

Serves 6 to 8.

Barbara Burney

Savory Broccoli Salad

Fresh broccoli buds to cover the bottom of 9x13-inch pan

Cook broccoli buds 3-4 minutes. Rinse in cold water and drain. Set aside.

1	cup olive oil	2	teaspoons dry mustard
6	tablespoons red wine vinegar	1	teaspoon basil
1	teaspoon salt		Fresh ground pepper
2	cloves garlic, crushed		

Mix above ingredients together to make marinade. Arrange broccoli in 2 large ziplock bags and pour marinade over. Marinate overnight in refrigerator, turning several times. Drain broccoli and place in a 9x13-inch pan.

½	cup mayonnaise	6	hard-cooked eggs, chopped
3	tablespoons sour cream		

Mix mayonnaise and sour cream; spread on top of broccoli. Sprinkle chopped eggs over mayonnaise mixture.

Lynne Rutkowski

German Coleslaw

8	cups finely shredded cabbage	1	medium yellow onion, finely chopped
½	medium green bell pepper, cored, seeded and minced		

Place cabbage, green pepper and onion in a large bowl and toss well to mix.

DRESSING

3	tablespoons sugar	½	teaspoon salt
3	tablespoons hot water		Pinch of pepper
3	tablespoons cider vinegar	¼	cup vegetable oil
½	teaspoon celery seed		

Combine sugar and hot water, stirring until sugar dissolves; stir in vinegar, celery seed, salt and pepper. Pour over slaw and toss well. Drizzle in oil and toss well again. Cover and let marinate in the refrigerator 2 or 3 hours before serving. Toss well again before serving.

"You will not go wrong in making German sweet-sour dishes if you use equal parts sugar, water and vinegar – whether pickling beets, making coleslaw, lettuce or potato salad."

Dot Rookard

My Best Friend's Chicken Salad

1	chicken breast with skin and bones	¾	cup Miracle Whip
1	chicken breast, boneless and skinless	1	medium onion, chopped
		1	carrot, chopped
¾	cup celery, chopped		Salt and pepper
⅓	cup grapes		Sugar, to taste
			Nuts, optional

Boil chicken until it begins to fall away from the bone. Remove chicken from broth, cool and cut in chunks. Mix chicken with next 7 ingredients. Top with any kind of nuts if desired.
Serves 4 to 6.

Carol Krause

Curried Turkey Salad

1½	cups mayonnaise	1½	cups seedless grapes
1	small can Mandarin oranges, drain and reserve 2 tablespoons syrup	1	cup chopped celery
		1	5-ounce can sliced water chestnuts, drained
2	teaspoons curry powder	½	cup pecans
2	teaspoons soy sauce		Lettuce leaves
4	cups diced turkey or chicken		

In large bowl combine mayonnaise, reserved syrup from oranges, curry powder, soy sauce and beat well. Add turkey or chicken, grapes, celery, water chestnuts and pecans. Toss well to coat, cover and chill. Serve on lettuce leaves. Garnish with Mandarin oranges. Best made the day before serving. Serves 6.

Bette Siler

Broccoli Salad

1	head of broccoli, cut in small pieces	½	cup chopped pecans
		1	cup raisins
7	strips crumbled bacon	½	cup red onion slices
⅜	cup sunflower seeds	1	cup fresh mushrooms, sliced

DRESSING

1	cup mayonnaise	2½	tablespoons vinegar
½	cup sugar		

Blanch and drain broccoli; add remaining ingredients and marinate in Dressing. Serves 10.

Sue Barnett

I *like a cook who smiles out loud when he tastes his own work. Let God worry about your modesty; I want to see your enthusiasm.*

Robert Farrar Capon

Tomato Basil Salad With Garlic Toasts

3	cups chopped, seeded, well-drained tomatoes	½	cup sliced kalamata olives, drained
2	cups (about 6 ounces) cubed Monterey Jack cheese		

2	cups Garlic Cheese Croutons		Grated Parmesan cheese
	Red leaf lettuce		

Combine tomatoes, cheese and olives in large bowl and gently mix in Dressing. When ready to serve, add croutons and toss. Spoon salad onto lettuce and sprinkle with Parmesan.
Serves 8.

DRESSING

2	tablespoons red wine vinegar	¼	teaspoon coarsely ground black pepper
2	tablespoons chopped fresh basil leaves or 2 teaspoons dried	¼	teaspoon salt or to taste
1	small garlic clove, minced	3	tablespoons olive oil or vegetable oil

Shake dressing ingredients in jar with tight lid and pour over tomato mixture.

GARLIC CHEESE CROUTONS

4	cups ¾-inch cubes of French bread	4	tablespoons olive oil or melted butter or margarine
1	small clove garlic, minced, or ¼ teaspoon garlic powder	2-4	tablespoons freshly grated Parmesan cheese

Spread bread cubes on ungreased baking sheet. Mix garlic with olive oil; pour mixture over bread cubes and toss. Sprinkle with Parmesan. Bake at 300 degrees for 30-45 minutes if you want the cubes crunchy throughout; bake at 425 degrees for about 10 minutes or until golden if you want them crunchy only on the outside. Cover and refrigerate or freeze any leftover croutons.
Yield: about 3 cups

The dressing can be doubled and chilled, cooked pasta added, 8 ounces of spiral or wheel recommended. In place of croutons, top with toasted pine nuts.

Janet Hietbrink

127

Provence Potato Salad

2½ pounds red potatoes

Cook potatoes in salted, boiling water for 35 minutes or until fork tender. Drain potatoes and cut into ⅓-inch slices. Toss gently with Marinade and refrigerate. Let stand up to 1 hour. Toss again and serve at room temperature. Serves 8 to 10.

MARINADE

¼ cup low salt chicken broth	1 clove garlic, minced
¼ cup dry white wine	¼ cup red bell pepper, chopped
¼ cup olive oil	8 kalamata olives, seeded and
4 green onions, chopped	coarsely chopped
2 tablespoons Dijon mustard	1 teaspoon white wine
2 tablespoons tarragon vinegar	Worcestershire sauce
2 tablespoons drained capers	½ teaspoon sugar
2 tablespoons chopped parsley	½ teaspoon salt

Mix all ingredients together and blend well.

Suzy Goldman

Marinated Tomatoes

1 clove garlic, crushed	1 teaspoon paprika
2 tablespoons salt	Scant ¼ cup canola or vegetable
½ cup cider vinegar	oil
½ cup water	Vine ripened tomatoes, sliced

Mix all ingredients together and pour over tomatoes. Mixture will be salty but tomatoes will sweeten it. Marinate for 2 hours. Marinade should cover tomatoes or you will have to stir after 1 hour. Plan 1 or 2 slices per person.

Charlene Soderstrom

He who giveth up olive oil gives up his good taste.

Provencal Proverb

Salad Greens & Citrus Fruit

Assortment of salad greens,
washed, drained and dried
2   fresh grapefruit, Texas Ruby
Red or pink

2   large navel oranges
½   large sweet Bermuda onion
or red onion, thinly sliced

Break greens into bite-size pieces and place in shallow bowl. Peel and section grapefruit and oranges; arrange on top of greens. Separate the thin onion slices and scatter them decoratively among the fruit segments. Chill until serving time. Coat with Honey Dressing or pass dressing separately.

Serves 6 to 8.

HONEY DRESSING

⅔   cup sugar
1   teaspoon dry mustard
1   teaspoon paprika
1   heaping teaspoon celery salt
⅓   cup honey

⅓   cup white vinegar
1   tablespoon fresh lemon juice
1   teaspoon grated onion
1   cup vegetable oil

Mix all ingredients except oil and blend well. Add oil very slowly, beating constantly. Can be done in blender. Best made ahead. Will keep indefinitely in tightly covered jar in refrigerator.

Yield: 2 cups

Nancy Colglazier

Cranberry-Raspberry Mold

2   cups boiling water
1   6-ounce package raspberry
gelatin

1⅓ cups sour cream
⅔   cup whole cranberry sauce

Pour boiling water over gelatin and stir well. Refrigerate until very thick but not set. Beat in sour cream and cranberry sauce. Pour into 5-cup mold. Refrigerate until firm. Unmold to serving dish.

Serves 8 to 10.

Evelyne Miller

129

Indian Spinach Salad

8	cups fresh, washed spinach, torn into pieces	½	cup golden raisins
1½	cups pared, thinly sliced red apple	½	cup nuts, peanuts or walnuts, chopped
		3	green onions, sliced

Combine and chill until ready to serve.

DRESSING

¼	cup cider vinegar	½	teaspoon salt
¼	cup olive oil	1½	teaspoons curry powder
2	tablespoons chutney	1	teaspoon dry mustard
2	teaspoons sugar		

Mix ingredients together and toss with salad just before serving.

Nancy Neuman

Summer Pasta Salad

3	cups cooked pasta, about 9 ounces before cooking	⅓	cup red wine vinegar
1	14½-ounce can stewed tomatoes, undrained, cut up	¼	cup green onion, sliced with tops
1	6-ounce jar marinated artichoke hearts, undrained and quartered	¼	cup Parmesan cheese, coarsely shredded
1	3¼-ounce can pitted ripe black olives, drained and quartered	1	teaspoon dried basil leaves or 1 tablespoon fresh basil
		½	teaspoon salt
		¼	teaspoon pepper

Combine all ingredients in large bowl. Mix well. Cover and refrigerate before serving.

Serves 6.

Recommended pasta: rotini, shells or bows

Debbie Leecock

Low Calorie Cherry Delite

2	3-ounce packages of sugar free raspberry or cherry flavored gelatin	1	20-ounce can crushed pineapple, drained
2	cups boiling water	1	can pitted tart cherries, drained and lightly chopped
2	cups ice cubes		Cream cheese (optional)

Place gelatin in 9x13-inch dish and slowly add boiling water while stirring. When gelatin is completely dissolved, add ice cubes and continue stirring. After gelatin thickens, remove any remaining ice cubes. Stir in remaining ingredients. Small bits of cream cheese may be added at this time if desired. Refrigerate until firm and serve cold.

Roberta Fields

Cucumber Celery Mold

3	envelopes unflavored gelatin	2	drops green food color (optional)
½	cup cold water		
2	cups boiling water	1	cup celery leaves, packed
½	cup sugar	2	cups finely chopped celery
2	teaspoons salt	3	cups cucumber, cored and chopped, with a bit of skin
¾	cup cider vinegar		

Soften gelatin in cold water. Stir in boiling water to dissolve gelatin; add sugar, salt, vinegar and food color. Chill until mixture begins to thicken and then blend in vegetables. Pour into oiled 7-cup mold.

DRESSING

1	pint sour cream	1	teaspoon sugar
4	tablespoons grated onion	3	tablespoons horseradish
1	teaspoon salt	2-3	dashes hot pepper sauce

Annie Stanton

Life is like an onion; you peel it off one layer at a time, and sometimes you weep.

Carl Sandburg

131

Copper Pennies (Marinated Carrots)

2	pounds carrots, sliced and cooked	1	teaspoon Worcestershire sauce
1	can tomato soup, undiluted	1	medium onion, chopped
1	cup sugar	1	medium green bell pepper, chopped
¼	cup vegetable oil		Celery, optional
¾	cup vinegar		Salt and pepper, to taste
1	teaspoon prepared mustard		

Mix all ingredients together and refrigerate for at least twenty-four hours.

Evelyne Miller

Curried Chicken Salad

4	whole chicken breasts, skinned and boned	½	teaspoon pepper
1	onion	1	cup sliced water chestnuts
1	bay leaf	½	cup scallions, cut on the diagonal
½	teaspoon salt		Rind of 2 limes, grated

DRESSING

1	cup mayonnaise	⅓	cup curry powder, or to taste
2	tablespoons soy sauce	1	cup mango chutney

Add onion, bay leaf, salt and pepper to enough water to cover breasts and poach chicken 10-15 minutes. Let chicken stand and cool. When cool cut into 1-inch square pieces and put in a bowl. Add water chestnuts, scallions and lime rind. Mix ingredients for dressing and pour over chicken. Gently toss to coat. Suggested condiments: chopped onions, parsley, ground peanuts, raisins, chopped green peppers, minced egg yolks and whites, grated coconut. Serves 6.

In India, each condiment for the curry dishes is served by a "boy." Some dinners had one hundred boy curries. This also denoted the importance of the host and guest. The more the boys, the more the importance.

Joan Keever

Cranberry Salad

3	8-ounce cans whole cranberries	1	3-ounce box of any red gelatin
1	8-ounce can crushed pineapple, drained, reserve juice	1	cup walnuts, chopped
		1	cup grapes, halved
			Celery to taste, chopped

Dissolve gelatin in $\frac{1}{2}$ cup of liquid using reserved pineapple juice. Add fruit and walnuts. Refrigerate.

Argie Grader

Surprise Shrimp Salad

2	pounds shrimp, cooked	1	tablespoon chopped olives
1	cup rice, cooked	3	tablespoons lemon juice
$2\frac{1}{2}$	cups cauliflower, finely chopped	1	cup mayonnaise
3	tablespoons chopped green onion	6	tablespoons French dressing
		$1\frac{1}{2}$	teaspoons salt
			Cracked pepper

Mix all ingredients together and let stand 8 hours before serving. Serves 6 to 8.

Margaret McCulloch

Weber Dressing

$\frac{2}{3}$	cup olive oil	3	cloves garlic, crushed
$\frac{1}{3}$	cup wine vinegar		Salt, to taste
36	shakes Maggi seasoning		

Mix ingredients together and serve over Boston lettuce or your choice of greens. Store in refrigerator.

Bobbie Weber

133

Blue Cheese Salad Dressing

2	cups light mayonnaise	½-1	teaspoon minced garlic
1	cup reduced fat sour cream	1-1½	tablespoons fresh lemon juice
½-¾	pound blue cheese, crumbled		Salt and freshly ground pepper, to taste

Thoroughly mix all ingredients and refrigerate for 24 hours before using.

Marcia DaPont

Poppy Seed Dressing

⅓	cup sugar	⅓	cup apple cider vinegar
1	teaspoon salt or to taste	1	tablespoon lemon juice
1	teaspoon dry mustard	1	cup canola oil
½	teaspoon grated onion or dried onion flakes	1½	tablespoons poppy seeds

Combine first 5 ingredients in jar. Shake thoroughly. Let sit for 5 minutes. Add last 3 ingredients. Shake thoroughly. Store in refrigerator. Will last several weeks. Shake well before using.

Yield: 2 cups

Great on assorted greens or spinach salad.

Bobbie Tooher

Roquefort Dressing

¼	cup vegetable oil	⅛	teaspoon pepper
¼	cup olive oil	½	teaspoon sugar
2	tablespoons wine vinegar	½	teaspoon paprika
2	tablespoons lemon juice	⅓	cup crumbled Roquefort cheese
½	teaspoon salt		
½	teaspoon celery seed		

Combine all ingredients in jar with tight fitting lid. Shake vigorously to combine. Refrigerate until ready to use. Shake again just before using.

Yield: 1 cup

Sarah Wyant

Main Dishes

meat
poultry
seafood
pasta
vegetarian

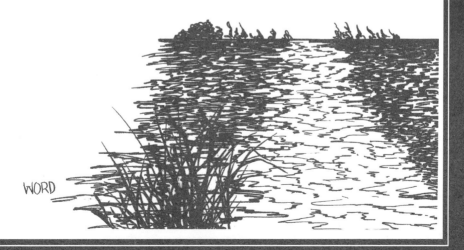

WORD

Joy's Game Time Chili

2	tablespoons olive oil	1	14½-ounce can tomato sauce
2	pounds lean ground round or ground turkey, as desired	3	tablespoons chili powder
1	large onion, chopped	1	teaspoon ground cumin
2	garlic cloves, thinly sliced	1	teaspoon ground coriander
1	14½-ounce can chicken broth	1	teaspoon paprika
		⅛	teaspoon cayenne pepper
1	28-ounce can diced tomatoes, undrained	1½	teaspoon salt, or to taste
		2-3	14½-ounce cans kidney beans, drained and rinsed
2	4.5-ounce cans diced green chiles, undrained		

Brown the ground meat in the olive oil, then drain off any excess grease. Add the onion and garlic and sauté 1-2 minutes or until onion is slightly softened. Stir in the chicken broth, tomatoes, diced chiles, tomato sauce, chili powder, ground cumin, ground coriander, paprika, cayenne pepper and salt. Cover and simmer about 30 minutes to marry flavors. Stir in drained and rinsed kidney beans and simmer an additional 15 minutes. Serve with a choice of traditional chili toppings: grated cheese, sour cream, tortilla chips, salsa, etc.

Serves 8.

This chili can easily be prepared several days in advance and reheated before serving.

Joy Borden

Swiss Meat Loaf

2	pounds meat loaf mixture	½	cup chopped onion
1½	cups shredded Swiss cheese	½	teaspoon paprika
2	beaten eggs	2	cups milk
½	teaspoon pepper	1	cup dry bread crumbs
1	teaspoon celery salt		

Preheat oven to 350 degrees.

Mix all ingredients together and make two loaves. Bake uncovered for 1½ hours. Freezes well.

Serves 6 to 8.

Priscilla Stahl

Chip's Chili

¾ pound lean ground beef
¾ pound sirloin steak, cut in bite-size cubes
1 pound chicken breast, cut in bite-size cubes
1 pound hot Italian sausage, removed from casing, broken in pieces
2 garlic cloves, minced
3 small onions, chopped
1 green bell pepper, diced
1 red bell pepper, diced
1 yellow or orange bell pepper, diced
1 poblano chile pepper, minced

1 jalapeño chile pepper, minced (devein, discard seeds)
½ pound corn kernels (optional)
1 large can tomato soup
2 16-ounce cans crushed tomatoes
1 15-ounce can tomato sauce
2 teaspoons Italian seasoning
3 15-ounce cans black beans
1 can kidney or pinto beans
1 teaspoon cumin
2 tablespoons chili powder or to taste
Hot pepper sauce, to taste
Salt, to taste

Brown meats in large stovetop pot. Degrease and add garlic, onion, peppers and cook until softened. Add remainder of ingredients; simmer 1-2 hours. Cool in refrigerator overnight.

Serves 10 to 12.

This chili is best the following day. If there are leftovers, put them in a casserole. Top with prepared cornbread mix, adding 1 cup cheddar cheese to batter. Spread batter over chili. Bake at 350 degrees for 30 minutes or until browned.

Suzy Goldman

Standing Rib Roast

Preheat oven to 375 degrees.

Meat should be at room temperature. Cook roast, seasoned to taste, in shallow pan, fat side up for 1 hour. Turn oven off. Before serving, turn oven on again for 40 minutes at 375 degrees. Never Open Oven Door.

Cook for the first time at least 3 hours before cooking the second time. If roast is small, cook only 35 minutes for second cooking. This makes rare to medium rare roast. Foolproof with delicious texture and flavor. Allow 2 servings per rib.

Connie M. Jones

Meat Loaf Burgundy

2	pounds ground beef	½	cup chili sauce
	(top round or sirloin)	3	eggs, beaten
1	pound ground veal	3	tablespoons chopped green
1	pound ground pork		bell pepper
1	cup cottage cheese		Salt and pepper, to taste
1	cup bread crumbs	½	cup Burgundy wine
1	cup chopped onions	1	cup tomato sauce

Combine beef, veal and pork. Mix thoroughly. Add cottage cheese, bread crumbs, onion, chili sauce, eggs, green pepper and season to taste. Shape into one large or two small loaves and put in baking pan. Pour wine over loaves and spread tomato sauce on top. Bake in 400 degree oven for 30 minutes, basting frequently with juices. Reduce heat to 350 degrees and bake 30 minutes longer. Delicious hot or cold. Can be frozen.

Serves 8 generously.

Char Hylbert

Meat Loaf

1	cup ketchup	¼	cup vinegar
¼	cup brown sugar	1	teaspoon mustard
1	egg, lightly beaten	2	pounds ground beef
1	minced onion	1½	teaspoons salt
¼	cup cracker crumbs		

Preheat oven to 350 degrees.

In a small bowl mix together ketchup, brown sugar, vinegar and mustard. Set aside. Mix remaining ingredients together adding ½ cup of sauce mixture. Place meat in 8x12-inch oblong baking dish. Pour remainder of the sauce on top of meat loaf and bake uncovered for 1 hour. Freezes well.

Serves 8 to 10.

Sheila Kautz

I feel a recipe is only a theme, which an intelligent cook can play each time with a variation.

Madame Benoff

138

Crunchy Topped Meatloaf

1	pound ground chuck	1	teaspoon Worcestershire
⅓	cup dry oatmeal		sauce
3	slices bread, torn into pieces	¼	teaspoon pepper
¾	cup chili sauce	3	saltine crackers, crumbled
1	egg	4	slices bacon
1	medium onion, chopped		

Preheat oven to 350 degrees.

Mix all ingredients and mound in a greased shallow baking pan or flat casserole dish. Spread crumbled crackers over meat and place strips of bacon on top. Bake for 1 hour.

Serves 6.

Joyce Englerth

Swedish Meatballs

1	pound ground beef	1	small onion, grated
½	cup fine dry bread crumbs	⅓	cup oil
1	cup milk	3	tablespoons flour
1	egg	1	package G. Washington
1	teaspoon salt		seasoning
⅛	teaspoon pepper	2½	cups water
⅛	teaspoon allspice		

Using a fork, thoroughly mix together the bread crumbs, milk, egg, salt, pepper, allspice and onion. Add the ground meat. Mix well with fork. Form into balls using two spoons or lightly form with your hands. Brown meatballs in hot oil in heavy frying pan. Remove. Pour off all but 3 tablespoons of the fat. Mix in flour. Add G. Washington seasoning and broth package. Heat until smooth and bubbling. While bubbling, add 2½ cups water all at once, stirring constantly to keep from getting lumpy (or add liquid slowly, stirring constantly). Cook until gravy thickens slightly. Add meatballs to gravy and continue cooking for at least another 15 minutes. Longer cooking time may be desired if using more than 1 pound of meat. Serve with mashed potatoes.

Serves 6.

A package of Herb-ox broth with seasonings may be substituted for the G. Washington seasoning and broth package.

Helen Lantz

Hamburger Chop Suey

1½ pounds ground chuck
1½ cups chopped celery
1½ cups chopped onion
½ cup chopped mushrooms
½ cup bean sprouts
½ cup uncooked rice, not
   instant

1 10¾-ounce can cream of
   mushroom soup
1 10¾-ounce can cream of
   chicken soup
1½ cups warm water
⅓ cup soy sauce
Chow mein noodles

Preheat oven to 350 degrees.

Brown meat, drain. Place in large greased casserole with vegetables and rice. Blend soups, water and soy sauce. Combine soup mixture with meat, vegetables and rice, mixing well. Bake uncovered 1 hour. Add noodles for last 15 minutes.

Serves 6.

Judy Stenzel

Hamburger Pie

1 pound ground chuck
¾ pound sharp cheddar cheese,
   grated
1 cup mayonnaise
1 cup milk
1 medium onion, chopped

4 eggs
4 tablespoons cornstarch
Dash pepper
2 8-inch pie shells, unbaked
   (optional)

Brown meat and onion and drain. Combine all other ingredients with meat and onion. Pour mixture into the two pie shells or into two greased pie plates if you wish a crustless pie. Bake at 400 degrees for 15 minutes. Reduce oven to 325 degrees and bake 30-40 minutes or until an inserted knife comes out clean.

Serves 12.

Julie Washenko

C uisine is when things taste like themselves.

Curnonsky

Savory Roast

1	3-pound boneless chuck roast, trimmed of fat	¾	cup sweet sherry
2	tablespoons white vinegar	¼	cup brewed coffee
1	teaspoon garlic salt	1	cup sliced mushrooms
¼	cup all-purpose flour	1	medium onion, sliced
2	tablespoons olive oil	4	carrots, cut in 1-inch pieces
½	package dry onion-mushroom soup	3	potatoes, cut in 1½-inch cubes

Preheat oven to 350 degrees.
Rub roast with vinegar. Cut 8-10 slits in roast; sprinkle garlic salt into slits. Dredge roast in flour. Brown roast on all sides in hot oil in a Dutch oven over medium heat. Stir together the soup mix, sherry and coffee; pour over roast. Add mushrooms and rest of vegetables. Cook covered for 3 hours. You may add more water as it cooks if you want more volume for the gravy.
Serves 6 to 9.

Alma Kloss

Mexican Salad

1	sweet red onion	1	teaspoon hot pepper sauce
1	head iceberg lettuce	1	10-ounce bag tortilla chips
1	head romaine lettuce	4	ounces sharp cheddar cheese, grated
1	avocado		
2	tomatoes	1	8-ounce bottle French dressing
1	pound ground beef or turkey		
1	15-ounce can kidney beans		

Chop and refrigerate the vegetables, keeping the tomato separate. Brown meat and drain off the fat. Add the beans and hot pepper sauce, salt if desired, and simmer until dry. Crush the tortilla chips in the bag. (May be made ahead to this point.) Mix everything together and toss with the French dressing.
Serves 8 to 10.

Carol Nasr

Beef Roulade

2	eggs, slightly beaten	½	teaspoon leaf oregano,
¾	cup bread crumbs		crumbled
½	cup ketchup	¼	teaspoon pepper
⅓	cup chopped parsley	1	clove garlic, crushed
½	teaspoon dried basil	2	pounds ground round
	Dry bread crumbs	3	cups shredded Swiss cheese
3	4-ounce packages ham slices		(¾ pound)
			Mustard Sauce

Preheat oven to 350 degrees.

Combine first nine ingredients. Mix lightly until well-blended and divide into two equal portions. Cut two 12x12-inch squares of foil. Sprinkle each with dry bread crumbs. Pat out each half of meat mixture on foil to 9x12-inch rectangle. Arrange ham slices on top of each to within ½-inch of edges. Sprinkle each with Swiss cheese. Using foil as an aid, roll up meat from long side, jelly roll fashion. Seal edges and ends. Place on foil-lined jelly roll pan. Bake for 50 minutes. Cool to room temperature. Serve sliced with Mustard Sauce. Can be prepared two days before serving.

Serves 8.

MUSTARD SAUCE

1	cup sour cream	1-3	teaspoons prepared
¼	cup mayonnaise		horseradish
2	tablespoons Dijon-style	¼	cup chopped green onion
	mustard		

Mix all ingredients until well-blended. Refrigerate until ready to use.

Marolyn Overton

Man is the only animal that eats when he is not hungry, drinks when he is not thirsty, and makes love at all seasons.

Anonymous

Beef Barbecue

6	pounds chuck roast	3	teaspoons vinegar
1	rib celery, chopped	1	teaspoon hot pepper sauce
3	large onions, chopped	2	teaspoons chili sauce
1	24-ounce bottle ketchup	2	teaspoons salt
3	tablespoons barbecue sauce	1	teaspoon pepper
1	green bell pepper, chopped	1½	cups water

Preheat oven to 300 degrees.

Cut beef in chunks. Place in roaster with all other ingredients. Heat on top of stove until boiling. Cover and bake in oven for 6 hours. Shred with fork and serve on heated buns. Meat will be so tender after cooking that you can easily remove any bones.

Serves 8 to 10.

Mary Ellen Fox

Boeuf Bourgignon

2	pounds of chuck, cubed	⅔	cups beef bouillon
	Flour	6	cloves
	Salt and pepper	2	bay leaves
1	pound mushrooms, sliced	1-2	cloves garlic
1⅓	cups red Burgundy wine	18	peeled small white onions

Preheat oven to 300 degrees.

Dredge beef in flour, salt and pepper. Brown in hot fat in Dutch oven. Pour off excess fat. Remove meat from pan and brown mushrooms. Return meat to pan, add wine, bouillon, cloves, bay leaves and a garlic clove or two. Add onions. Simmer a few minutes stirring up from bottom of pan. Cook uncovered in oven for 2 hours. Serve with rice or noodles.

Serves 8.

Best if made day before serving.

Theresa Sullivan

A host is like a general: It takes a mishap to reveal his genius.

Horace

Beef Burgundy

3	pounds chuck, cut in chunks	1	bottle of beer or equal
1	packet dry onion soup mix		amount of red wine
1	can cream of mushroom	1½	pounds mushrooms
	soup	1	clove garlic, minced
1	can cream of celery soup		Chopped parsley

Preheat oven to 320 degrees.
Blend soups with beer or wine and pour over chuck. Cover and bake for 2½ hours. Add mushrooms and garlic; sprinkle with parsley and continue to cook for 30 more minutes. Serve over Noodles.
Serves 8 to 10.

NOODLES

1	pound wide egg noodles, cooked and drained	1	cup chopped green onions
			Worcestershire sauce, to taste
4	cups sour cream		Hot pepper sauce, to taste
4	cups small curd cottage cheese	4	tablespoons poppyseeds
			Parmesan cheese

Mix all ingredients together except for Parmesan cheese. Sprinkle cheese on top of noodle mixture and bake until hot.
Serves 24.

Gail Andrus

Hoosier Beef

2	pounds cubed sirloin	¼	teaspoon pepper
2	tablespoons butter	2	tablespoons brown sugar
1	medium onion, chopped	½	cup ketchup
½	teaspoon dry mustard	2	cups beef broth
¼	teaspoon salt	1	pound carrots, sliced

Preheat oven to 325 degrees.
Brown meat in butter; add onion. Add all ingredients except carrots. Stir well over medium heat. Add sliced carrots. Bake in greased casserole for 3 hours.

Anita Madigan

Bifteck Marchand de Vin

2½ pounds steak, 2-inches thick
    (sirloin, porterhouse, T-bone,
    filet or rib)
2   tablespoons butter
1   tablespoon shallots, chopped
1   teaspoon flour

1   cup dry red wine
1   teaspoon lemon juice
Salt and freshly ground pepper,
    to taste
1   tablespoon cream
1   teaspoon chopped parsley

Melt butter in a saucepan and sauté the chopped shallots. Blend in the flour, wine, lemon juice, salt and pepper. Simmer until liquid is reduced to ½ cup. Stir in cream and simmer a few seconds longer. Trim excess fat from steak, score edges and pan broil in a heavy skillet over high heat to desired doneness. Remove steak with its juices onto a heated platter. Spoon on the sauce, sprinkle with chopped parsley and serve.

Serves 4.

Marie R. Cappuccio

Teriyaki Tenderloin

½   cup dry sherry
¼   cup soy sauce
2   tablespoons dry onion soup
    mix

2   tablespoons brown sugar
1   to 2 pounds beef tenderloin

Combine first four ingredients. Place beef in plastic bag and place bag in a deep bowl. Add marinade to beef. Chill 8 to 24 hours. Occasionally press bag against meat to distribute marinade.

Preheat oven to 425 degrees.

Place meat on rack in roasting pan. Bake for 50 minutes. Baste occasionally with half the marinade. Bring rest of marinade and 2 tablespoons water to boiling. Slice meat and spoon sauce over.

Serves 6.

Using a meat thermometer, the internal temperature for well-done should read 160 degrees; for rare, 130 degrees. Cooking time may need to be adjusted depending on the degree of doneness you prefer.

Estelle Franz

Brazilian Tenderloin With Chimichurri

6   tenderloin steaks, about   **Fresh Cilantro Marinade**
    8 ounces each, trimmed

Combine the marinade and steaks in a large bowl. Cover and let marinate in the refrigerator for about 3 hours. Turn the steaks over occasionally. Cook to desired doneness and serve with Chimichurri.

FRESH CILANTRO ADOBO (MARINADE)

1½ cups fresh cilantro, leaves   1   tablespoon salt
    and stems   ½   cup coarsely chopped white
3   bay leaves   onion
2   teaspoons ground cumin   ¼   cup coarsely chopped garlic
2   teaspoons dried oregano   1   cup distilled white vinegar
2   teaspoons dried thyme   ½   cup vegetable oil
2   teaspoons pepper

Place all the ingredients, except the vegetable oil, in a blender. Purée on high speed. Transfer the mixture to a mixing bowl and whisk in the vegetable oil. Yield: approximately 2½ cups

CHIMICHURRI

6   cloves garlic   ½   cup finely minced flat-leaf
3   bay leaves   parsley
2   jalapeño chiles, coarsely   ¼   cup finely minced fresh
    chopped, with seeds   oregano leaves
1½ tablespoons salt   ¼   cup distilled white vinegar
½   cup finely minced fresh   ⅓   cup extra virgin olive oil
    parsley

Mash the garlic, bay leaves, jalapeños and salt with a mortar and pestle until a smooth paste is formed. (You can also purée with a small amount of vinegar in blender.) Transfer to a mixing bowl and add the herbs. Whisk in the vinegar and olive oil until well-mixed and set aside.

Oscar Mejia
Executive Chef
The Landings Club

Peggy Taylor's Beef Tenderloin

1   whole beef tenderloin

Remove from refrigerator one hour before baking.
Preheat oven to 500-550 degrees.
Trim fat from tenderloin placing some on top of meat for added flavor. Rub the tenderloin with salt, pepper, garlic salt, lemon pepper – your favorite seasonings.
Melt one stick of butter and pour it over the tenderloin. Bake for five minutes. DO NOT OPEN THE OVEN DOOR! Turn the oven off. Leave the tenderloin in the oven for another 30 minutes. Remove meat from oven. Make a slit in the center to check doneness. The tenderloin will continue to cook as it cools. Make a tent out of aluminum foil and tuck it in around the tenderloin to slow cooling and retain moisture. Serve with Horseradish Mousse.

HORSERADISH MOUSSE

Use oil or cooking spray to grease 4-cup mold.

1	**envelope unflavored gelatin**	**½**	**cup water**
¼	**cup fresh lemon juice**	**2**	**tablespoons creamy**
4	**eggs**		**horseradish**
¾	**cup sugar**	**1**	**cup whipping cream,**
3	**tablespoons Dijon mustard**		**whipped**
½	**teaspoon salt**	**2**	**tablespoons finely chopped**
½	**cup cider vinegar**		**parsley**

Sprinkle gelatin over lemon juice. Slightly beat eggs in a medium saucepan. Add sugar, mustard, salt, vinegar and water. Beat with wire whisk until blended. Add gelatin to mixture. Add horseradish. Stir constantly over heat until thickened but do not boil. Refrigerate until thickened and almost set. Fold in whipped cream and parsley. Pour into mold and refrigerate.

Gail Andrus

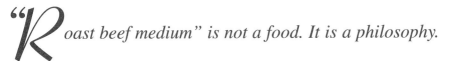

oast beef medium" is not a food. It is a philosophy.

Edna Ferber

M.K.'s Filet In Sauce

12	filets of beef cut 1-1½ -inches thick	4	teaspoons tomato paste
2	large cloves garlic, crushed	1	teaspoon garlic, crushed
1	tablespoon salt	2	cups chicken broth
½	teaspoon pepper	1	cup beef broth
1	stick of butter plus 2 tablespoons, divided	1½	cups dry red wine
		½	teaspoon Worcestershire sauce
4	tablespoons cognac	4	tablespoons currant jelly
6	tablespoons flour	1	pint mushrooms, sliced

In small bowl make a paste of the 2 garlic cloves, salt and pepper. Rub seasoning on both sides of steaks. Heat 2 tablespoons of butter in hot skillet and sear filets on both sides. Take steaks out and place in casserole. Add cognac to skillet, cooking over medium heat. Scrape pan and add the stick of butter. When butter is melted and foamy, stir in flour. Reduce heat to low, stirring constantly until mixture is golden. Stir in tomato paste and 1 teaspoon garlic. Remove from heat, add chicken and beef broths and wine. Return to heat and bring to boil. Stir. Reduce heat and simmer for 10 minutes until reduced approximately one-third. Stir in Worcestershire sauce and jelly. When jelly is melted, stir in mushrooms. Sauce should be coating consistency – if too thick, thin down with wine – and cool completely. Pour sauce over steaks that have been placed in a casserole dish and refrigerate overnight or freeze. Bring to room temperature. Preheat oven to 400 degrees. Bake 15-20 minutes, uncovered, for medium rare.

Serves 12.

Steaks cut 1-inch thick will be medium rare. Steaks 1½-inch thick will be rare. Freezing may improve flavor.

M. K. Maxon

Barbecued Flank Steak

¼	cup soy sauce	¾	cup salad oil
3	tablespoons honey	1	finely chopped green onion
2	tablespoons vinegar	1	large flank steak
1½	teaspoons chopped fresh ginger		

Mix soy sauce, honey and vinegar; add ginger, oil and onion. Pour over meat in shallow pan. Let stand in refrigerator for 4 hours or more. Broil or grill.

Leslie McCloskey

Pampered Beef Filets

6	large fresh mushroom crowns	2	tablespoons butter or margarine
6	beef filets, cut 1 inch thick		

For fluted effect on mushrooms, cut V-shaped pieces out of tops. Set crowns aside: reserve mushroom pieces for Royal Mushroom Sauce. Heat butter in heavy skillet till golden brown and bubbling. Quickly brown steaks on both sides over high heat, about 1 minute per side. Place filets on individual squares of heavy foil on baking sheet. Allow to cool slightly.

Prepare Royal Mushroom Sauce. Spoon a generous 3 tablespoons sauce over each filet; top each with a mushroom crown. Bring corners of each foil square up over steak, twist gently, and seal. Refrigerate packets. (May be done to this point the day before or in the morning of party.)

Before baking filets, open tops of packets slightly. Bake in 500 degree oven for 14-15 minutes for rare, 16-18 minutes for medium. If packets have not been refrigerated, bake a few minutes less.

Serves 6.

ROYAL MUSHROOM SAUCE

½	cup chopped fresh mushroom stems and pieces	½	cup water
¼	cup chopped green onion	2	tablespoons minced parsley
4	teaspoons cornstarch	1	teaspoon salt
1	cup Burgundy wine		Dash of pepper

Add the half cup mushroom stems and pieces and the onions to drippings remaining in skillet after filets have been browned. Cook vegetables till tender, but not brown. Blend in cornstarch. Add remaining ingredients and dash of pepper; cook and stir till thickened and bubbly. Cook 1 minute more.

Joy Bollman

There is no one who has cooked but has discovered that each particular dish depends for its rightness upon some little point which he is never told.

Hillaire Belloc

149

Spiced Apple Butter Pork Roast

1	2-pound boneless center-cut lean pork loin roast or boneless lean pork sirloin roast	2	tablespoons cider vinegar
		2	tablespoons lemon juice
		2	tablespoons prepared horseradish
1	1-pound, 13-ounce jar apple butter (about 2⅔ cups)	1	teaspoon Dijon mustard
		¼	teaspoon salt
¼	cup apple brandy or apple juice	¼	teaspoon coarsely ground pepper

Place roast in a zip-top plastic bag. Combine apple butter with apple brandy or apple juice, vinegar, lemon juice, horseradish, mustard, salt and pepper in a bowl; stir well. Reserve 2 cups apple butter mixture; cover and chill. Pour remaining apple butter mixture over roast; seal bag and marinate in refrigerator 8 hours.

Preheat oven to 350 degrees.

Line a shallow roasting pan with heavy-duty foil. Remove roast from bag; place roast in prepared pan and drizzle with marinade. Insert meat thermometer into thickest portion of roast. Bake for 55 minutes or until meat thermometer registers 150 degrees (pork will be slightly pink). Let stand 10 minutes before slicing.

Place reserved 2 cups apple butter mixture in a small saucepan. Place over low heat and heat thoroughly. Serve with roast.

Yield: 8 3-ounce servings with ¼ cup apple butter mixture

Theresa Sullivan

Pork Roast

1	3-pound boneless pork roast	1	can whole cranberry sauce
1½	tablespoons ground sage	½	cup apricot preserves
	Salt and pepper		

Preheat oven to 350 degrees.

Rub roast with ground sage and sprinkle with salt and pepper. Combine cranberry sauce and apricot preserves in small pan over low heat until blended. Put roast in small roasting pan, pour cranberry mixture over. Cover and bake for 2 hours.

Serves 8.

Marolyn Overton

Pork With Camembert

1	pound pork filet	4	ounces Camembert cheese,
Freshly ground black pepper			remove rind (2½ ounces
1	tablespoon butter		without rind)
3	tablespoons dry white wine	1½	teaspoons Dijon mustard
½	cup whipping cream		Fresh parsley, to garnish
1	tablespoon chopped fresh		
	mixed herbs, such as		
	marjoram, thyme and sage		

Slice the pork filet crossways into small steaks about ¾-inch thick. Place between two sheets of greaseproof paper or clear film and pound with the flat side of a meat mallet to flatten to a thickness of ½-inch. Sprinkle with pepper.

Melt the butter in a heavy frying pan over a medium-high heat until it begins to brown, then add the meat. Cook for 5 minutes, turning once, or until just cooked through and the meat is springy when pressed. Transfer to a warmed dish and cover to keep warm. Add the wine and bring to a boil, scraping the base of the pan. Stir in the cream and herbs and bring back to a boil. Add the cheese and mustard and any accumulated juices from the meat. Add a little more cream if needed and adjust the seasoning. Serve the pork with the sauce and garnish with parsley.

Serves 3 to 4.

Kurt Faxon

Grilled Pork Tenderloin

4	pork tenderloins	¼	cup light soy sauce
1	6-ounce can pineapple juice	⅛	cup dry sherry
3	tablespoons rice wine	3	shakes cayenne pepper
	vinegar with roasted garlic		

Marinate tenderloins in marinade for at least one hour. Preheat grill and grill at medium setting for 10 minutes on each side.

Serves 8.

Patricia Eilender

A t a dinner party one should eat wisely but not too well, and talk well but not too wisely.

W. Somerset Maugham

151

Pork Tenderloin With Mustard Sauce

¼   cup soy sauce   2   1½-pound packages pork
¼   cup bourbon   tenderloin
2   tablespoons brown sugar

Preheat oven to 325 degrees.
Combine first 3 ingredients in an 11x7-inch baking dish; add tenderloin.
Cover and refrigerate at least 2 hours, turning occasionally. Remove from
marinade, discarding marinade. Place tenderloin on a rack in a shallow
roasting pan. Bake for 45 minutes or until a meat thermometer reaches 160
degrees. Can also be cooked on outdoor grill. Serve with Mustard Sauce.
Serves 8.

MUSTARD SAUCE

⅔   cup sour cream   ⅔   cup mayonnaise
2   tablespoons dry mustard   3-4 green onions, chopped

Combine all ingredients; cover and chill.
Yield: 1⅓ cups

Mary Ann Schmitt

Lowfat Vidalia Onion & Sausage Casserole

2   sleeves of lowfat Ritz   1   8-ounce package of lowfat
    crackers   cheddar cheese
2   boxes Healthy Choice   1   8-ounce package of part-
    sausage patties   skim mozzarella cheese
3   medium to large Vidalia   1   can lowfat cream of
    onions   mushroom soup

Preheat oven to 350 degrees.
Spray bottom and sides of an 8x8-inch casserole dish with nofat spray. Crush the Ritz
crackers and layer on the bottom, spray lightly with nofat spray. Cook sausage per
package instructions. Cut sausage patties into small cubes. Layer ⅓ of the sausage on
the crackers. Thinly slice onions, separating into individual rings. Layer ⅓ of them
over mixture. Cover with ⅓ of cheeses. Repeat the layers twice. In a separate bowl,
mix cream of mushroom soup with 1 soup can of water, blending well. Pour mixture
over the layers. Lightly spray with nofat spray. Bake 45 minutes.
Serves 4.

Marcia Wilk

Pork Chops With Orange-Rice Stuffing

6   pork chops, 1½-inch thick   2   cups water
    (full rib cut)   1   chicken bouillon cube
Salt and pepper   1   cup long grain white rice,
Milk   uncooked
Flour   2   oranges, peeled and sliced
3   tablespoons fat or oil   ½   cup orange juice plus
½   cup raisins   additional for basting

Preheat oven to 350 degrees.

Season chops with salt and pepper. Dip in milk and coat lightly with flour. Brown chops in hot fat; drain. Plump raisins in hot water and drain. Cook rice in two cups of water in which bouillon cube has been dissolved. Cook 14 minutes at lowered heat after water reaches boil. Add raisins and cut up orange pieces to rice. Mix with ½ cup orange juice and warm in pan used to brown chops. Stuff chops with rice mixture. Cover and bake for 1 hour or until tender. Remove cover and bake 10 minutes longer, basting with additional orange juice.

Serves 6.

Honey may be added to orange juice used for basting for extra sweetness and glaze.

Marie R. Cappuccio

Peachy Pork Chops

4   pork loin chops, ½-inch   1   tablespoon soy sauce
    thick   ¼   cup whole berry cranberry
1   teaspoon salt   sauce
4   peach halves, drained from   1   tablespoon packed brown
    can, reserve 2 tablespoons   sugar
    syrup

Preheat oven to 375 degrees.

Place pork chops in ungreased baking dish. Sprinkle both sides with salt. Mix reserved syrup and soy sauce; brush over pork chops. Cover and bake 40 minutes. Mix cranberry sauce and brown sugar. Remove pork chops from oven; turn. Top each pork chop with a peach half and 1 tablespoon cranberry mixture. Bake, uncovered, basting once, until chops are tender, 15-20 minutes.

Serves 4.

Anonymous

153

Stifado (Stew)

2	tablespoons vegetable or olive oil	1	tablespoon tomato paste
2	pounds lean lamb, veal or beef, cut into cubes	1	tablespoon sugar
1	medium onion, chopped	¼	cup chopped parsley
2	small cloves garlic, sliced	½	stick cinnamon
¼	cup dry red wine	6	whole cloves
¼	cup red wine vinegar	2	large bay leaves
4	canned plum tomatoes, chopped	2	pounds small white onions, peeled but left whole (white boiling onions)
		3	tablespoons butter

If oven baking, preheat oven to 325 degrees.

Heat oil in a large stew pot or Dutch oven. Sear the meat in batches until well-browned and remove from pot. Add chopped onion and garlic to pot and cook until softened, about 5 minutes. Add the wine, vinegar, tomatoes, tomato paste, sugar and parsley. Stir until smooth. Put cinnamon stick, cloves and bay leaves in a cheesecloth bag and add to pot. Return meat to pot. In separate pan, brown the whole onions in the butter. Cook stew for about 1 hour, add onions and cook for another hour. Stew may also be cooked in oven for about 1½ hours covering pot and stirring occasionally. Serve with orzo, rice or mashed potatoes.

Serves 6 generously.

Anna M. Nichols

Simple Rack Of Lamb

1	small rack of lamb, 6-8 chops	Butter, softened
		Salt and pepper
Garlic		Parsley, finely chopped

Preheat oven to 400 degrees.

Rub the lamb with garlic, butter, salt and pepper. Put it to roast on a rack in a shallow pan. Cook 20 minutes for medium rare, 23-25 minutes for pink center. Transfer to warm platter and allow to rest 5 minutes. Carve into separate chops. Sprinkle with chopped parsley. Don't forget the mint jelly! Serves 2.

Onnie Duffie

Osso Bucco Alla Linda
(Braised Veal Shanks)

6	2½-inch veal shank crosscuts		1	peeled tomato, chopped
Salt and pepper			2	chicken or beef bouillon
½	cup butter or margarine,			cubes
	divided		2	cups hot water
1	medium onion, minced		¼	cup dry white wine
1	pared carrot, diced		1	teaspoon dried rosemary
1	celery rib, diced		½	teaspoon salt
1	clove garlic, minced		⅛	teaspoon pepper
2	tablespoons flour		1	tablespoon snipped parsley

Sprinkle veal with salt and pepper. In Dutch oven, brown veal in ¼ cup hot butter. Remove pieces as they brown. Add onion, carrot, celery and garlic to Dutch oven. Sauté, stirring occasionally until tender, about 5 minutes. Return meat to Dutch oven. Combine ¼ cup butter and flour and add to meat; add tomato, bouillon cubes which have been dissolved in the 2 cups of water, wine, rosemary, salt and pepper. Stir well. Simmer, covered, 2 hours or until meat is tender. Just before serving, stir in snipped parsley.

Serves 6.

Bev McCamman

Italian Stew

4	sweet Italian sausages,		2	red bell peppers, chopped
	halved		1	orange bell pepper, chopped
4	hot Italian sausages, halved		1	green bell pepper, chopped
⅓	cup olive oil		1	28-ounce can Italian peeled
1	large clove garlic, chopped			tomatoes with basil, puréed
1	red onion, chopped		Salt and pepper, to taste
1	yellow bell pepper, chopped		Oregano, to taste

Brown sausage in small amount of olive oil. Set aside. In separate pan, heat ⅓ cup of olive oil and sauté garlic, onion and peppers until soft. Add sausage and puréed tomatoes. Add salt, pepper and oregano to taste. Simmer 45 minutes. Serve with Italian bread and/or pasta. Can be made ahead.

Serves 6.

Dotty Greer

Company Corned Beef

4-5 pounds corned beef (2 small
    briskets can be used)
2   bay leaves
5   peppercorns
6   large sprigs parsley

Several ribs of celery, including
    leaves
1   large onion, diced
Whole cloves

Wash corned beef thoroughly to remove brine. (If corned beef comes packaged with seasoning as it so often does, use it also.) Place in large pan and cover with cold water. Add bay leaves, peppercorns, parsley, celery and onion. Cover and simmer 3¾ hours. The cooking time remains the same whether cooking one large brisket or two small ones. Remove hot beef to shallow baking dish or oven pan. Insert whole cloves to your liking. Preheat oven to 350 degrees.

4   tablespoons butter or
    margarine
2   tablespoons prepared
    mustard
⅔   cup brown sugar

⅔   cup ketchup
6   tablespoons white or apple
    cider vinegar
6   tablespoons water

Melt butter; add remaining ingredients and mix thoroughly. Cook over medium heat until ingredients are well-blended. Pour half of sauce over corned beef and bake for 30 minutes basting with the sauce every ten minutes. The balance of the sauce can be heated and served in a gravy bowl as option for each person to use over individual slices. Can be prepared a day or two ahead and reheated at 225 degrees before serving. Reheat sauce also.

Suzie Moore

Ribs In Bag

2   slabs spare ribs

1   pint barbecue sauce

Preheat oven to 250 degrees.
Put ribs in baking bag. Add sauce. Bake 5 hours. Longer will not matter.

Phyllis Huffer

Louisiana Red Beans Over Rice

1	pound dried red kidney beans	1	cup yellow onion, chopped
2	quarts liquid, half water, half lowfat chicken broth or all water	½	cup green onions, chopped
		1½	cups celery, chopped
1	ham bone or 2 smoked ham hocks	1	bay leaf
		1½	teaspoons salt, or to taste
1	pound smoked sausage, cut in ½-inch pieces	1	teaspoon Worcestershire sauce
3	cloves garlic, pressed	Hot pepper sauce, to taste	
⅔	cup green bell pepper, chopped	1	tablespoon fresh parsley, minced

Rinse and drain beans. Place beans in a large pot with lid and cover with liquid. Add ham bone or hocks and bring to a boil. Reduce heat and simmer for 1 hour. Add sausage, cover, and cook 1 hour. Stir occasionally. Add garlic, green pepper, onions, celery and bay leaf. Continue cooking, covered, 1 hour longer or until beans are soft. Add salt, Worcestershire, hot pepper sauce and parsley. Simmer 5 minutes. Remove bay leaf. Serve over rice. Best made ahead. Beans can be frozen.

Serves 6 generously.

Carol Browning

Sausage Casserole

1	pound Polish sausage	1	can small peas
1½	cups uncooked rice	1	pound Swiss cheese, cut into cubes
1	can cream of celery soup		
2½	cups water		

Slice and brown the sausage in a large saucepan. Add the uncooked rice and the soup, stirring until blended. Continuing to stir, gradually add water. Bring to a boil, turn heat down and simmer for 15 minutes with lid on. After most of the liquid is absorbed, add the peas and cheese. Stir gently over low heat until the cheese is melted. Freezes well.

Serves 8.

Barbara Barker

Cheese & Spinach Pie

1	pound sweet Italian sausage links, chopped	⅔	cup ricotta cheese
6	eggs	½	teaspoon salt
2	10-ounce packages frozen, chopped spinach, thawed and well drained	1	10- to 11-ounce package piecrust mix
1	16-ounce package mozzarella cheese, shredded (4 cups)	1	tablespoon water

Preheat oven to 375 degrees.

In 10-inch skillet, cook sausage, stirring frequently until well browned, about 10 minutes. Spoon off fat. Reserve 1 egg yolk. In large bowl, combine remaining eggs and egg white with sausage, spinach, mozzarella, ricotta and salt. Prepare piecrust for two crust pie. Make one crust slightly larger than 9-inch pie plate. Spoon sausage over the crust in the pie plate then add the spinach/egg mixture. Put remaining crust over filling. Press gently around edges of crust to seal. Cut slits in pastry top. Mix egg yolk with water. Brush top of pie with egg yolk mixture. Bake for 1¼ hours. Let stand 10 minutes. Cut into wedges.

Serves 10.

Marie R. Cappuccio

Sausage Puff

2	eggs	1	pound bulk sausage
1	cup milk	2	tablespoons butter
1	cup flour	2	tablespoons chopped chives

Preheat oven to 425 degrees.

Lightly beat eggs in mixing bowl. Alternately add milk and flour, beating well after each addition. Refrigerate at least 1 hour. Brown sausage in skillet. Place butter in shallow baking pan and put in oven until it sizzles. Stir chives in butter. When butter is hot, pour in batter and sprinkle evenly with sausage. Bake at 425 degrees for 15 minutes and then lower temperature to 350 degrees and bake 10 more minutes or until well-browned.

One pound of kielbasa, cut in ¼-inch slices may be used in place of sausage. Brown as for sausage.

Carol Toth

158

Turkey Tetrazzini

1	8-ounce package thin spaghetti	½	teaspoon grated nutmeg
5	cups cooked turkey (or chicken), diced	½	cup mayonnaise
		½	cup sherry
½	cup slivered almonds	½	cup whipping cream
1	teaspoon margarine	½	pound fresh mushrooms, sliced
2	10¾-ounce cans cream of mushroom soup	½	cup Parmesan cheese, grated
2	teaspoons Worcestershire sauce		

Preheat oven to 350 degrees.

Cook spaghetti as directed on package; drain. Put cooked spaghetti in a greased 3-quart casserole dish. Spread turkey over top. In small skillet, lightly toast almonds in margarine, then sprinkle over turkey. Blend soup, Worcestershire sauce, nutmeg, mayonnaise and sherry together. Whip cream until soft peaks form; fold gently into the soup mixture. Pour sauce evenly over top of casserole; top with mushroom slices and cheese. Bake 30 minutes until hot and bubbly.

Serves 8 to 10.

Jerriann Kirkwood

Barbecued Chicken In Oven

1	3-4 pound chicken, cut up, or boned breasts	1	cup ketchup
		1	cup water
½	cup flour	2	tablespoons brown sugar
¼-½	cup oil	2	tablespoons Worcestershire sauce
1	onion, sliced		
½	cup celery, minced	1	teaspoon salt

Preheat oven to 350 degrees.

Dredge chicken in flour and fry in oil until brown. Place in casserole dish. Brown onion and celery. Add remaining ingredients and pour over chicken. Bake for 1-1½ hours. Can be made ahead.

Serves 6.

Melissa Parrish

159

Lime Turkey Cutlets

⅓	cup flour	½	cup chicken broth
½	teaspoon freshly ground	3	tablespoons fresh lime juice
	pepper	¼	teaspoon dried dill
16	turkey breast cutlets, about	1	tablespoon chopped fresh
	2 pounds		parsley
3	tablespoons butter or		Lime slices
	margarine		

Combine flour and pepper; dredge turkey cutlets. Lightly coat a large skillet with vegetable cooking spray. Add butter to skillet and place over medium heat until butter melts. Add turkey and cook 2 to 3 minutes on each side or until browned; set aside. Dry skillet with paper towels. Combine chicken broth, lime juice and dill in skillet. Add turkey, cover and simmer over low heat 10 minutes or until turkey is tender. Remove to a warm platter. Sprinkle with parsley and garnish with lime slices.

Serves 6 to 8.

Argie Grader

Roasted Herb Turkey Breast On Grill

1   (4- to 5-pound) turkey breast

HERB DRESSING

¼	cup olive oil	½	teaspoon lemon rind
3	tablespoons Italian parsley	¼	teaspoon salt
1	teaspoon thyme leaves	¼	teaspoon pepper
1	teaspoon marjoram		

Preheat oven to 350 degrees or Weber Grill at Medium-Off-Medium. Whisk together herb dressing. Rinse the turkey breast and pat dry with a paper towel. Using fingers, gently separate skin from breast meat and pour about 2 tablespoons of dressing over meat and pin skin around edges with small skewer. Brush remaining dressing over entire breast. Roast turkey with lid to grill closed for 1½ hours or cook for the same amount of time in oven.

June Beerman

Rock Cornish Hens

¾ cup butter
¾ cup dry white wine
1 tablespoon dried tarragon
6 Cornish hens
6 garlic cloves

6 teaspoons dried tarragon
1½ teaspoons salt
¾ teaspoon pepper
Garlic salt

Preheat oven to 400 degrees.

Melt butter, add wine and dried tarragon. In each hen, place 1 clove of garlic, 1 teaspoon dried tarragon, ¼ teaspoon salt and ⅛ teaspoon pepper. Sprinkle outside of each hen with garlic salt. Place hens in shallow roasting pan. Bake for 1 hour and 15 minutes or until well-browned and drumstick twists easily. Baste several times while cooking with the melted butter, wine and tarragon sauce.

Serves 6.

Pat Butterfield

Cornish Hens In Cherry Sauce

2 Rock Cornish hens
2 teaspoons salt
½ teaspoon black pepper
1 stick butter, divided
3 tablespoons wine vinegar
3 tablespoons sugar

1 cup port wine
1 teaspoon cornstarch
2 tablespoons water
1½ cups canned pitted black cherries

Preheat oven to 375 degrees.

Season the hens with salt and pepper. Melt ½ the butter in a shallow baking pan and pour into the hens. Bake 50 minutes or until hens are browned and tender, basting frequently. Cut in half, arrange on a serving platter.

Cook the vinegar and sugar until caramel colored. Put aside. Add port wine to pan juices and reduce to half over high heat, scraping up the glaze from the pan. Stir in caramelized vinegar and sugar. Mix the cornstarch with cold water and stir into the pan, cooking until thickened. Mix in cherries and remaining butter and cook over low heat 5 minutes.

Serves 4.

Hens can be cooked, but not browned, in the morning. One-half hour before serving, return to oven to warm and brown.

Theresa Sullivan

Spicy Mustard Game Hens

¼	cup Dijon mustard	¾	teaspoon salt
3	tablespoons cream sherry	¼	teaspoon freshly cracked
2	tablespoons freshly grated		black pepper
	lemon zest	4	Cornish game hens, about
1	tablespoon butter, melted		1 pound each

Preheat oven to 450 degrees.

Combine mustard, sherry, lemon zest, butter, salt and pepper. Brush hens with marinade and place breast side up on rack set in roasting pan. Reduce oven temperature to 350 degrees. Roast hens 1 hour.

Remove the skin from the hens before cooking to save 99 calories and 5 grams of fat.

Katelyn S. and Larry Owens

Hunan Chicken

1½	teaspoons vegetable oil	1	ounce snow peas, strings
½	pound chicken breast, boned		removed
	and skinned, cut into cubes	1	tablespoon soy sauce
2	fresh mushrooms, sliced	⅛	teaspoon garlic powder
1	green onion, sliced on angle		Pinch of crushed red pepper
¼	red bell pepper, seeded,		flakes
	cored and cut into strips	1½	teaspoons cornstarch
1	clove garlic, chopped	1	tablespoon water
½	cup bok choy, sliced	2	tablespoons unsalted
1	ounce bean sprouts		cashews

Heat oil in large skillet or wok. Stir fry chicken about 10 minutes. Set aside. In same pan, cook mushrooms, green onion, red pepper, garlic and bok choy. Stir constantly for 5 minutes. Add bean sprouts and snow peas. Cook for 2 minutes. Stir in chicken, soy sauce, garlic powder and red pepper flakes. Cook for 2 minutes or until chicken is heated thoroughly. Blend in cornstarch mixed with water. Stir until thickened. Add cashews. Serve over hot rice.

Serves 4.

Barbara Burney

Orange Chicken With Sesame & Ginger

1	cup fresh orange juice	3	tablespoons grated orange
½	cup fresh lemon juice		peel
⅓	cup mango chutney	1	tablespoon sesame oil
¼	cup chopped, peeled, fresh	½	teaspoon dried crushed red
	ginger		pepper
3	tablespoons seasoned rice		
	vinegar		
¼	cup sesame seeds	6	tablespoons butter, divided
10	boneless chicken breast		
	halves, with skin		

Preheat oven to 400 degrees.
Combine first 8 ingredients in medium bowl. Whisk until blended. Pour mixture into 13x9-inch baking dish. Place sesame seeds in small bowl. Sprinkle chicken with salt and pepper. Place skin side down on seeds, coating skin. Melt 3 tablespoons butter in large nonstick skillet over high heat. Add 5 breasts, skin side down, to skillet and cook until golden, about 3 minutes. Turn chicken over; cook 2 minutes longer. Place chicken, skin side up, in marinade in baking dish. Wash skillet. Repeat with 3 tablespoons butter and 5 chicken breasts. Cover chicken with foil; bake until cooked through, about 20 minutes. Remove foil; let chicken cool 1 hour, uncovered, in marinade. Cover and chill overnight. Let stand 1 hour at room temperature before serving.
Serves 10.
Couscous is a nice accompaniment.

Betsy Contino

Chicken Atherton

8	chicken breasts	1	can whole cranberry sauce
6	chicken legs	1	package dry onion soup mix
1	8-ounce bottle French		
	dressing		

Place chicken pieces with meaty part down in a 9x13-inch baking dish. Mix together dressing, cranberry sauce and soup mix. Pour over chicken. Bake for approximately 1 hour and 15 minutes.

Pat Dickinson

163

Chicken Broccoli Casserole

1	bunch green onions, chopped	½	teaspoon pepper
2	tablespoons butter	1	8-ounce package spaghetti,
4	chicken breast halves,		cooked and drained
	cooked and chopped	2½	cups sharp cheddar cheese,
1	bunch broccoli, steamed and		grated, divided
	chopped	¾	cup whipping cream
1	teaspoon salt		Paprika

Preheat oven to 375 degrees.

In large skillet, sauté onions in butter. Add chicken, broccoli, salt and pepper. Cook 5 minutes over low heat. Put spaghetti in 3-quart baking dish and cover with half the cheese. Pour cream over cheese. Add chicken mixture. Top with remaining cheese. Sprinkle with paprika. Bake for 30 minutes.

Monica de Guzman

Chicken Brunswick Stew

1	large onion, chopped	⅛	cup Worcestershire sauce
3	chicken breast halves	2	tablespoons butter, cut up
1	15-ounce can cream style	1	tablespoon cider vinegar
	corn	1	teaspoon dry mustard
1	14-ounce can crushed	¼	teaspoon salt
	tomatoes	¼	teaspoon pepper
1	7-ounce can chicken broth,	¼	teaspoon hot pepper sauce
	or equivalent bouillon	1	box frozen baby limas
1	6-ounce bottle salsa	1	box frozen chopped okra

In the bottom of a crock pot, place onion, then chicken, then corn, then rest of ingredients except frozen vegetables. Cook on high for 4 hours. Remove chicken and shred it. Cook frozen vegetables while shredding chicken and add both chicken and vegetables to the stew continuing to cook for 30 minutes more.

Karen Sellick

Stir Fry & Sauce

2   tablespoons cornstarch
1¼ cups water
⅓   cup soy sauce
⅓   cup corn syrup, light or dark
½   teaspoon crushed dried red
    pepper

1   pound boneless chicken, beef
    or pork
Assorted fresh vegetables, cut up
4   tablespoons vegetable oil,
    divided

In bowl, mix cornstarch and water until smooth. Stir in soy sauce, corn syrup and red pepper. In wok or large skillet, heat 2 tablespoons vegetable oil over medium to high heat. Add meat of choice. Stir fry 5 minutes until tender. Remove meat. Heat remaining oil in wok and add cut fresh vegetables. Stir fry 1 minute until vegetables are tender crisp. Return meat to skillet with vegetables. Add sauce to skillet. Stirring constantly, bring to boil for 1 minute. Serve over rice.

Serves 4 to 6.

Anne Faxon

Chicken Cacciatore

2   pounds boned, skinned
    chicken breasts, cubed
½   cup flour
1   teaspoon salt
½   teaspoon pepper
¼   cup olive oil
¼   cup butter
1   cup onions, chopped

3   cups fresh mushrooms,
    sliced
½   cup parsley, chopped
1   clove garlic, minced
1   teaspoon basil
1   28-ounce can tomato pieces
1   cup white wine

Preheat oven to 350 degrees.

Combine flour, salt and pepper in paper bag. Shake chicken pieces in flour mix, coating well. Heat oil and butter in large skillet. Brown chicken on all sides. Remove from pan and drain. Brown onions and mushrooms in same skillet, add parsley, garlic and basil and cook 5 minutes. Add tomatoes and wine. Place chicken mixture in 4-quart casserole, cover and bake 45-60 minutes. Serve over rice or noodles.

Serves 8.

Jane Heiser

Poulet Maman Dupont

1   package (3 cups) herb   1   cup water or chicken broth
    stuffing   ½   cup melted butter

Combine and spread ½ the mixture in a 9x13-inch pan.

2½ cups cooked chicken, cubed   ½   cup celery, chopped
½   cup onion, chopped   ½   cup mayonnaise
½   cup green onion tops,   ¾   teaspoon salt
    chopped

Combine ingredients and spread over stuffing mixture.

2   eggs   1½ cups milk

Beat eggs with milk. Mix with the leftover half of the stuffing mixture. Pour this over the chicken mixture in the casserole. Cover and refrigerate several hours or overnight.

1   can cream of mushroom or   ¼   cup dry vermouth
    cream of chicken soup   Cheddar cheese, grated

One hour before baking, combine soup and vermouth. Pour over casserole. Preheat oven to 325 degrees. Bake, uncovered, for 40-50 minutes. Top with cheddar cheese 10 minutes before removing from oven.

Chopped mushrooms, almonds or water chestnuts may be added to chicken mixture if desired.

Jackie Linder

Chicken In A Pot

1   chicken, about 3 pounds   2   teaspoons salt
2   carrots, quartered   ½   teaspoon pepper
2   medium onions, quartered   ½-1 cup water
2   celery stalks with leaves   ½-1 teaspoon basil

Put everything in crockpot and cook on low setting for 7-10 hours, or on high setting for 2½-3 hours.

Pat Dickinson

166

Sautéed Chicken Breasts
With Mustard & Tarragon

3	tablespoons unsalted butter, divided	1	cup chicken stock
2	tablespoons oil, divided	2	minced cloves garlic
2	whole large chicken breasts, boned, skinned and halved	3	tablespoons grainy mustard
		½	cup cream, optional
2	medium shallots, finely chopped	1	tablespoon fresh tarragon, chopped
Tomato and mushrooms, optional		1	teaspoon fresh thyme, chopped
½	cup white wine	½	teaspoon salt and pepper

In large skillet, heat 2 tablespoons butter and 1 tablespoon oil over medium-high heat. Sauté breasts until golden on both sides. This ensures that the juices will be seared in. Remove from skillet to dish and cover. Add remaining butter and oil to skillet. Add shallots and sauté 2 minutes. Add wine, stock and garlic and boil until reduced to ¾ to ½ cup. Whisk in mustard (and ½ cup cream if you wish) and bring to boil. Add herbs and spices. Return breasts and their juices to skillet and cook 5 minutes until warmed. Garnish with fresh parsley.

Serves 4 to 6.

May be prepared up to 2 hours ahead until time to whisk in mustard, and kept at room temperature. Add a chopped tomato or mushroom with shallots for variation.

Betsy Contino

Skinny Chicken Delight

4	chicken leg quarters, skin removed	⅓	cup soy sauce
		⅓	cup lemon juice
Minced garlic			

Place leg quarters in microwave safe baking dish. Rub chicken with minced garlic. Mix soy sauce with lemon juice and pour over chicken. Marinate for 15 minutes or more. Cover dish with waxed paper and microwave for 15 minutes at power level 10. Remove to turn pieces over and microwave for 10 minutes more.

Serves 4.

Marie Scheuermann

167

Hot Chicken Salad

16 SERVINGS		4 SERVINGS	
8	cups chicken breasts, cooked and diced	2	cups chicken breasts, cooked and diced
8	cups celery, diced	2	cups celery, diced
2	cups blanched almonds	½	cup blanched almonds
2	teaspoons salt	½	teaspoon salt
4	tablespoons lemon juice	1	tablespoon lemon juice
2	cups mayonnaise	½	cup mayonnaise
2	cups cream	½	cup cream
8	teaspoons onion, chopped	2	teaspoons onion, chopped
2	cups cheddar cheese, shredded	½	cup cheddar cheese, shredded

Preheat oven to 350 degrees.

Mix all ingredients together with exception of cheese. Place in a baking dish and top with cheese. Bake 20-30 minutes for 4 servings. Bake 1 hour plus if one large casserole dish is used for serving 16.

Suzanne Reid

Chicken & Wild Rice

2	6-ounce boxes long grain and wild rice mix	½	cup chopped parsley
6	whole chicken breasts or 12 halves	½	cup chopped pimiento
1	large can sliced mushrooms	3	cans cream of mushroom soup
1	can sliced water chestnuts	¾	cup cream sherry

Preheat oven to 425 degrees.

Simmer chicken in water for about 20 minutes. Save broth from chicken. Cut cooked chicken into cubes. Cook rice according to package directions. Combine all other ingredients and place in a large pot. Heat slowly. Add milk or chicken broth if too thick. Place in large casserole dish. Bake 30 minutes. Serves 10 to 12.

Joan Kassebaum

Baked Chicken

1	3-pound fryer, cut up	1	can cream of mushroom
Salt and pepper, to taste			soup
½	cup flour	1	cup sour cream
1	teaspoon paprika	1	cup cheddar cheese,
1	teaspoon baking powder		shredded
1	teaspoon poultry seasoning		
1	6-ounce can sliced mushrooms		

Preheat oven to 350 degrees.

Combine all dry ingredients in a brown bag. Shake chicken in dry mixture. Brown chicken in small amount of oil. Arrange in 13x9-inch baking dish. Drain mushrooms, reserving liquid. Add water to reserved mushroom liquid to make ½ cup. Combine soup, mushrooms, mushroom liquid and sour cream; blend well and pour over chicken. Bake for 1 hour or until chicken is tender. Sprinkle with cheese. Bake for 3 minutes longer or until cheese is melted.

Serves 6.

May be made ahead of time, refrigerated and reheated just before serving. Good served with rice.

Bobbie Stabe

Grilled Chicken

6	chicken breasts, skinless and boneless

MARINADE

6	tablespoons olive oil	3	tablespoons grainy mustard
4	tablespoons cider vinegar	2	cloves garlic, minced
4	tablespoons lemon juice	½	teaspoon salt
½	cup brown sugar, packed		

Mix together. Marinate chicken for at least 2 hours in refrigerator before grilling.

Serves 6.

Lois Flanagan

Orange Chicken

6	chicken breast halves, boneless and skinless	1½	tablespoons fresh lemon juice
3	egg whites, beaten	1½	tablespoons lemon zest
¾	cup dry bread crumbs	2½	teaspoons Worcestershire sauce
3	tablespoons olive oil		
1	cup orange juice	2	cloves garlic, crushed
1	cup orange marmalade	1½	tablespoons Dijon mustard

Lightly pound chicken breasts to prevent shrinkage. Dip each piece of chicken in egg white and then in bread crumbs, coating evenly. In large skillet, heat oil and sauté each breaded breast over medium heat until golden. Remove from pan. Combine all other ingredients in skillet. Cook over medium heat, stirring until smooth. Add chicken, cover and cook 10 more minutes.

Onnie Duffie

Drunken Chicken

4	whole chicken breasts, halved, boned and skinned	1	28-ounce can tomato wedges, undrained
Salt and freshly ground pepper to taste		½	teaspoon ground cinnamon
		¼	teaspoon ground cloves
1	cup all-purpose flour	¼	cup packed light brown sugar
2	tablespoons olive oil		
2	tablespoons butter	1	cup dry sherry or vermouth
1	large onion, finely chopped	½	cup golden raisins
2	tablespoons minced fresh parsley	½	cup slivered almonds

Preheat oven to 375 degrees.

Season chicken with salt and pepper and dredge with flour. In large skillet, brown chicken in oil and butter. Place browned chicken in shallow 3-quart casserole dish. In same pan, cook onions until transparent. Add parsley, tomatoes with liquid, cinnamon, cloves, brown sugar, sherry and raisins and simmer uncovered for 15 to 20 minutes, stirring occasionally. Pour over chicken and sprinkle with almonds. Bake for 30 minutes.

Serves 6.

To serve 8, double the sauce and use 6 whole chicken breasts.

Ann Robertson

Chicken Breast Saltimbocca

12	split, skinless chicken breasts	¼	teaspoon garlic salt
12	paper thin slices ham	¼	cup flour
¼	pound Swiss cheese, slices	1	beaten egg
2	tablespoons Parmesan	4	tablespoons butter
	cheese	½	cup sherry
¾	cup bread crumbs	½	cup chicken broth

Preheat oven to 350 degrees.

Lay ham and Swiss cheese on flattened chicken breast. Roll lengthwise and fasten with toothpicks. Mix together Parmesan cheese, bread crumbs and garlic salt. Set aside. Dip chicken in flour, shake off excess. Dip in egg; roll in bread crumb mixture. Brown in butter, put in baking dish and cover with sherry and chicken broth. Bake uncovered for 30-45 minutes.

SAUCE

1	tablespoon cornstarch	½	cup regular strength
1	tablespoon water		chicken broth
		½	cup sherry

Dissolve cornstarch in water. Add broth and sherry. Heat and stir until thickened. Pass with chicken.

Arlene Gilligan

Chicken Supreme

8-10	chicken breast halves	1	package dry onion soup
1	can mushroom soup	1	soup can white wine
1	6-ounce jar mushroom	¼	cup water
	pieces or caps		

Preheat oven to 350 degrees.

Arrange chicken breasts in 13x9-inch or 9x15-inch baking dish. Mix all ingredients and pour over chicken. Bake for 1-1½ hours. Serve with rice. Use remaining sauce as gravy over chicken or rice.

Sue Winship

Chicken Casserole

7	ounces thin spaghetti	2	cans (or 1 family-size) cream	
½	pound mushrooms, sliced		of chicken soup	
½	cup butter	⅓	cup dry white wine	
4	whole chicken breasts,	2	tablespoons Parmesan	
	cooked		cheese, grated	
2	cups lowfat sour cream	8	ounces mozzarella cheese,	
			shredded	

Preheat oven to 300 degrees.

Break spaghetti into 1-inch pieces and cook until tender. Sauté sliced mushrooms in butter. Cut chicken into bite-size pieces. Combine all but cheeses. Pour mixture into 9x12-inch pan which has been greased with cooking spray. Top with cheeses using mozzarella first and then Parmesan. Bake 45-60 minutes.

Serves 8 to 10.

Recommend making 24 hours ahead to blend flavors. May be frozen.

Mary Stewart

Joan's Chicken

8	chicken cutlets	½	can cream of celery soup	
8	ounces Swiss cheese, sliced	½	can cream of chicken soup	
8	slices prosciutto, diced	1	cup white wine	
5	slices boiled ham, diced	2	cups packaged herbed	
16	ounces fresh mushrooms,		stuffing mix	
	sliced	1	stick butter	

Preheat oven to 350 degrees.

Spray glass baking dish with cooking spray. Cut chicken cutlets into pieces and cover the bottom of the pan with chicken. Do not leave spaces. Cover the chicken with Swiss cheese. Sprinkle prosciutto and boiled ham generously over cheese. Layer mushrooms densely over the ham and prosciutto. Whisk soups and wine together and heat. Pour hot soup mixture over mushrooms. Top with stuffing mix and drizzle with melted butter. Bake 45-50 minutes.

Serves 8 to 10.

Joan Kassebaum

Chicken Andalusia

8	boneless chicken breast halves	2-3	cloves garlic, pressed or minced
Flour		½	cup sliced almonds
2-3	tablespoons olive oil	½	cup raisins
½	cup pimiento-stuffed green olives, sliced	1	cup port or sherry wine (not cooking sherry)
½	cup green onions with tops, sliced	Salt and pepper, to taste
		1-2	tablespoons brown sugar

Preheat oven to 325 degrees.

Dredge chicken breasts in flour and sauté in olive oil until browned. Remove from skillet. Using same pan, sauté olives, green onions and garlic in oil about 5 minutes. (Add additional oil by tablespoon if skillet is too dry.) Add almonds and continue to sauté additional 5 minutes.

Heat raisins in port or sherry in separate pot until raisins are plump. Add raisins and liquid to skillet of sautéed vegetables. Make a thin roux of 1 tablespoon flour and ⅓ cup of water and stir into mixture. Stir in seasonings and sugar, adding enough water or wine to make about 2 cups liquid total, including original liquid. Return chicken to skillet and transfer all to casserole. Bake covered for 45 minutes and uncovered 15-20 minutes more. Serve with rice.

Serves 8.

A small amount of saffron added to rice will give it color and complete this dish using native Spanish ingredients.

Sally Robyn

Hot Chicken Salad

2	cups cooked chicken, cubed	1	cup mayonnaise
2	cups diced celery	½	cup slivered almonds
2	teaspoons grated onion	½	cup grated cheddar cheese
2	tablespoons lemon juice	1	cup potato chips, crushed

Preheat oven to 450 degrees.

Mix first six ingredients together and pile lightly in baking dish. Sprinkle with cheese and top with potato chips. Bake 20 minutes.

Serves 5 to 6.

Katie Wood

Tuscan Chicken

1	pound boneless, skinless, chicken breasts, cut into 1-inch cubes	1	26-ounce jar chunky garden spaghetti sauce
2	tablespoons olive oil	½	pound frozen whole green beans
2	cloves garlic, minced	1	teaspoon dried basil or Italian seasoning
4	medium potatoes, cut into ½-inch cubes		Salt and pepper, to taste
1	medium green bell pepper, diced		

Sauté chicken in oil. Add garlic and sauté. Add potatoes and pepper. Cook 5 minutes. Add spaghetti sauce, beans and seasonings. Simmer 35 minutes until chicken and potatoes are done.

Serves 6.

Elayne Blecker

Parmesan Chicken Breasts

6	boneless, skinless chicken breast halves, about 2 pounds, marinated in white wine for 20 minutes	¼	cup dry bread crumbs
		1	teaspoon dried oregano leaves
6	tablespoons melted margarine	1	teaspoon parsley flakes
½	cup grated Parmesan cheese	¼	teaspoon paprika
		¼	teaspoon salt
		¼	teaspoon pepper

Preheat oven to 400 degrees.

Spray a 15x10x1-inch baking pan with cooking spray. Remove chicken from wine and dip in melted margarine. Coat with combined remaining ingredients. Place into prepared pan. Bake 20-25 minutes or until tender. Freezes well.

Serves 6.

Marcia Wilk

P oultry is for the cook what canvas is for the painter.

Brillat-Savarin

Chicken & Rice Casserole

1	cup rice, uncooked	¾	cup mayonnaise
2	cups sliced celery	¾	cup water
2	cups finely chopped carrots	½	cup dry white wine
1	cup chopped onion	2	teaspoons curry powder
1	cup sliced fresh mushrooms	8	chicken breast halves,
1	10-ounce can cream of		skinned and boned
	mushroom soup		Paprika

Preheat oven to 350 degrees.

Place rice in greased 8x12-inch glass baking dish. Combine vegetables and put over rice. Mix soup, mayonnaise, water, wine and curry powder in a blender. Pour half of soup mixture over rice and vegetables. Place chicken breasts on top and cover with remaining soup mixture. Sprinkle with paprika. Cover and bake for 30 minutes. Remove cover and bake another 30 minutes or until bubbly. If it seems dry, add a little more wine or water.

Serves 8.

This dish does not freeze well. Can be prepared one day ahead of baking.

Patty Boggs

Chicken Pot Pie

2	pie crusts, unbaked	1	can cream of mushroom
4	chicken breast halves		soup
1	small onion, chopped	⅓	cup white wine or sherry
8	ounces fresh mushrooms,	½	teaspoon poultry seasoning
	sliced	1	small box or bag of frozen
			peas

Preheat oven to 425 degrees.

Place one pie crust in 10-inch pie plate. Cook chicken, cool and cut into bite-size pieces; set aside. Sauté onions until soft; add mushrooms. Add soup, blending well. Stir in wine and add poultry seasoning, peas and chicken. When mixture is heated, pour into pie shell. Cover with second pie crust, making slashes on top. Bake at 425 degrees for 10 minutes. Reduce heat to 375 degrees and continue to cook for 25 minutes. Freezes well.

Serves 4.

Bobbie Tooher

Chicken Fajita Feta-Chini

2	teaspoons chili powder	2	cups combined red, green
1	teaspoon ground cumin		and yellow bell pepper strips
1	teaspoon oregano	1	medium onion, sliced
2	tablespoons fresh lime juice	1	cup mild or medium hot
3	boneless, skinless chicken		salsa
	breast halves, cut into	6	ounces feta cheese
	2x3-inch strips	8	ounces fettuccine, cooked
2	tablespoons olive oil		and drained

In medium bowl, combine chili powder, cumin, oregano and lime juice. Add chicken and stir to coat. Set aside while you prepare other ingredients. Heat 1 tablespoon oil in large skillet, add chicken and cook 5 minutes or until done. Remove chicken and add peppers and onions to same skillet. Cook and stir 5 minutes or until tender/crisp. Stir in salsa, bring to boil. Add chicken and ¾ cup feta cheese; heat through. Spoon over pasta, toss and sprinkle remaining cheese over dish.

Serves 6 to 8.

This dish is good hot, cold or at room temperature. Other pastas can be used. Penne is suggested.

Margaret McCulloch

Chicken Breast Gourmet

1	cup corn flakes	1	cup pineapple juice
1	teaspoon salt	1	tablespoon cornstarch
¼	teaspoon thyme	1	tablespoon sugar
¼	teaspoon marjoram	¼	teaspoon curry powder
¼	teaspoon paprika	1	tablespoon lemon juice
2	whole chicken breasts, cut in	3	tablespoons sherry
	half		Slivered almonds, browned
1	egg, slightly beaten		

Preheat oven to 300 degrees.

Combine corn flakes with salt, thyme, marjoram and paprika. Dip chicken in egg and roll in seasoned crumbs. Brown in butter. Place in casserole in single layer. Mix pineapple juice, cornstarch, sugar, curry and lemon juice. Pour over chicken and cover with heavy foil. Bake for 1 hour. Before serving, pour sherry over and top with almonds.

Linda Shaw

176

Chicken Strudel With Mushroom Sauce

1	2½-3 pound broiler-fryer or breast meat	2	tablespoons chopped parsley
1	teaspoon salt	½	teaspoon pepper
Water		½	cup butter
1	8-ounce package Muenster cheese, shredded	Phyllo, about ½ pound	

SAUCE

3	tablespoons butter	2	tablespoons all-purpose flour
½	pound mushrooms, thinly sliced	½	cup milk
1	green onion, thinly sliced	1	2-ounce jar diced pimiento, drained

Preheat oven to 375 degrees.

Night before or about 2½ hours before serving: Rinse chicken, giblets and neck in running cold water. Place chicken, breast side down, in 5-quart saucepan or Dutch oven; add giblets, neck, 1 teaspoon salt, and 2 inches water; over high heat, heat to boiling. Reduce heat to low; cover and simmer 35 minutes or until chicken is fork tender. Remove chicken to large bowl; refrigerate 30 minutes or until easy to handle. Reserve ½ cup broth. Discard skin and bones; cut meat and giblets into bite-size pieces. In same large bowl, toss chicken pieces with cheese, parsley and ½ teaspoon pepper.

Grease large cookie sheet. In 1-quart saucepan, over low heat, melt ½ cup butter. Cut two 24-inch lengths of waxed paper; overlap two lengthwise sides about ½-inch; fasten with cellophane tape. On waxed paper, place one sheet of phyllo; brush with some melted butter. Layer two more sheets of phyllo, brushing each sheet with butter. Cut sheets into two, 6½-x9-inch rectangles, and spoon about ⅔ cup chicken mixture onto center of a narrow end of each. Starting at same narrow end, roll phyllo, jelly roll fashion or make a package shape. Fold ends under. Repeat with remaining phyllo and chicken to make 6 "packages." Place phyllo packages on cookie sheet, seam side down. Brush each with more melted butter. Bake 20-25 minutes or until golden brown.

In 3-quart saucepan, melt 3 tablespoons butter; add mushrooms and green onion and cook until vegetables are tender, stirring occasionally. With slotted spoon, spoon vegetables into small bowl. Into remaining liquid (or add more butter), stir flour until blended. Gradually stir in milk, reserved chicken broth, ½ teaspoon salt, ⅛ teaspoon pepper. Cook over medium heat until slightly thickened, stirring. Add mushroom mixture and pimiento. Sauce is served with phyllo. Make 1½ amount of sauce if you like a more generous serving. Serves 6.

Joyce Blanke

177

Mediterranean Saffron Chicken

12	chicken pieces, breasts, thighs, legs		Pinch of sage
3	tablespoons olive oil	2	bay leaves
3	tablespoons butter or margarine	1	28-ounce can whole tomatoes, drained and cut into chunks
1½	teaspoons saffron	¾	cup white wine
1	tablespoon lemon juice	¾	cup chicken broth
2	garlic cloves, sliced		Salt and pepper, to taste
½	teaspoon tarragon, or 1 tablespoon fresh	¾	cup pitted green olives, about 36
¼	teaspoon thyme, or 1 tablespoon fresh		Chopped parsley

Sauté chicken in olive oil and butter until browned. Soak saffron in lemon juice and add to chicken along with garlic, herbs, tomatoes, wine, chicken broth and salt and pepper. Bring to a simmer, cover and allow to simmer about 30 minutes or until chicken is tender. Add olives the last 10 minutes of cooking. Garnish with parsley. Serve with rice. Easily doubled. Can be made ahead and reheated. Serves 6.

June Hutchinson

Chicken Reuben

4	chicken breasts, skinned and boned	8	slices Swiss cheese
1	can (or fresh) sauerkraut, drained and rinsed	1	8-ounce bottle Thousand Island salad dressing

Preheat oven to 375 degrees.
Fold chicken breasts in half rounds. Place in ungreased 8x11-inch baking dish. Top each breast with sauerkraut and a slice of cheese. Cover all with salad dressing. Cover and bake 40 minutes.

Linda Shaw

I have Henri-Paul Pellaprat on my shelf but Fannie Farmer in my heart.

178   Robert Farrar Capon

Make Ahead Chicken

3	whole chicken breasts	1	10½-ounce can cream of
3	ounces chipped beef		mushroom soup
Salt		1	pint dairy sour cream
Pepper			

Preheat oven to 250 degrees.

Remove skin and bones from chicken and cut breasts in half. Blanch chipped beef in boiling water. Drain beef and cut slices in half. Lay beef slices on bottom of greased casserole dish. Put chicken in single layer on top of beef. Sprinkle with salt and pepper to taste. Mix undiluted soup and sour cream. Spread mixture over chicken, cover and bake 4 hours. Serve with rice which has been cooked separately.

Karen Blado

Chicken Marsala

4	skinless chicken breasts	2	cloves garlic, minced,
4	tablespoons butter, divided		divided
3	tablespoons olive oil, divided	¾	cup Marsala wine, divided
1	medium onion, diced	1	tablespoon tomato paste
		12	ounces sliced mushrooms

Pound chicken flat between waxed paper. Dredge chicken in flour to lightly coat. In a large skillet, sauté chicken in 2 tablespoons of butter and 1 tablespoon olive oil until lightly browned. Set aside to drain on paper toweling. Sauté the onions and 1 clove of garlic in 2 tablespoons of olive oil until golden. Place chicken back into the skillet with the cooked onions and garlic. Pour ½ cup of the Marsala wine into the skillet and stir in the tomato paste. Let simmer.

In a separate skillet, sauté the mushrooms with a clove of minced garlic in 2 tablespoons of butter and ¼ cup Marsala wine. Cook until the liquid is absorbed. Pour mushrooms over chicken and serve over cooked noodles, rice or with garlic mashed potatoes.

Serves 4.

Vikki Alpher

*W**hen you are on the verge of calling the whole thing off, calm yourself with a poultry recipe.*

Unknown

179

Scampi

1	teaspoon olive oil	1¼	pounds large shrimp, peeled
5	garlic cloves, minced		and deveined
2	28-ounce cans whole	1	cup crumbled feta cheese
	tomatoes, drained and		(4 ounces)
	coarsely chopped	2	tablespoons fresh lemon
½	cup chopped fresh parsley,		juice
	divided	¼	teaspoon fresh ground
			pepper

Preheat oven to 400 degrees.

Heat oil in a large Dutch oven over medium heat. Add garlic; sauté 30 seconds. Add tomatoes and ¼ cup parsley. Reduce heat; simmer 10 minutes. Add shrimp; cook 5 minutes. Pour mixture into a 13x9-inch baking dish; sprinkle with cheese. Bake for 10 minutes. Sprinkle with ¼ cup parsley, lemon juice and pepper.

Serves 6.

Chris Aiken

Shrimp Creole

½	cup onion, chopped	1	teaspoon sugar
½	cup celery, chopped	1	tablespoon Worcestershire
1	clove garlic, minced		sauce
1	16-ounce can (2 cups)	1	teaspoon cornstarch
	tomatoes, chopped,	2	teaspoons cold water
	undrained	½	cup green bell pepper,
1	8-ounce can seasoned tomato		chopped
	sauce	¾	pound raw, cleaned shrimp
1½	teaspoons salt		

Cook onions, celery and garlic in hot fat until tender but not brown. Add tomatoes, tomato sauce and seasonings. Simmer, uncovered, 45 minutes. Mix cornstarch with water; stir into sauce. Cook and stir until mixture thickens. Add green pepper and shrimp. Cover. Simmer until done, about 5 minutes. Serve over cooked rice.

Serves 5 to 6.

Carolyn A. Brooks

Shrimp With Sweet & Sour Dipping Sauce

2	pounds large or jumbo shrimp	1	teaspoon freshly ground pepper
¾-1	cup vegetable oil	1	teaspoon Worcestershire sauce
1	cup lemon juice		
2	teaspoons Italian salad dressing mix	¼	cup packed brown sugar
		2	tablespoons soy sauce
2	teaspoons seasoned salt	½	cup chopped green onions

Rinse the shrimp well. Peel and devein the shrimp. Drain on paper towels.

Mix the vegetable oil, lemon juice, salad dressing mix, seasoned salt, pepper and Worcestershire sauce in a bowl. Place the shrimp in a large bowl. Add the marinade. Marinate, covered, in the refrigerator for 2 to 4 hours, stirring occasionally.

Drain the shrimp, reserving the marinade. Bring the reserved marinade to a boil in a saucepan. Boil for 1-2 minutes. Thread the shrimp onto skewers and place on a hot grill rack. Grill for 7-10 minutes, turning once and brushing with some of the heated marinade. Add the brown sugar, soy sauce and green onions to the remaining marinade. Bring to a boil. Boil 1-2 minutes, stirring frequently. Serve with the shrimp for dipping.

Serves 5.

Betsy Smith

Fabulous Fish

2	tablespoons olive oil	1	tomato, chopped
3-4	leeks, washed, dried and chopped	1	cup white wine
		3	pounds fish filets, halibut or salmon
1	large onion, chopped		
2	garlic cloves, minced		Salt and pepper, to taste
1	green bell pepper, chopped	1	cup white grapes, halved

In large sauté pan, "sweat" the leeks in olive oil. Add onion and garlic and sauté slowly until onion is transparent. Add green pepper and tomato and cook 5-7 minutes, covered. Remove lid and add wine. Cook until wine reduces. Push vegetables to side of pan and add fish. Pile vegetables over fish. Salt and pepper. Add grapes and a little extra wine. Cover and poach until fish is cooked through. Serve hot or cold.

Serves 6.

Norma Rappaport

Chilled Caribbean Black Beans With Shrimp

2	15-ounce cans black beans, drained and rinsed	1⅓	cups picante sauce
1	large green bell pepper	½	cup fresh lime juice
1	cup sliced celery	¼	cup canola oil
1	medium red onion, peeled, sliced, separated into rings	¼	cup honey
¼	cup chopped fresh cilantro	¼	teaspoon salt
		1	cup fresh or frozen corn kernels
3	cups water	1	pound medium shrimp, in shells
2	level tablespoons Old Savannah Seafood Seasoning		Lettuce leaves
			Grape tomatoes, halved

Combine beans, bell pepper, celery, red onion, cilantro, picante sauce, lime juice, oil, honey and salt. Add corn. Toss to blend. Cover and chill 8-10 hours.

Heat seasoning spices and water to boiling. Add shrimp and cook 3-5 minutes until shrimp are pink. Drain and rinse with cold water. Chill one hour. Peel and devein. Can all be prepared a day ahead to this point.

Line individual serving plates with lettuce leaves and spoon black bean mixture in center. Arrange shrimp and tomatoes on top.

Serves 4 to 6.

Suzy Goldman

Low Country Boil (Frogmore Stew)

¼	cup Old Bay seasoning	6	ears corn, halved
4	pounds small red potatoes	4	pounds unpeeled large fresh shrimp
2	pounds kielbasa sausage, cut into 1½-inch slices	1	large onion, optional

Fill a 6- to 8-quart pot halfway with water. Add Old Bay seasoning (and onion, if using) and bring to a boil. Add potatoes, return to a boil and cook 10 minutes. Add kielbasa and corn, return to a boil and cook 10 minutes. Add shrimp; cook until shrimp are pink, 3-5 minutes. Remove meat and vegetables from broth with a slotted spoon or by pouring mixture into a colander and place on a serving platter. Serve with cocktail sauce.

Serves 6 to 8 generously.

Joy Borden

Shrimp With Tomato & Feta Cheese Sauce

1	medium-sized onion, chopped		Freshly ground pepper, to taste
3	tablespoons olive oil	1	teaspoon dried oregano or
2	garlic cloves, minced		3 tablespoons fresh
1½	pounds ripe tomatoes,	2	tablespoons capers
	peeled, seeded and chopped		Cayenne pepper or red pepper
	or 3 cups canned, drained		flakes, to taste
½	cup dry red or white wine	2	pounds unshelled shrimp
½	cup chopped parsley leaves	¾	pound feta cheese, crumbled
	Coarse salt, to taste		Fresh basil leaves

Preheat oven to 400 degrees.

Cook onion in olive oil until soft. Add garlic, tomatoes, wine, parsley, salt, pepper, oregano, capers, cayenne or red pepper flakes. Meanwhile, peel and clean shrimp. Add the feta cheese to the tomato mixture, and stir in shrimp. Bake about 15 minutes or until the shrimp are cooked, stirring once. Be extra careful not to overcook the shrimp. Garnish with fresh basil leaves. Serve with rice.

Serves 4.

Use a pan that will go on top of the stove and in the oven. A cast-iron skillet works well.

Paige Word

Seattle Salmon

4	salmon fillets	1	lemon
2	large oranges	1	stick butter
2	limes		

Melt butter in baking dish until just liquid. Grate zest from oranges and limes into the butter. Add juice of one orange, one lime and half of a lemon to the butter and mix. Slice the remaining citrus into ¼-inch slices and set aside. Cover heated grill with foil so fish won't stick. Put fish on foil with skin side down and cover with fruit slices. Brush generously with butter mixture, splashing a little over the coals to create smoke for a better flavor. Cover and cook. Generously brush with the butter mixture several times during the cooking. Remove from the grill when fish is opaque and flakes. Brush with butter mixture one more time before serving and garnish with remaining citrus slices.

Serves 4.

Pat Palmer

183

Curried Shrimp

3   pounds raw shrimp

Boil shrimp in crab boil or a broth made of:

Sufficient water to cover shrimp		½	bay leaf
1	small onion, sliced	6	peppercorns
¼	teaspoon mace	1	slice lemon
1	clove garlic, minced	⅛	teaspoon pepper
1	teaspoon salt		

1½	tablespoons cornstarch	1	quart heavy cream or
¼	teaspoon curry powder		½ evaporated milk and
¾	teaspoon salt		½ cream
¼	teaspoon cayenne pepper	½	cup sherry

Cook shrimp and peel. Mix together the cornstarch, curry powder, salt and cayenne. Bring heavy cream to a boil. Add cornstarch mixture and stir until thick. Add sherry and shrimp. Heat only until hot. Serve over rice.

Serves 6 to 8.

Accompaniments to top shrimp at serving: chutney, bacon bits, chopped peanuts, fresh coconut.

Betty Stroup

Poached Cod With Egg Sauce

1½	pounds cod fillets, or other white fish	3	hard-cooked eggs, chopped
Milk		1-2	tablespoons coarsely chopped parsley
6	tablespoons melted butter	Salt, to taste	
3	tablespoons flour	Paprika	
1-2	teaspoons dry mustard		

Place cod, in a single layer, in well-greased large skillet. Pour in enough milk to just cover the fish. Bring the milk just to boiling. Immediately reduce the heat and simmer until fish flakes easily, about 15 minutes. Remove fish to a warm platter. Blend butter, flour and mustard; stir into the milk, cooking until thickened. Add eggs, parsley and salt. Pour sauce over cod and sprinkle with paprika.

Serves 4.

Karen Blado

Cheesy Shrimp & Wild Rice Casserole

2	tablespoons margarine	1	tablespoon Worcestershire
1	small onion		sauce
1	small bell pepper, chopped	2	teaspoons lemon juice
2	pounds or more cleaned		Cream of mushroom soup
	shrimp		(enough for desired
	Dash of garlic powder		consistency)
2	teaspoons Dijon mustard	1½	cups cheddar cheese, grated,
	Salt and pepper, to taste		divided
	Dash of dill weed	2	boxes long grain and wild
	Dash of oregano		rice mix, cooked

Preheat oven to 400 degrees.

Sauté onion, bell pepper and shrimp in margarine. Add all remaining ingredients except rice and 1 cup of cheese. Place in greased casserole dish; add the cooked rice and mix well. Bake for 20 minutes adding remaining cheese during the last 10 minutes.

Robin Pulaski

Folly Island Shrimp & Grits

1	14½-ounce can chicken	2	tablespoons milk or half-
	broth		and-half
1	soup can water	½	cup chopped green onions
3	tablespoons butter, divided	⅔	pound large shrimp, peeled,
¾	cup white grits		deveined
3	tablespoons cream cheese	2	tablespoons fresh lime juice

Combine chicken broth and water and 1 tablespoon butter in heavy medium-size saucepan and bring to boil. Stir in grits. Reduce heat, cover, and simmer 5 minutes, stirring occasionally. Mix cream cheese and milk into grits. Cover and simmer mixture until almost all liquid is evaporated and grits are tender, stirring frequently, about 7 minutes. Stir in green onions. Remove mixture from heat.

Melt remaining 2 tablespoons butter in heavy large skillet over medium-high heat. Add shrimp and sauté just until shrimp are cooked through, about 3 minutes. Stir in lime juice. Remove skillet from heat. Spoon grits onto center of plate. Top with shrimp and drizzle with lime butter from skillet. Serves 2.

Shelby and Peter Schavoir

Shrimp Brochettes Adriatic Style

1½	pounds large or jumbo shrimp	¾	teaspoon salt
4	tablespoons olive oil		Freshly ground pepper
3	tablespoons vegetable oil		Lemon wedges
½-¾	cup fine, dry unflavored bread crumbs	1	red bell pepper, optional
1	teaspoon very finely chopped garlic	1	green bell pepper, optional
2	teaspoons finely chopped parsley	4	large metal flat skewers or small wooden skewers that have been soaked in water to prevent burning of the ends

Clean shrimp and pat thoroughly dry with paper towels. Put shrimp in a large mixing bowl. Add as much of the oil and bread crumbs as you need to obtain an even, light creamy coating on all the shrimp. Add the garlic, parsley, salt and pepper to shrimp and toss. Allow shrimp to steep in the marinade for at least 20 minutes at room temperature. Have ready flat edge skewers. Skewer the shrimps lengthwise. As you skewer the shrimp, curl and bend one end inward so that the skewer goes through the shrimp at three points. This prevents shrimps from slipping. Alternate with red and green peppers if desired. In a hot broiler or on a hot grill cook rapidly 2-3 minutes per side. Serve hot on the skewers or remove from skewers and serve on a large platter with lemon wedges.

Serves 4.

Patricia Eilender

Smith Island Crab Cakes

1	pound lump crab meat	1	teaspoon prepared mustard
2	eggs, beaten	1½	slices toasted white bread, made into crumbs
1	teaspoon Old Bay seasoning		
2	tablespoons mayonnaise		

Whisk all together except crab meat. Slowly add crab meat and stir with hands just until blended. Shape into 4 large patties. Fry in half oil and half butter until golden brown.

Carol McClelland

Crustless Crab Quiche

½	pound sliced mushrooms	2	tablespoons margarine or	
½	cup chopped onion		butter	
4	eggs	4	tablespoons flour	
1	cup lowfat sour cream	1	teaspoon onion powder	
1	cup lowfat cottage cheese	¼	teaspoon salt	
½	cup grated Parmesan cheese		Dash of hot pepper sauce	
2	cups Monterey Jack cheese, or 1 cup Gruyère and 1 cup Monterey Jack	6	ounces crab meat	

Preheat oven to 350 degrees.

Sauté mushrooms and onion in margarine or butter and drain on paper towel. In food processor, blend the next 8 ingredients. Pour into a large bowl and add cheese and crab meat. Pour into a 9- or 10-inch pie plate or quiche dish. Bake for about 40 minutes or until knife comes out clean.

Serves 8.

Ham, bacon, spinach or any combination you like can be substituted for crab meat. Quiche can be frozen before baking. Thaw and bake as indicated. If baking frozen quiche, oven temperature remains the same but extend cooking time.

Posy Merz

Scalloped Oysters

1	package Uneeda Biscuits (about 20-24 unsalted)	½	cup melted butter	
1	egg	1	pint oysters or 2 cans, undrained	
2	cups milk			

Preheat oven to 350 degrees.

Break up biscuits, add egg and milk. Add oysters and liquid. (If fresh oysters use only ¼ cup liquid.) Add half the butter and salt and pepper to taste. Place in casserole dish and top with the remaining butter. Cover and cook 1 hour. Remove cover last 10 minutes of baking time.

Sandy Trice

Savannah Crab Cakes

1	pound jumbo lump crab meat	½	teaspoon hot pepper sauce, optional
½	sleeve saltine crackers	1	egg white
1	cup mayonnaise		Freshly ground pepper
1½	teaspoons Worcestershire sauce	3	ounces peanut oil
			Honey Mustard Sauce

In a medium-size mixing bowl, add crackers and crush well. Add mayonnaise, Worcestershire sauce, hot pepper sauce, egg white and pepper, mix well. Fold in crab meat. If not moist enough, add a tablespoon of mayonnaise. Form into 3-ounce patties. In a heavy bottomed frying pan, over medium heat, add peanut oil and brown patties lightly on both sides. Put crab cake into 350 degree oven for 10 minutes. Serve with Honey Mustard Sauce.

HONEY MUSTARD SAUCE

1	cup mayonnaise	2	tablespoons honey
1½	tablespoons Dijon mustard		

Mix all ingredients together until well-blended.

Oscar Mejia
Executive Chef
The Landings Club

Gingered Shrimp

2	pounds shrimp (15-20 count)	¼	cup finely chopped fresh ginger
½	cup butter		
½	cup finely chopped green onion	2	cloves garlic, minced
		¼	cup finely chopped parsley
			Salt and black pepper

Clean shrimp and remove shells, leaving tails intact. In a heavy skillet, heat the butter and sauté the shrimp until they are pink. Remove shrimp from skillet and set aside. Add green onion, ginger and garlic; sauté 2-3 minutes. Add the shrimp, toss well, sprinkle with parsley. Season to taste with salt and pepper. Serves 10 to 12.

Anonymous

Crab Cakes

1½ cups soft bread crumbs
2 egg whites, lightly beaten
4 tablespoons mayonnaise
2 tablespoons fresh parsley
1 teaspoon prepared mustard
½ teaspoon celery salt
½ teaspoon ground pepper
¼ teaspoon salt

1¾ pint containers of fresh lump crab meat, drained and flaked
2 tablespoons vegetable oil, or to taste
Salad greens, optional
Lemon slices, optional

Combine first 9 ingredients. Shape into 12 patties, 2-inches wide and ¾-inch thick. Chill one hour. Can be made early in day, covered with wrap and refrigerated until ready to fry. Cook patties in oil in a nonstick skillet over medium heat 3 minutes on each side or until golden brown. Drain on paper towels. Arrange some salad greens and crab cakes on individual plates; top with Dijon Dressing. Garnish with lemon slices, if desired.

DIJON DRESSING

1 cup mayonnaise
¼ cup Dijon mustard

1 teaspoon Worcestershire sauce

Suzie Moore

Crab Cakes

1 pound crab meat
1 teaspoon Dijon mustard
1 teaspoon Old Bay seasoning
3 tablespoons bread crumbs

1 tablespoon mayonnaise
1 egg
½ teaspoon Worcestershire sauce

Separate crab meat with fork and set aside. Combine remaining ingredients in a bowl and mix with crab meat until smooth. With wet hands, pat out into four cakes. Pan fry in vegetable oil, browning on both sides, about 4 minutes per side. Serve with slices of lemon or your favorite sauce.

Charlene Soderstrom

189

Grilled Salmon Filets

SALAD SEASONING

1	teaspoon sesame seed	½	teaspoon garlic powder
1	teaspoon poppy seed	½	teaspoon paprika
½	teaspoon salt	½	teaspoon Parmesan cheese

Mix all ingredients together.

MARINADE

Soy sauce	Melted butter
Lemon juice	Salad Seasoning

Mix all ingredients together. Amount of each ingredient will depend on the number of salmon filets you will be marinating. Marinate filets at least 30 minutes. Place on heavy aluminum foil, skin side down. Place foil with filets on hot grill and cover. Cook 10 minutes. Lift off, leaving skin, and serve with Dill Sauce.

DILL SAUCE

½	cup mayonnaise	½-1	teaspoon dill weed
½	cup sour cream	1	tablespoon cider vinegar
1	teaspoon dry mustard	1	tablespoon onion flakes
½	teaspoon salt	¾	teaspoon sugar

Mix all ingredients together until well-blended. Flavor improves if made 1 to 2 hours ahead.

Betty Stroup

Red Wine Marinade For Grilling Fish

½	cup red wine (a hearty Burgundy is good)	¼	teaspoon garlic salt
		½	teaspoon dried basil
½	cup teriyaki sauce	½	teaspoon dried parsley
¼	cup olive oil		Grated rind of 1 small lemon

Mix all ingredients. Pour over fish steaks and marinate no more than 2 hours. Suggested fish: tuna, swordfish, bluefish, mahi mahi.

Lynda Ibach

Sesame Crusted Salmon With Ginger Vinaigrette

1 large English cucumber, peeled and coarsely chopped	1 teaspoon hot sauce
½ cup rice wine vinegar	½ teaspoon ground coriander
⅛ teaspoon salt	½ teaspoon dark sesame oil
2 tablespoons sugar	4 4-ounce salmon filets
¼ cup water	1 tablespoon sesame seeds, toasted
¼ cup low-sodium soy sauce	1 large English cucumber, thinly sliced
2 tablespoons rice wine vinegar	Ginger Vinaigrette
1 tablespoon honey	Fresh mint sprigs for garnish

Preheat oven to 450 degrees.

Position knife blade in food processor bowl; add chopped English cucumber. Process until smooth, stopping once to scrape down sides. Line a large wire-mesh strainer with cheesecloth or a coffee filter; pour cucumber mixture through strainer, discarding pulp. Stir ½ cup vinegar and salt into cucumber liquid; set aside. Combine sugar and water in a small saucepan; cook over medium heat, stirring often, until mixture boils. Remove from heat, and stir into cucumber liquid mixture; set aside. Combine soy sauce and next 5 ingredients; brush over salmon. Place salmon in a lightly greased 13x9x2-inch baking pan; sprinkle with sesame seeds. Bake for 10-12 minutes or until fish flakes when tested with a fork. Arrange salmon filets and sliced cucumber evenly in 4 pasta bowls. Spoon cucumber liquid mixture evenly into each dish. Drizzle with a small amount of Ginger Vinaigrette. Garnish, if desired. Serves 4.

GINGER VINAIGRETTE

1 1½-inch long piece fresh ginger, peeled	1 tablespoon honey
1 clove garlic	⅛ teaspoon dried crushed red pepper
2 tablespoons rice wine vinegar	¼ cup peanut oil
1 tablespoon low-sodium soy sauce	½ teaspoon dark sesame oil

Position knife blade in food processor bowl; add fresh ginger and garlic. Process until smooth, stopping once to scrape down sides. Add vinegar and next 3 ingredients; process 30 seconds. Slowly pour peanut oil and sesame oil through food chute with processor running, blending just until smooth.

Yield: ½ cup

Andy Borden

191

Salmon With Caper Sauce

2   salmon steaks, 4 ounces each   Lemon slices for garnish
2   tablespoons dry white wine

CAPER SAUCE

2   tablespoons lowfat plain   1   tablespoon lemon juice
    yogurt   1   tablespoon fresh dill,
2   tablespoons lowfat   chopped, or 1 teaspoon
    mayonnaise   dried
1   tablespoon capers, drained

Preheat oven to 350 degrees.
Rinse salmon under cold water; pat dry. Spray an 8x8-inch baking dish with cooking spray. Place salmon in dish and sprinkle with wine. Cover and bake for 15-20 minutes, or until fish is flaky but not dry.
In a small pan, combine all the ingredients for the caper sauce and warm over low heat. When ready to serve, pour caper sauce over each salmon steak and garnish with lemon slices.
Serves 2.

Betsy Smith

Fish "N" Vegetable Skillet Dinner

¼   cup margarine   ½   teaspoon dried dill weed
1   cup carrots, sliced ½-inch   ¼   teaspoon pepper
    thick   2   teaspoons lemon juice
1   medium potato, sliced   ½   pound white fish; if using
    ¼-inch thick   frozen fish, thaw and pat dry
1   small onion, cut in rings   1   medium tomato, cut into
½   teaspoon salt   1-inch pieces

In 10-inch skillet, melt margarine. Add all ingredients except fish and tomato. Cover. Cook over medium heat, stirring until vegetables are crispy tender, 9-11 minutes. Place fish in skillet, arranging vegetables on top of fish. Cover, cook on low 5 minutes. Add tomato on top. Cover and cook until tomato is heated through, 1-2 minutes.
Serves 2.

Carol Krause

Grilled Salmon With Ginger-Orange Mustard Glaze

¼ cup fresh orange juice
¼ cup tamari or soy sauce
¼ cup cream sherry
¼ cup Dijon mustard
2 tablespoons grated peeled fresh ginger or 2 teaspoons ground ginger

2 tablespoons honey
4 6-ounce salmon fillets (about 1-inch thick)
Cooking spray

Combine first 6 ingredients in a large zip-top plastic bag. Add salmon to bag; seal and marinate in refrigerator 30 minutes. Remove salmon from bag, reserving marinade. Prepare grill or broiler. Place salmon on grill rack or broiler pan coated with cooking spray. Cook 6 minutes on each side or until fish flakes easily when tested with a fork, basting frequently with reserved marinade. Place remaining marinade in a saucepan; heat and serve over salmon if desired.

Chris Aiken

Salmon Bake With Pecan Crunch Coating

4 (4- to 6-ounces each) salmon fillets
⅛ teaspoon salt
⅛ teaspoon pepper
2 tablespoons Dijon mustard
2 tablespoons butter or margarine, melted

1½ tablespoons honey
¼ cup soft bread crumbs
¼ cup finely chopped pecans
2 teaspoons chopped fresh parsley

Preheat oven to 450 degrees.

Sprinkle salmon with salt and pepper. Place skin side down in lightly greased 9x13-inch pan. Combine mustard, butter and honey; brush on fillets. Combine bread crumbs, pecans and parsley; spoon mixture evenly on top of each fillet. Bake for 10 minutes or until fish flakes easily when tested with a fork.

Serves 4.

Amberjack, grouper or any firm fish can be used in place of salmon.

Mary Ann Schmitt

Firecracker Grilled Alaska Salmon

4   (4- to 6-ounces each) Alaska
    salmon steaks, thawed if
    necessary
¼   cup peanut oil
2   tablespoons soy sauce
2   tablespoons balsamic
    vinegar
2   tablespoons chopped green
    onions

1½ teaspoons brown sugar
1   clove garlic, minced
¾   teaspoon grated ginger
½   teaspoon red chili flakes, or
    more to taste
½   teaspoon sesame oil
⅛   teaspoon salt

Place salmon steaks in a glass dish. Whisk together remaining ingredients and pour over salmon. Cover with plastic wrap and marinate in refrigerator 4-6 hours. Remove salmon from marinade and place on a well-oiled grill 5 inches from coals. Grill for 10 minutes per inch of thickness, measured at thickest part, or until fish just flakes when tested with a fork. Turn halfway through cooking.

Serves 4.

Jan Hazel

Baked Tuna Chow Mein Casserole

1   cup chopped celery
¼   cup onion
2   tablespoons green bell
    pepper, chopped
1   tablespoon butter
1   6-ounce can of tuna

1   10½-ounce can mushroom
    soup
¼   cup milk
¼   cup water
1½ cups chow mein noodles
    Salt and pepper, to taste
¾   cup salted cashews

Preheat oven to 350 degrees.

Sauté celery, onion and green pepper in butter. Mix together the soup, milk and water until well-blended. Reserve ⅓ cup chow mein noodles. Mix all ingredients together and pour into 1½-quart baking dish. Sprinkle with remaining noodles. Bake 45 minutes.

Serves 4 to 6.

A 6-ounce can of chicken can be used in place of tuna.

Sue Winship

Blackened Fish By Will Ferrari

BLACKENING SPICE

Equal measures (1x) of black pepper, white pepper, oregano, basil, cayenne pepper, onion powder, garlic powder, Old Bay seasoning. Double measures (2x) of paprika and salt.

COOKING FISH

Suggested fish: salmon, grouper, sword, mahi mahi, tuna

Pull the skin off the side of salmon and other fish that has skin on one side. (If you insist on leaving this skin on, blacken the "skin on" side in next step.) Sprinkle a thin layer of spice mix on foil or wax paper. Lay one side of fish on top of seasoning and how much adheres is a good starting point to determine how much blackening suits your taste. Can also sprinkle a little on top side according to taste.

Preheat oven to 400 degrees.

On stove, preheat a very thin layer of oil in an ovenproof frying pan and sear seasoned side of fish for about 4-5 minutes. DO NOT TURN FISH. Place frying pan in oven and let it bake/sizzle for 12-15 minutes, longer for very thick fish. Don't use too much oil for searing or it may splatter all over oven. Fish seems to stay relatively moist cooking with this method so don't worry too much about overcooking. Serve immediately.

After seasoning, fish can be cooked more easily and quickly on preheated outdoor grill but it will not be as good. Rack of grill should be sprayed with cooking spray or oil before heating.

Save extra blackening seasoning for future use with fish, scallops, shrimp or chicken.

Bob Ferrari

White Wine Marinade For Grilling Fish

1 cup white wine
¼ cup vegetable oil
¼ teaspoon garlic salt
Dash of pepper

½ teaspoon dried parsley
½ teaspoon dill weed
Grated rind from 1 small lemon

Mix all ingredients. Pour over fish steaks and marinate no more than 2 hours. Suggested fish: salmon, halibut, bass, swordfish, shark.

Lynda Ibach

195

Buridda (Baked Assorted Fish, Tomatoes & Onions Genova Style)

⅓ cup olive oil
2 large onions, thinly sliced
3 anchovy fillets, finely chopped
3 cloves garlic, finely minced
2 pounds ripe, juicy tomatoes, cut into ¼-inch rounds
Salt and freshly ground pepper

1 pound firm-fleshed fish, cut into 4 serving pieces ¾-inch thick
4 ounces sea scallops
4 ounces medium-size shrimp, peeled and deveined
2 tablespoons chopped fresh parsley

Preheat oven to 350 degrees.

Heat ¼ cup of the oil in a large skillet over medium heat. Add the onion and cook, stirring until the onion begins to cook, 5-6 minutes. Add the anchovies and garlic and cook, stirring, about 1 minute. Spread half of the onions in the bottom of a baking dish, top the onions with half of the tomatoes, and season lightly with salt and pepper.

Arrange the fish and shellfish over the tomatoes and top with the remaining onions, spreading them evenly with the remaining tomatoes, season again lightly with salt and pepper and sprinkle with parsley. Pour the remaining oil over the tomatoes and bake 25-30 minutes. Let the dish settle for a few minutes; then, with a large spoon, remove some of the excess oil and water juices from the pan and serve.

Serves 4 to 6.

Sea bass, halibut or mahi mahi are the fish recommended. Anchovy paste can also be used in place of anchovy fillets. Dish can be assembled several hours ahead and baked just before serving.

Dorothy Pero

Swordfish Steak

2 tablespoons Dijon mustard
2 tablespoons lime juice
½ cup olive oil
2 shallots, chopped

1½ teaspoons dry or
2 tablespoons fresh rosemary
4 swordfish steaks

Mix first 5 ingredients and whisk until creamy. Marinate swordfish 1-4 hours. Grill approximately 4 minutes per side or until flaky.

Mary Cassady

Baked Seaman's Catch

9	lasagna noodles, cooked and drained	1	10-ounce package frozen spinach
1	large onion, chopped	2	tablespoons vegetable oil
3	ounces cream cheese, softened	1	teaspoon Italian herb seasoning
1	cup creamed cottage cheese		Salt and pepper, to taste
1	egg, beaten		
1	10¾-ounce can condensed cream of celery soup	8	ounces shrimp, cooked
⅓	cup milk	1	pound fish filets, cubed
3	tablespoons grated Parmesan cheese	2	tablespoons seasoned bread crumbs, fine
⅓	cup grated sharp cheddar cheese		Butter or margarine

Preheat oven to 350 degrees.

Arrange 3 noodles over bottom of lightly buttered 13x9-inch casserole dish. Set aside. Sauté onion in vegetable oil until soft. Thaw spinach; chop well; press to remove all moisture. Add to onion.

Add cream cheese, cottage cheese, egg, Italian herb seasoning and salt and pepper to spinach mixture. Mix well and spread ⅓ of mixture over noodles in dish.

Combine soup, milk, shrimp and fish filets and spread ⅓ fish mixture over cheese layer. Repeat these three layers twice.

Combine Parmesan cheese and bread crumbs and sprinkle over casserole. Bake 45 minutes. Sprinkle cheddar cheese over top; dot with butter and bake an additional 5 minutes. Let stand 20 minutes before serving.

Serves 6 to 8.

After 45 minutes of cooking the dish seems juicy. Do not drain; liquid seems to be absorbed while resting the 20 minutes after removing from the oven. Can be made the day before and baked the next day.

Janet Hietbrink

197

Rotolo

ROTOLO PASTA

1	cup flour	½	teaspoon olive oil
1	egg, beaten	2-3	tablespoons flour for
3	tablespoons water		kneading

Stir together egg, water and olive oil. Stir egg mixture in flour all at once, mixing well until combined. Sprinkle kneading surface with some flour. Knead until smooth, 8-10 minutes. Add more of remaining flour as needed. Let rest for 10 minutes.

FILLING

1	10-ounce package frozen chopped spinach	½	cup Parmesan cheese, grated
		8	slices prosciutto
1	egg, beaten	8	slices mozzarella cheese
1	cup ricotta cheese	½	cup butter, heated until
¼	teaspoon nutmeg		lightly browned
⅛	teaspoon pepper		

Thaw spinach, drain well. Combine egg, ricotta cheese, nutmeg and pepper. Stir in spinach and Parmesan cheese. Set aside. Roll out dough on floured surface to 18x11-inches. Spread filling evenly over dough to within ½-inch on all sides. Layer prosciutto and mozzarella slices over filling. Moisten short edge with water. Roll up beginning with short edge. Wrap roll in a layer of cheesecloth; tie loosely. In Dutch oven, bring about 1½-inches of water to a boil. Carefully add roll; reduce heat. Simmer covered for 30-35 minutes. Remove from water; cool slightly, about 10 minutes. Remove cheesecloth. Place roll on plate; cover and chill for several hours.

To serve, preheat oven to 450 degrees. Cut roll into 12 slices; place on baking sheet. Brush with browned butter. Bake for 5 minutes. Turn over and brush with browned butter and bake for additional 5 minutes.

Serves 5.

Mary Lou Deeney

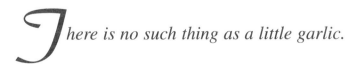

here is no such thing as a little garlic.

Arthur Baer

Rigatoni With Sausage & Broccolini

1	pound sweet Italian sausage links	1	16-ounce package rigatoni or ziti macaroni
1	large onion, chopped	½	cup fresh Parmesan cheese, grated
1	pound broccolini (broccoli rabe)	½	teaspoon coarsely ground black pepper
1	teaspoon salt		
2-3	cans diced tomatoes		

In 12-inch skillet over medium-high heat, heat sausages and ¼ cup water to a boil; reduce to low heat, cover and simmer 5 minutes. Remove cover and cook sausages turning until brown and water evaporates, about 20 minutes. With slotted spoon, remove sausages to plate; cool slightly then cut into ½-inch slices.

In hot sausage drippings, over medium high heat, cook onion just until tender, about 5 minutes. Discard tough stems from broccolini, coarsely chop and add to onion with 1 teaspoon salt. Cook until tender crisp, stirring occasionally. Add tomatoes and bring to a boil. Reduce heat and simmer while preparing pasta according to package directions. Drain pasta and add to tomato sauce with sausage slices, cheese and pepper, tossing to mix well.

Serves 6 to 8.

Carole Michna

Chicken Spaghetti

1	cup chopped onion	1	cup chopped celery
1	cup chopped bell pepper		

½	cup green olives, sliced	1	pound Velveeta cheese (Mexican)
½	cup black olives, sliced		
1	can Rotel tomatoes with chiles	4-5	cups cooked chicken
1	cup chicken broth	1	12-ounce package spaghetti, cooked
1	can mushroom soup		

Preheat oven to 350 degrees.

Sauté onion, bell pepper and celery in butter or olive oil. Mix in all remaining ingredients. Bake 30-40 minutes. Freezes well.

Margaret McCulloch

199

Springtime Noodles – Pasta Primavera

¼   cup butter or margarine
½   pound asparagus, cut into
     1-inch pieces keeping tips
     whole
½   pound mushrooms, sliced
¼   cup prosciutto or baked
     ham, slivered
1   medium carrot, thinly sliced
1   medium zucchini, diced
1   8-ounce package thin
     noodles

3   green onions, tops included,
     sliced
½   cup frozen tiny green peas,
     thawed
½   teaspoon dry basil
½   teaspoon salt
Dash nutmeg
1   cup whipping cream or half-
     and-half
¼   cup Parmesan cheese,
     freshly grated
Fresh parsley, chopped

Before you begin cooking, have all the vegetables cut and ready to use. The sauce cooks quickly.

In a wide frying pan, over medium heat, melt butter or margarine. Add asparagus, mushrooms, prosciutto, carrot and zucchini. Cook, stirring occasionally, for 3 minutes. Cover pan and cook 1 minute more. Meanwhile, cook pasta until al dente. Drain. To vegetable mixture add green onions, peas, basil, salt, nutmeg and cream. Increase heat and cook until liquid boils all over and forms large shiny bubbles. Return noodles to pot in which they were cooked, pour sauce over, mix gently. Add Parmesan cheese and mix again. Sprinkle with parsley and serve at once. Offer additional Parmesan.

Serves 4 to 6.

Carol Browning

A man who lost his goatskin filled with milk, found it only to discover cheese. Bless him, the chicken, and the glutton who gave the world pasta.

Unknown

Pasta With Tomatoes & Zucchini

6	ounces of your favorite pasta, cooked and drained	4	medium tomatoes, peeled, seeded and cut into strips
4	ounces butter	¼	cup parsley, chopped
½	cup chopped onion	½	cup Parmesan cheese, grated
1	green pepper, seeded and cut into thin strips	½	cup Swiss cheese, grated
2-3	cups zucchini, sliced	½-1	teaspoon salt
		½	teaspoon pepper

Preheat oven to 325 degrees.

Melt butter in skillet and sauté onion and green pepper for about 5 minutes. Combine with remaining ingredients, reserving a few tablespoons Parmesan cheese for top. Place in buttered 2-quart casserole dish and top with cheese. Cover and bake for 30 minutes. Do not overbake.

Serves 6.

Works well as either a side dish or main dish.

Barbara Schroeder

Spaghetti Pizza

1	7-ounce package spaghettini	1	cup mozzarella cheese, shredded
2	eggs		
½	cup milk	¾	teaspoon garlic salt
		½	teaspoon salt

TOPPING

1	32-ounce jar spaghetti sauce	1	3½ to 4-ounce package pepperoni slices
1½	teaspoons oregano leaves		
3	cups mozzarella cheese, shredded		

Preheat oven to 400 degrees.

Cook spaghettini, drain and cool. Beat eggs slightly and stir in milk, cheese, garlic salt and salt. Add cooked spaghettini and stir together. Grease a 9x13-inch pan. Spread spaghettini mixture into pan. Bake 15 minutes. Remove from oven and reduce heat to 350 degrees. Spread spaghetti sauce over crust. Sprinkle with oregano and 3 cups cheese. Add sliced pepperoni on top. Bake 30 minutes. Let sit at room temperature for 5 minutes before cutting.

Serves 10 to 12.

Judy Hanna

Chicken, Zucchini & Leek Lasagna

1	tablespoon plus 1 teaspoon margarine, divided	2½	cups 2% lowfat milk
1½	pounds skinned, boned chicken breast, cut into bite-size pieces	1½	cups grated fresh Parmesan cheese, divided
		1	cup nonfat ricotta cheese
4	cloves garlic, divided, crushed	½	teaspoon dried whole basil
		¼	teaspoon pepper
6	cups sliced fresh mushrooms (about 1 pound)	¼	teaspoon salt
		12	lasagna noodles, uncooked
6	cups thinly sliced leeks		Vegetable cooking spray
3	tablespoons all-purpose flour	5	cups coarsely shredded zucchini (about 1¼ pounds)

Melt 1 teaspoon margarine in a large skillet over medium heat. Add chicken and 2 cloves garlic; sauté 4 minutes or until chicken is done. Remove from skillet; set aside. Add remaining 2 cloves garlic and mushrooms; sauté 10 minutes or until liquid evaporates. Set aside.

Melt remaining 1 tablespoon margarine in a large saucepan over medium heat; add leeks. Cover and cook 30 minutes, stirring occasionally. Sprinkle with flour, stirring until well-blended. Gradually add milk, stirring with a wire whisk. Cook over medium heat 8 minutes or until thickened, stirring constantly. Add chicken, ½ cup Parmesan cheese, ricotta cheese, basil, pepper and salt. Stir well.

Arrange 4 noodles in bottom of a 13x9x2-inch baking dish coated with cooking spray. Top with half of zucchini, ⅓ cup Parmesan cheese, half of mushroom mixture, and 2 cups chicken mixture. Repeat layers, ending with noodles. Spread the remaining 2 cups chicken mixture over noodles; sprinkle with remaining ⅓ cup Parmesan cheese. Cover and chill 8 hours. Bake, covered, at 350 degrees for 1 hour. Uncover and bake 15 minutes. Let stand 5 minutes before serving. Must be made day before serving.

Serves 9.

Use only uncooked noodles in this dish. While it chills overnight, the uncooked noodles absorb the liquid from the vegetables. The noodles tend to soften while baking, producing a creamy lasagna. Using pasta that has been cooked results in a watery lasagna.

Chris Aiken

he trouble with eating Italian food is that five or six days later you're hungry again.

George Miller

Pasta With Bay Scallops

1	pound bay scallops	½	cup chopped fresh parsley
Juice of ½ lemon		1	tablespoon finely chopped
4	tablespoons butter, divided		lemon zest
1	pound linguini		

SAUCE

4	tablespoons olive oil	1	cup puréed canned Italian
4	tablespoons butter		plum tomatoes
8	shallots, sliced fine	12	ounces clam juice
½	cup white wine	½	teaspoon fennel seed
		Salt and pepper, to taste	

Marinate scallops in lemon juice for 30 minutes. Prepare sauce. In a skillet, heat oil and butter and sauté shallots until they begin to turn color. Add wine, tomatoes, clam juice, fennel, salt and pepper. Bring to a boil, lower heat and simmer for 10 minutes. Drain scallops and sauté in 2 tablespoons butter over high heat for 3 minutes. Add to the sauce. Cook the pasta, drain, and return to the pot. Add remaining butter and toss lightly. Add the sauce with the scallops, the parsley, the lemon zest and serve.

Serves 4 to 6.

Christie Ann Pattin

ꟻish, to taste right, must swim three times – in water, in butter, and in wine.

Polish Proverb

203

Speedy Shrimp & Scallop Lasagna

1   tablespoon oil, preferably
    olive oil
1   medium onion, chopped
2   10-ounce packages frozen
    chopped spinach, thawed
    and squeezed dry
½   teaspoon salt
¼   teaspoon nutmeg
1   8-ounce package mozzarella
    cheese, shredded and divided

4   tablespoons Parmesan
    cheese, grated and divided
½   pound medium shrimp,
    peeled and cooked
¾   pound uncooked sea
    scallops, halved horizontally
1   26-ounce jar tomato and
    basil flavored pasta sauce
9   oven ready lasagna noodles
    from one 8-ounce package

Preheat oven to 375 degrees.

In nonstick skillet, heat oil over medium-high heat. Add onion and cook until softened, 3 to 4 minutes. Add spinach, salt and nutmeg. Cook until heated through and excess moisture evaporates, about 2 minutes. Remove from heat and cool 5 minutes. Stir in 1 cup mozzarella cheese and 2 tablespoons Parmesan cheese until combined. Set aside. Spread ¾ cup pasta sauce over bottom of 13x9-inch baking dish. Top with 3 noodles; spread with ½ of spinach mixture, all of shrimp and ¼ cup mozzarella cheese. Top with 3 noodles, spread with ¾ cup of pasta sauce. Top with remaining spinach mixture; arrange scallops over the spinach and top with ¼ cup mozzarella cheese and 2 tablespoons Parmesan cheese. Cover with remaining 3 noodles and then the remaining pasta sauce and mozzarella cheese. Coat sheet of foil with cooking spray, cover lasagna with spray coated side down. Bake 40 minutes. Remove foil and bake until cheese begins to brown, 5 to 10 minutes. Cool slightly on rack before cutting.

Serves 8.

Jerriann Kirkwood

he most indispensable quality in a cook is punctuality, and no less is required of a guest.

Brillat-Savarin

Chicken Spaghetti

7	ounces cracked pepper spaghetti, cooked	1	small green bell pepper, chopped
1	cup shredded jack cheese, divided	1	small onion, chopped
1½	cups cooked chicken, chopped	1	10¾-ounce can lowfat celery soup
1	2-ounce jar diced pimiento, undrained	½	cup chicken broth

Preheat oven to 350 degrees.

Combine spaghetti, ¾ cup of cheese, chicken, pimiento, green pepper, onion, soup and broth. Mix well. Grease 8x12x2-inch baking dish with cooking spray. Spoon mixture into dish. Sprinkle with remaining ¼ cup cheese. Bake 45 minutes. Serves 8.

Can be made ahead and cooked just before serving. Regular spaghetti and ¼ teaspoon black pepper may be used instead of black pepper spaghetti. Works well with reduced fat cheese. Microwaves well also.

Karen G. Hickman

Beverly's Macaroni & Cheese

1	8-ounce package macaroni twists	3	tablespoons flour
1	pound bulk Italian sausage	½	teaspoon salt
½	cup onion, chopped	2	cups milk
½	cup sweet red bell pepper, cut in strips	2	cups Vermont extra sharp cheddar cheese, shredded, divided

Preheat oven to 350 degrees.

Cook macaroni in salted water for 7-8 minutes. Brown sausage, drain fat reserving 2 tablespoons. Set aside. Sauté onion and red pepper in reserved fat and cook 2-3 minutes. Stir in flour and salt. Slowly add milk, cooking over medium heat and stirring until thick. Stir in 1½ cups of cheese reserving ½ cup. Place macaroni and ½ of sausage into a greased 3-quart casserole dish. Pour cheese mixture over top of macaroni and sausage. Place the remaining sausage over top. Sprinkle remaining ½ cup cheese over sausage. Bake 30-40 minutes or until hot and bubbly. Serves 8.

Priss Wentworth

205

Vodka Sauce Pasta ala Ferrari/Gasperoni

6-8	cloves garlic, crushed	¼	cup sugar
½	cup olive oil	1	tablespoon Crazy Salt
1	28-ounce can whole peeled tomatoes	1	tablespoon black pepper
		½	cup vodka
1	28-ounce can crushed tomatoes	16	ounces vermicelli spaghetti
		½	cup Romano or Parmesan cheese, grated
½	cup fresh basil, chopped		

Lightly brown crushed garlic in the olive oil. Crush whole tomatoes with "clean hands" using only the juice inside the tomatoes. Combine these hand crushed tomatoes with the canned crushed. Stir into this tomato mixture the basil, sugar, salt, pepper and vodka. Pour this mix into the heated olive oil and garlic. Stir well and simmer for about 20 minutes.

Cook the spaghetti al dente in boiling water with salt. Drain spaghetti in colander and rinse with hot water. Place spaghetti in large bowl and toss with some sauce to avoid sticking before serving. Add remaining sauce to individual servings of spaghetti as desired and add "lots" of grated Romano or Parmesan cheese to taste.

Bottled sweet basil can be used to supplement if you are short of fresh and prepared chopped garlic can be used in place of the crushed cloves of garlic. Less olive oil, according to your taste, can also be used for browning the garlic.

Bob Ferrari

Quick Pasta

1	pound spaghetti	1	can chopped tomatoes
¼	cup extra virgin olive oil		Red pepper flakes, to taste
1	clove garlic		

Cook spaghetti and drain. In heated, large frying pan, sauté crushed garlic in olive oil. Add tomatoes and sprinkle in pepper flakes. Continue cooking for 3 minutes. Stir in spaghetti until completely coated with sauce. Serve at once.

Gerald Fields

No man is lonely while eating spaghetti – it requires so much attention.

Christopher Morley

Pasta Sauce Raphael

2   6-ounce jars marinated
    artichoke hearts in oil
¼   cup olive oil
2   cups onions, chopped
2   tablespoons garlic, minced
½   teaspoon dried oregano
½   teaspoon dried basil
1   tablespoon coarsely ground
    black pepper, or to taste

½   teaspoon salt
    Pinch of dried red pepper flakes
1   28-ounce can plum tomatoes,
    undrained
¼   cup freshly grated Parmesan
    cheese
¼   cup Italian parsley, chopped

Drain the artichoke hearts, reserving the marinade. Heat the olive oil in a large saucepan. Add the onions, garlic, oregano, basil, black pepper, salt, red pepper flakes, and reserved artichoke marinade. Sauté over medium-low heat until the onions and garlic are soft and transparent, about 10 minutes. Add tomatoes and simmer for 30 minutes. Add the artichoke hearts, Parmesan cheese and parsley. Stir gently and simmer another 5 minutes.

Serves 6.

Can be prepared ahead through simmering the tomatoes. Reheat and add remaining ingredients. Enough sauce for 1 pound of pasta. Especially good over tortellini.

Jackie Buggy

Linguine With Shrimp

¼   cup sliced shallots or
    scallions
2   tablespoons olive oil
1   14.5-ounce can diced
    tomatoes in olive oil, garlic
    and spices
1   generous tablespoon
    chopped fresh basil

⅓   cup heavy cream or coffee
    cream
    Cooked shrimp, 7 per serving
⅛   teaspoon cayenne pepper
8   ounces linguine or angel hair
    pasta, cooked
    Basil leaves for garnish

Sauté shallots in oil until soft, about 4 minutes. Add tomatoes and basil. Simmer 5 minutes. Add cream; boil 2-3 minutes to thicken. Add shrimp and cayenne. Heat until hot. Pour over hot pasta. Sprinkle basil over all.

Serves 2.

Bobbie Tooher

Penne With Blue Cheese & Broccoli

2	tablespoons olive oil	4	ounces blue cheese,
1	large clove garlic, peeled and		crumbled
	minced	2	tablespoons grated Romano
¼	teaspoon crushed red pepper		or Parmesan cheese
	flakes	2	tablespoons finely chopped
1	pound broccoli, cut into		basil or 2 teaspoons dried
	florets, rinsed well		basil
¼	teaspoon salt		Freshly ground black pepper, to
2	cups penne pasta		taste

In a large skillet, heat the olive oil over medium heat. Add garlic and red pepper flakes, stirring 30 seconds. Add broccoli with water still clinging to the florets. Sprinkle with salt, cover and cook about 4-5 minutes, until broccoli is just tender when pierced. Transfer to a bowl. Chop the broccoli coarsely using a fork and small paring knife.

Bring a large pot of water to a boil. Add the pasta and cook according to package directions. Reserve ¼ cup of the cooking water, then drain the pasta. Put back into the hot pan. Add the broccoli, blue cheese, grated cheese, basil, pepper and enough reserved cooking water to make moist, creamy sauce. Serve immediately.

Serves 4.

Donna Pfeifer

Cheese Noodles

3	cups uncooked fine noodles	2	teaspoons Worcestershire
1	cup sour cream		sauce
1	cup cottage cheese		Pinch of salt
½	cup diced onion	1	cup sharp cheddar cheese,
			shredded

Preheat oven to 350 degrees.

Cook noodles for 7 minutes and drain. Mix noodles with all other ingredients except cheddar cheese. Put in casserole dish and bake, covered, for 45 minutes. Uncover and top with cheddar cheese. Put under broiler for a few minutes until cheese is bubbly.

Evelyne Miller

Nancy's Lenten Lasagna

9 oven ready lasagna noodles
½ cup stewed tomatoes or spaghetti sauce
2 eggs, slightly beaten
2 cups cottage cheese
2 cups ricotta cheese
1½ teaspoons dried Italian seasoning, crushed
2 tablespoons margarine
2 cups sliced fresh mushrooms
1 small onion, chopped
3 cloves garlic, minced
2 tablespoons flour
½ teaspoon pepper

1½ cups milk
1 10-ounce package frozen chopped spinach, thawed, well-drained
1 10-ounce package frozen chopped broccoli, thawed, well-drained
1 carrot, shredded (½ cup)
¾ cup Parmesan cheese, divided
8 ounces shredded part-skim mozzarella cheese
1 1-pound can salmon, drained and picked over

Combine eggs, cottage cheese, ricotta cheese and Italian seasoning in medium bowl. In large skillet, cook mushrooms in hot margarine for 5 minutes. Add onion and garlic cooking until much of liquid has evaporated. Stir in flour and pepper. Cook 1 minute. Add milk all at once and cook, stirring, until thickened and bubbly. Remove from heat. Stir in spinach and/or broccoli, carrot and ½ cup Parmesan cheese.

To assemble: Grease a 13x9-inch dish. Evenly spread tomato sauce on bottom. Place 3 pieces of lasagna over sauce. Top with ⅓ of cottage cheese mixture, then ⅓ of vegetable mixture. Sprinkle with ⅓ of mozzarella. Repeat layers one more time, after second layer, add salmon pieces evenly. Repeat layers again making sure that top layer of dried lasagna noodles is covered completely. Sprinkle top with remaining Parmesan cheese. Bake lasagna immediately or chill up to 24 hours. Bake uncovered in a 350 degree oven for 45-60 minutes. Let stand 10 minutes before cutting.

Serves 8 to 10.

If you prefer, all broccoli or all spinach can be used in place of combining the vegetables.

Nancy Craig

Basil Tomato Tart

½ of a 15-ounce package folded refrigerated unbaked pie crust (1 crust)
1½ cups shredded mozzarella cheese (6 ounces), divided
5 Roma or 4 medium tomatoes
1 cup loosely packed fresh basil leaves

4 cloves garlic
½ cup mayonnaise or salad dressing
¼ cup grated Parmesan cheese
⅛ teaspoon ground white pepper
Fresh basil leaves (optional)

Unfold pie crust according to package directions. Place in a 9-inch quiche dish or glass pie plate. Flute edge; press with the tines of a fork, if desired. Pre-bake according to package directions. Remove from oven. Sprinkle with ½ cup of the mozzarella cheese. Cool on a wire rack.

Cut tomatoes into wedges; drain on paper towels. Arrange tomato wedges atop melted cheese in the baked pie shell. In a food processor bowl, combine basil and garlic; cover and process until coarsely chopped. Sprinkle over tomatoes.

In a medium mixing bowl, combine remaining mozzarella cheese, mayonnaise, Parmesan cheese and pepper. Spoon cheese mixture over basil mixture, spreading to evenly cover the top. Bake for 35-40 minutes or until top is golden and bubbly. Serve warm. If desired, sprinkle with basil leaves.

Yield: 4 main-dish servings or 8 appetizer servings.

Chris Aiken

Cheddar Cheese Soufflé

1 tablespoon sweet butter
6 eggs
½ cup heavy cream
1 teaspoon Dijon mustard
Salt and pepper, to taste

½ pound sharp cheddar cheese, grated
¼ cup Parmesan cheese, grated
11 ounces cream cheese

Preheat oven to 375 degrees.

Butter a 5-quart soufflé dish. Put eggs, cream, mustard, salt and pepper in blender. Blend until smooth. Add cheddar and Parmesan cheese in small batches and blend. Add cream cheese in small chunks and blend. Bake for 45-50 minutes.

Serves 2 to 4.

This soufflé can be made one day in advance and refrigerated.

Joan Keever

Stuffed Portobello Mushroom

8 large or 12 medium portobello mushrooms	1 cup couscous, uncooked, or contents of 2 6-ounce boxes
Non-stick cooking spray	Salt and pepper, to taste
2 tablespoons garlic flavored oil	16 ounces baby spinach (approximately 1½ bags)
1 large red bell pepper, diced	½ cup grated Parmesan cheese
⅔ cup minced shallots or onion	
3 cups boiling water with mushroom flavoring packet from couscous box added or 3 cups chicken broth with thyme or rosemary added, to taste	

Preheat oven to 450 degrees.

Clean mushrooms with damp paper towel. Cut off stems and discard. Scrape out and discard mushroom gills. Place mushroom caps, rounded side up, on a baking sheet and coat caps with cooking spray. Bake 5 minutes. Remove from oven.

Meanwhile, heat oil in a large deep skillet over medium high heat. Add red bell pepper and shallots. Sauté 5 minutes. Bring broth to a boil and add to skillet. Stir in couscous, thyme or rosemary, salt and pepper. Remove from heat and cover. Cook spinach in saucepan until wilted. Drain spinach well and add to skillet. Stir well and cover. Let stand 5 minutes or until liquid is mostly absorbed. Turn mushrooms over and fill with couscous mixture. Sprinkle cheese on top. May be prepared ahead and refrigerated. Just before serving, broil 4 inches from heat until cheese is golden brown.

Serves 8.

Patricia Eilender

A book of verses underneath the bough,

A jug of wine, a loaf of bread – and thou
Beside me . . .

Omar Khayyam

Zucchini & Onion-Filled Crêpe Stack

10	crêpes, pre-made	2	tablespoons chopped parsley
3	tablespoons butter, divided	1½	teaspoons oregano
3	tablespoons oil, divided	1½	teaspoons salt
4	large onions, sliced	¼	teaspoon pepper
6	zucchini	1	cup shredded Swiss cheese

Preheat oven to 350 degrees.

Heat 2 tablespoons butter and 2 tablespoons oil in large skillet. Sauté onion until tender. Remove with slotted spoon to bowl. Shred zucchini and sauté in remaining butter and oil until zucchini is tender and juices have evaporated. Add zucchini to onion, stir in parsley, oregano, salt and pepper.

Butter a shallow baking dish or pie plate. Place one crêpe in dish, spread with ⅓ cup zucchini filling, 2 tablespoons sauce and sprinkle with grated Swiss cheese. Continue stacking and filling, repeating sequence. Pour remaining sauce over all and top with a few sprinkles of cheese. Bake for 30 minutes.

SAUCE

2	tablespoons butter	1½	cups milk
3	tablespoons flour	2	eggs
½	teaspoon salt	¼	cup Parmesan cheese

Melt butter in pan; stir in flour and salt. Gradually add milk, cook, stirring constantly until sauce thickens. Beat eggs in medium bowl; gradually beat in half of hot sauce; pour back in saucepan. Stir in Parmesan cheese.

Carol Toth

*T*hree things on the earth are accounted precious: Knowledge, grain and friendship.

Japanese Proverb

Sides

potatoes
rice
vegetables
fruits
et cetera

WORD

Parmesan Potato Cakes

2½ pounds potatoes, grated
2 ounces egg yolk
¼ cup heavy cream

½ cup chopped parsley
¾ cup grated Parmesan cheese
Salt and pepper, to taste

Combine all ingredients and place about 3 ounces on flat surface. Shape into 3-inch rounds and repeat until all is used. Place scoops of filling mixture on a potato cake and cover with another cake. Repeat until all is used. Sauté in butter until crispy on both sides.

Yield: about 8 potato cakes

FILLING

8 ounces feta cheese
8 ounces cream cheese

8 ounces grated cheese blend
of your choice

Combine all ingredients until well-blended.

Charles P'Ablaing
Chef, The Landings Club

Glorious Potatoes

5 pounds potatoes or
12 potatoes, cooked and
mashed
2 cups heavy cream, whipped

2 cups mayonnaise
1¼ cups grated Parmesan
cheese
Salt and pepper, to taste

Preheat oven to 325 degrees.

Put mashed potatoes into a greased 9x13-inch casserole dish. Gently mix together remaining ingredients and cover mashed potatoes. Bake for 55 minutes or until golden brown on top. Can assemble the night before and cook when needed.

Serves 12 to 16.

Sharon Williams

Cabernet Whipped Potatoes

2	pounds Yukon Gold potatoes, peeled and sliced ½-inch thick	1	tablespoon minced garlic
		½	cup heavy cream
1½	cups Cabernet Sauvignon wine	4	tablespoons unsalted butter, room temperature
2	tablespoons minced shallots		Salt and freshly ground pepper
		2	tablespoons chopped chives

Put the potatoes in a large pot of lightly salted water and bring to a boil. Reduce the heat to a simmer and cook for 20 to 30 minutes until the potatoes are tender. Combine the wine, shallots and garlic in a small non-corrosive saucepan and bring to a boil over high heat. Cook mixture for 7-8 minutes until the liquid is reduced to about ⅓ cup. Set aside.

Drain the potatoes and return them to the pan. Stir over medium high heat for about 1 minute to dry them out. Add the reduced red wine mixture and mash the potatoes with a fork or potato masher, mixing in the wine. (You can also press the potatoes through a potato ricer into a bowl, add the wine mixture, and blend well.)

Heat the cream in a saucepan over medium high heat until scalded but not boiling. Add the butter and cream to the potatoes, salt and pepper to taste and mash with the fork or potato masher until smooth. Stir in the chives. Serve immediately or keep warm until ready to serve.

Serves 4.

Bev Brucher

Cheesy Potatoes

2	pounds frozen hash brown potatoes, thawed	½	cup chopped onion
		1	can cream of chicken soup
¼	cup margarine, melted	1	soup can milk
1	teaspoon salt	½	pint sour cream
¼	teaspoon pepper	2	cups grated cheddar cheese

Preheat oven to 350 degrees.

Mix together all ingredients but potatoes. Add potatoes and blend together, stirring well. Place mixture in oiled 9x13-inch baking dish. Bake for 45 minutes.

Serves 6 to 8.

Marcia DaPont

Potatoes Romanoff

5	cups potatoes, cooked, peeled and diced	1	small clove garlic, finely chopped
1	teaspoon salt	½	cup American cheese, shredded
2	cups creamed cottage cheese		
1	cup sour cream		Paprika
¼	cup finely chopped green onions		

Preheat oven to 350 degrees.

Cook potatoes until tender. Cool. Sprinkle with 1 teaspoon salt. Combine cottage cheese, sour cream, onion and garlic. Fold in potato cubes and pour into a buttered 1½-quart casserole dish. Top with shredded cheese and sprinkle with paprika. Bake for 40-45 minutes.

Serves 6.

Linda Powers

Cheese Potatoes

4½	cups water	1	tablespoon minced onions
6	tablespoons margarine	1	tablespoon chopped black olives
1	teaspoon salt		
4½	cups instant mashed potatoes	1	tablespoon chopped chives
1	cup sour cream		Paprika, for garnish
1	cup shredded cheddar cheese		Parsley, for garnish

Preheat oven to 350 degrees.

Boil water, margarine and salt. Remove from heat and add potatoes, sour cream, cheese, onion, olives and chives. Place in greased 9x13-inch baking dish. Sprinkle with paprika and parsley. Bake for 10 minutes uncovered.

Serves 10.

This dish can be prepared up to two days before serving. Cover with foil and refrigerate. When ready to bake, uncover and bake at 350 degrees for 30 minutes. Also can be frozen before baking. To bake frozen dish, thaw and then bake at 350 degrees for 30 minutes.

Jane Roach

Morning Potatoes

4	large potatoes	½	teaspoon salt
4	garlic cloves, minced	½	teaspoon black pepper
¼	cup onion, chopped	2	tablespoons finely chopped
2	tablespoons olive oil		fresh parsley
1	tablespoon butter	2-3	teaspoons chopped fresh
2	small sweet green, red or		rosemary
	yellow bell peppers, cut in		
	strips		

Peel potatoes and cut into 1-inch chunks. Cook potatoes in boiling water until almost tender, about 5 minutes. Drain and set aside.

In a 12-inch skillet, cook and stir garlic and onions in oil and butter over medium heat until soft; toss in pepper strips. Cook and stir 1 minute. Add potatoes and cook until golden brown and crisp around edges, about 15 minutes, stirring occasionally. Season with salt and pepper. Sprinkle with fresh herbs.

Serves 8.

Judy Pelok

Roasted Potatoes With Artichokes & Feta

2	pounds small red potatoes, quartered	1	tablespoon olive oil
2	14-ounce cans artichoke hearts, drained and halved	½	teaspoon salt, Kosher preferred
2	tablespoons fresh thyme or 2 teaspoons dried	½	teaspoon black pepper
		½	cup feta cheese, crumbled

Preheat oven to 425 degrees.

Coat a 13x9-inch pan with cooking spray. Combine all ingredients, except feta, in pan. Cook 40 minutes until potatoes are tender. Add cheese and toss gently.

Serves 4.

Linda Torpie

The eye is harder to please than the stomach.

Japanese Proverb

217

Potatoes Baked & Stuffed

2	baking potatoes	¼	teaspoon pepper
1	zucchini, grated	4	ounces Gruyère or other
2	tablespoons butter		Swiss cheese, grated
½	teaspoon salt		

Bake potatoes until soft. Cut a thin slice, lengthwise, off top of each potato. Scoop out pulp. Grate enough zucchini to equal the amount of potato and sauté in butter. Mix potato, salt and pepper with zucchini and stuff potato shells. Top with grated cheese. (At this point may be covered and refrigerated for 6 to 8 hours.) Bake in 425 degree oven long enough to reheat and melt cheese, about 5 to 10 minutes.

Serves 2.

Barbara Schroeder

Potato Casserole

6	medium potatoes	⅓	cup onion, chopped
¼	cup butter	¼	cup pimiento, drained
¼	cup flour	1	8-ounce carton sour cream
1	cup chicken broth	1	cup cheddar cheese, grated
⅓	cup light cream	½	cup butter, melted
½	teaspoon salt, divided	½-1	cup corn flake crumbs
½	cup celery, chopped		

Preheat oven to 325 degrees.

Boil unpeeled potatoes until almost tender, about 15 minutes. Drain and cool. Melt ¼ cup butter; stir in flour and add broth. Stir in cream, ¼ teaspoon salt and cook, stirring until thick. Remove from heat and cool. Peel and grate potatoes. Add celery, onion, pimiento and ¼ teaspoon salt. Stir in sour cream and cheese. Add to flour and broth mixture and turn into a 9x13-inch casserole. Combine melted butter and cornflakes and sprinkle over top. Bake 1 hour. Can be prepared a day ahead.

Serves 6.

Joan Robinson

W̶hat I say is that, if a fellow really likes potatoes, he must be a pretty decent sort of fellow.

A. A. Milne

Lemon Sweet Potatoes

4	pounds sweet potatoes, cooked, peeled, mashed	½	stick softened butter
		2	egg yolks
3	tablespoons fresh lemon juice		Lemon juice, to taste
			Salt and pepper, to taste
1	teaspoon salt		Lemon slices

Preheat oven to 325 degrees.

Combine sweet potatoes, lemon juice and salt. Beat in butter, egg yolks, lemon juice, salt and pepper. Place mixture in a buttered 1½-quart casserole and top with lemon slices. Brush the top with melted butter. Bake for 45 minutes.

Serves 8.

Onnie Duffie

Mary's Sweet Potato Casserole

2½	pounds sweet potatoes, peeled and cubed	1½	cups sugar
		¼	cup milk
½	stick margarine	1	teaspoon vanilla
3	eggs, separated	¾-1	cup of pecan pieces

Preheat oven to 350 degrees.

Cook potatoes in boiling water 20 minutes. Drain. Add margarine and let stand until melted. With mixer on medium speed, beat potatoes, sugar and egg yolks until smooth. Blend in milk and vanilla. In separate bowl, beat egg whites until peaks form. Fold egg whites into potato mixture. Spoon into greased 2-quart casserole. Sprinkle with pecans. Bake 30 minutes or until lightly browned.

Mary Schoenwald

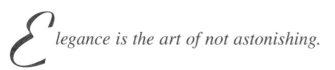

Elegance is the art of not astonishing.

Jean Cocteau

Pam's Sweet Potatoes

8	medium sweet potatoes	½ cup water
1¼	cups brown sugar, packed	½ cup raisins
½	cup apple juice	¼ cup butter or margarine

Preheat oven to 350 degrees.

Cook and peel potatoes. Allow to cool. Slice and place in a greased 2½-quart baking dish. In a small saucepan, combine remaining ingredients. Bring to a boil, stirring frequently. Pour over potatoes. Bake, uncovered, for 45 minutes. Serves 8.

Monica de Guzman

Sweet Potato Casserole

3	cups mashed sweet potatoes	2	eggs
1	cup sugar	1	teaspoon vanilla
½	cup milk		Dash of nutmeg
⅓	cup butter		

1	cup coconut (optional)	⅓	cup flour
1	cup chopped pecans	⅓	cup butter, melted
1	cup brown sugar		

Preheat oven to 375 degrees.

Combine first seven ingredients and pour into baking dish. Blend coconut, pecans, brown sugar and flour. Add melted butter and sprinkle over potatoes. Bake 25 minutes until brown.

Serves 6 to 8.

Linda Shaw

No spectacle on earth is more appealing than a beautiful woman . . . cooking dinner for someone she loves.

Thomas Wolfe

Broccoli Rice Casserole

1	cup chopped onions	1	stick butter
½	cup chopped celery	1	16-ounce jar of Cheez Whiz
2	packages frozen chopped broccoli, thawed	1	can cream of celery soup
		2½	cups rice, cooked

Preheat oven to 375 degrees.

In large skillet over medium heat, sauté onion, celery and thawed broccoli in butter for 3-5 minutes. Stir in cheese and soup until smooth. Place rice in a greased 3-quart casserole dish. Pour cheese mixture over and stir all ingredients together. Bake for 25-30 minutes or until hot and bubbly.

Serves 8.

Donna Elwell

Vidalia Onion Risotto

2	teaspoons vegetable oil	½	cup (2 ounces) crumbled feta cheese, divided
2	cups chopped Vidalia or other sweet onion	⅓	cup chopped fresh flat-leaf parsley
2	large garlic cloves, minced	¼	cup (1 ounce) grated fresh Parmesan cheese
1½	cups uncooked Arborio or other short-grain rice		Freshly ground black pepper
2	14½-ounce cans vegetable broth		Flat-leaf parsley sprigs (optional)

Heat oil in a saucepan over medium heat. Add onion and garlic; sauté 1 minute. Stir in rice. Add ½ cup broth, cook until liquid is nearly absorbed, stirring constantly. Add remaining broth, ½ cup at a time, stirring constantly until each portion of broth is nearly absorbed before adding the next (about 20 minutes total). Remove from heat; stir in ¼ cup feta, parsley and Parmesan. Spoon into a serving bowl; top with ¼ cup feta and pepper. Garnish with parsley sprigs, if desired.

Yield: 5 servings (serving size: 1 cup)

Carol Diver

O ne meal without rice mars domestic happiness for a week.

Japanese Proverb

221

Green Rice

1 stick butter	2 cups minute rice, cooked
1 medium onion, chopped	½ cup Parmesan cheese
1 package frozen spinach, thawed and drained	Salt and pepper, to taste

Preheat oven to 350 degrees.
Melt butter in pan and brown the chopped onion. Remove from heat and add spinach and rice mixing in cheese, salt and pepper. Bake, covered, in small casserole dish for 40 minutes. Easily doubled.
Serves 4.

Donna Meterko

Risotto

3 tablespoons olive oil	24 ounces chicken broth
1 small onion, chopped	3 plum tomatoes, chopped
1 cup risotto (arborio rice)	Parmesan cheese, to taste

Sauté onion in saucepan in olive oil. Add risotto and stir to coat with oil. Add half of broth, stirring constantly. Continue to gradually add the rest of the broth, stirring continuously. When all liquid is absorbed, add chopped tomatoes and grated Parmesan cheese.
Serves 4.

Mary Schoenwald

Rice Milanese

2 tablespoons margarine	Pinch turmeric or saffron
1½ cups long grain rice	4 cups chicken bouillon or broth
3-4 green onions, finely chopped	1 tablespoon grated Parmesan cheese
¼ cup dry white wine	
½ cup chopped mushrooms	

Melt margarine in a heavy saucepan. Add rice and green onions and cook slowly, stirring with a wooden spoon, until rice is milky. Add wine and continue cooking and stirring until it is absorbed. Lower heat and stir in remaining ingredients. Cover and simmer slowly for about 20 minutes.
Serves 6.

Jean Morris

Gorgonzola & Red Pear Risotto

1½	cups canned vegetable broth	2	tablespoons chopped fresh sage or 2 teaspoons dried rubbed sage
1	cup dry white wine		
1½	tablespoons olive oil		
1	cup arborio rice or medium grain white rice (arborio is better)	⅓	cup crumbled Gorgonzola cheese (about 2 ounces)
		1	ripe unpeeled red-skinned pear, halved, cored, diced

Bring vegetable broth and white wine to simmer in heavy small saucepan over medium heat. Reduce heat to low; keep mixture warm.

Heat oil in heavy medium saucepan over medium heat. Add rice and sauté until translucent, about 2 minutes. Add all but ½ cup broth mixture to rice. Simmer uncovered 15 minutes, stirring often. Mix in sage. Cook until rice is tender but still firm to bite and risotto is creamy, adding remaining broth mixture, ¼ cupful at a time if risotto is dry, about 5 minutes longer. Mix in Gorgonzola and pear. Cook until cheese melts and pear is heated through, about 1 minute. Season with salt and generous amount of pepper.

Serves 2, can be doubled.

Do not freeze. Can be reheated in microwave.

Donna Pfeifer

Wild Rice & Mushrooms

½	pound wild rice or combination of wild and long grain rice	2	tablespoons flour
		½	pint whipping cream
		¼	cup sherry
1	stick butter		Buttered bread crumbs
¾	pound fresh mushrooms		

Preheat oven to 350 degrees.

Cook rice according to package directions. Sauté sliced mushrooms in butter. Add flour and cream, stirring constantly. When well-blended remove from heat, add cooked rice and stir in sherry. Put in a 9x13-inch or 7x11-inch well-greased casserole dish and top with buttered bread crumbs.

Bake 30-45 minutes.

Serves 10 to 12.

Ann Robertson

Lemon Risotto

4	cups vegetable stock, garlic broth or defatted chicken stock	¼	cup dry white wine
			Salt, to taste
1	tablespoon olive oil		Juice of 1 large lemon (4-5 tablespoons)
½	small onion, minced		Grated zest of ½ lemon
2	garlic cloves, minced or put through a press	1	egg, beaten
		¼	cup freshly grated Parmesan cheese, or more
1	cup Italian arborio rice, washed		Freshly ground pepper

Have the stock simmering in a saucepan.

Heat the oil in a wide, heavy-bottomed, frying pan and sauté the onion and garlic over medium-low heat until the onion is golden. Add the rice and continue to sauté, stirring, until all the grains are separated and coated with oil. Stir in the white wine and salt and cook over medium heat, stirring all the while. The wine should bubble but not too quickly. You want some of the flavor to cook into the rice before it evaporates.

When the wine has just about evaporated, stir in a ladleful of the stock. It should just cover the rice and should bubble slowly like the wine. Cook, stirring constantly, until it is just about absorbed. Add another ladleful of the stock and continue to cook in this fashion, not too fast but not too slowly, adding more broth when the rice is almost dry. After 25-35 minutes, the rice should be cooked al dente, firm to the bite.

Beat together the lemon juice, lemon zest, egg and Parmesan. Add another ladleful of stock so that the rice is not completely dry and remove from the heat. Immediately stir in the lemon mixture. Taste and adjust seasonings, adding salt and pepper to taste. Return to the heat and stir for a few seconds, then serve at once.

Serves 2 as a main dish or 4 as a side dish.

Dorothy Pero

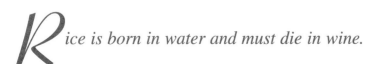

ice is born in water and must die in wine.

Old Italian Proverb

Anita's Artichoke Pie

3	tablespoons olive oil		Freshly ground black pepper, to
2	medium onions, finely		taste
	chopped	1	cup ricotta cheese
2	8-ounce packages frozen	8	eggs, divided
	artichoke hearts		Pastry for a 10-inch double crust
	Boiling salted water		pie
1½	cups freshly grated		
	Parmesan cheese		

Preheat oven to 450 degrees.

Heat the oil in a small, heavy skillet and sauté the onions until translucent but not browned. Cook the artichoke hearts in boiling, salted water in a covered saucepan until they are crisp-tender. Drain and cut into bite-size pieces. Combine the onion, artichokes, Parmesan cheese, pepper, ricotta cheese and four of the eggs, lightly beaten. Mix well. Line a 10-inch pie plate with half the pastry. Fill the pie with the artichoke mixture. Make four depressions in the artichoke mixture and break the remaining eggs into them. Roll out the remaining pastry and cover the pie. Seal the edges and decorate. Make steam holes in the crust. Bake the pie 10 minutes, reduce the oven heat to 400 degrees and bake about 30 minutes longer or until the pastry is done. Allow the pie to stand 10 minutes before cutting.

Serves 6 to 8.

Theresa Sullivan

Lima Beans

4	1-pound cans lima beans	1	tablespoon molasses
½	cup butter, melted	1	teaspoon dry mustard
1	cup sour cream		Dash of salt
1	cup brown sugar		

Preheat oven to 300 degrees.

Drain beans. Add remaining ingredients. Mixture will be soupy. Turn into a 3-quart casserole. (This can be made a day ahead up to this point.) Bake for one hour or more. Good served with ham.

Serves 8.

Bobbi Gerner

225

Asparagus In Zucchini Holders

40 asparagus spears, cleaned,
    with bottom 2-3 inches
    removed
2   zucchini cut in napkin
    holder size pieces, remove
    seeds to form rings

1   roasted red bell pepper cut
    into strips
    Lemon juice, optional

In a large skillet, cook the asparagus and zucchini rounds in a small amount of water until tender, about 6 minutes. Do not overcook. (Cooking time will vary depending on the size of your asparagus.) Drain vegetables and let stand 5 minutes. Group 5-6 asparagus spears together and insert into each zucchini ring. Place 2 strips of the roasted pepper on top of each zucchini ring. Cover and set aside. When ready to serve, heat in microwave 2 minutes. Place one package on each plate to serve. Sprinkle with lemon juice if desired. Serves 8.

Patricia Eilender

Old Settler's Beans

½   pound bacon, diced
½   pound lean ground beef or
    ground turkey
1   large onion, chopped
1   24-ounce can pork and
    beans
1   15-ounce can kidney beans,
    drained

1   15-ounce can butter beans,
    drained
¼   cup brown sugar
¼   cup ketchup
2   tablespoons molasses
½   teaspoon dry mustard
    Dash Worcestershire

Cook bacon. Add ground beef to bacon and brown. Drain. Combine all ingredients in a Dutch oven and cook slowly on top of stove 1 to 3 hours to blend flavors. Can also be cooked for 8 hours in a crockpot set on low. Serves 6 to 8+.

Patti Iott

re we going to measure or are we going to cook?

Mimi Sheraton

Red Cabbage With Carrots

2	tablespoons butter	¼	cup cider vinegar
2	tablespoons olive oil	1	teaspoon sugar
1	medium onion, thinly sliced	1	carrot, grated
½	head red cabbage, thinly sliced		Salt and pepper, to taste
		1	teaspoon caraway seeds
¼	cup water		

Sauté onion in butter and olive oil. Stir in cabbage. Stirring over medium heat add water and vinegar and cook, covered, 5 minutes. Stir in carrots and seasonings continuing to cook, covered, until carrots are crisp-tender. Add caraway seeds and cook 5 minutes more, uncovered.

Serves 6.

Very good reheated.

Anita Madigan

Sally's Broccoli Soufflé

1	16-ounce package frozen broccoli buds	10	ounces sharp cheddar cheese, grated
3	tablespoons butter	¾	teaspoon salt
3	tablespoons flour	½	teaspoon pepper
1	cup milk	3	eggs, separated
		1	large onion, chopped

Preheat oven to 350 degrees.

Cook broccoli in small amount of water until tender. Drain well. Melt butter in large pan and when bubbly, whisk in flour. When butter and flour are blended, whisk in milk and cook over medium heat, stirring constantly until thickened. (Mixture will be very thick.) Add grated cheese, salt and pepper; continue to stir until mixture is smooth. Remove from heat. Beat egg yolks slightly; stir small amount of cheese sauce into yolks and then yolk mixture into rest of sauce. Process the broccoli and onion in food processor until very finely chopped and add to cheese mixture. Beat egg whites until stiff and fold into broccoli. Spoon into greased soufflé or casserole dish. Place dish in pan of water and bake approximately 45 minutes or until browned on top.

Serves 8 to 10.

Sally Robyn

Peas Extraordinaire

1	pound frozen baby peas, thawed and uncooked	¼	cup onion, chopped
½	cup bacon cooked, crumbled	1	cup cream of celery soup
1	8-ounce can water chestnuts, drained and chopped	1	cup herb stuffing
		2	tablespoons melted butter
		¼	cup sherry

Preheat oven to 350 degrees.

Spread peas over bottom of greased 1-quart casserole dish. Combine bacon, water chestnuts, onion and soup. Spoon mixture over peas. Sprinkle stuffing over mixture. Drizzle butter over stuffing. Pour sherry over top. Bake for 30 minutes.

Serves 6.

Agi Sutton

Broccoli Soufflé

3	tablespoons butter	5	egg yolks
3	tablespoons flour	1	cup, or more, chopped broccoli
1	cup milk		
1	teaspoon salt	6	egg whites
¼	teaspoon pepper	½	cup Parmesan cheese, grated, divided
1	teaspoon Worcestershire sauce		

Preheat oven to 350 degrees.

To prepare the soufflé dish, butter a 1½-quart straight-sided baking dish. Sprinkle ¼ cup grated Parmesan cheese over the bottom of the dish.

Melt the butter in a saucepan. Add the flour and cook, stirring, until golden and bubbly. Add the milk all at once and cook, over high heat, stirring constantly, until thick and smooth. Remove from heat. Add the salt, pepper and Worcestershire. Add the egg yolks, one at a time, stirring well after each addition. Stir in the chopped broccoli.

Beat the egg whites until stiff but not dry. Fold into the broccoli mixture. Pour into the soufflé dish. Sprinkle with ¼ cup Parmesan cheese.

Bake for 30-35 minutes. Serve immediately.

Jackie Linder

Broccoli Puff

6	ounces broccoli buds	¼	cup milk
4	ounces artichoke hearts, rinsed and drained	¼	cup mayonnaise
1	can cream of mushroom soup	1	beaten egg
2	ounces shredded Swiss cheese	¼	cup dry bread crumbs
		1	tablespoon butter, melted

Preheat oven to 350 degrees.

Cut broccoli and artichokes to bite-size. Steam broccoli until almost done (do not overcook) and drain. Place vegetables in 8-inch square pan. Stir together soup, cheese, milk, mayonnaise and egg. Pour over broccoli and artichokes. Combine bread crumbs and butter, sprinkle evenly over soup mixture. Bake for 45 minutes until crumbs are brown.

Serves 6.

Anne Armel

Broccoli Casserole

2	packages frozen chopped broccoli	1	cup mayonnaise
2	teaspoons minced onion	1	cup celery soup, undiluted
2	beaten egg yolks	¾	teaspoon salt
2	beaten egg whites		Dash pepper
2	teaspoons Worcestershire sauce		Buttered bread crumbs

Preheat oven to 350 degrees.

Cook broccoli according to package directions. Drain and cool. Mix with all other ingredients except bread crumbs. Sprinkle buttered bread crumbs on top and bake in greased casserole dish for 45 minutes.

Serves 6 to 8.

Estelle Franz

Broccoli & Corn Casserole

1	10-ounce package frozen chopped broccoli	½	box "Chicken in a Biscuit" crackers, crushed
1	can white corn	½	stick butter or margarine, melted
1	can yellow corn		

Defrost and drain broccoli. Mix with the two cans of corn. Mix crackers with melted butter and add ½ of cracker mixture to vegetables. Pour into baking dish. Place rest of crackers on top and bake for 35 minutes.
Serves 6.

Jamie Lee Scholten

Brussels Sprouts With Hazelnuts

2	pints Brussels sprouts	½	teaspoon salt
6	tablespoons butter	¼	teaspoon pepper
½	cup chopped skinned hazelnuts		

Cook Brussels sprouts for 10 minutes in boiling water, or until tender. Cut in halves or quarters if large. Melt butter in skillet and add hazelnuts. Sauté for 5 minutes or until golden brown, stirring often. Add salt and pepper. Mix in Brussels sprouts, tossing to coat. Heat through, 2-4 minutes.

Gail Andrus

Carrots Denali

1½	pounds carrots, peeled and julienned	2	teaspoons dried tarragon Salt and pepper, to taste
2	tablespoons butter or margarine	½	cup white wine
		¼	cup brandy or amaretto

Steam carrots in a steamer in a saucepan until crisp-tender. Drain and plunge into cold water; drain. Melt the butter or margarine in skillet over medium-high heat. Add the tarragon, salt, pepper, white wine and brandy. Bring to a boil and add the carrots; cook, stirring, until heated through.
Serves 12.

Anonymous

Zesty Carrots

1½	pounds carrots, peeled	1	tablespoon horseradish
¼	cup water reserved from cooking carrots	½	cup mayonnaise
		¼	cup grated sharp cheese
2	tablespoons grated onions and juice	½	teaspoon salt
		¼	teaspoon pepper

TOPPING

1	cup fresh bread crumbs	1	teaspoon paprika
¼	cup butter, melted		

Preheat oven to 350 degrees.

Slice carrots ¼-inch thick. Cook in small amount of water for 5 minutes. Drain and reserve ¼ cup water for sauce. Combine water, onion, horseradish, mayonnaise, cheese, salt and pepper. Add carrots and spoon into 2-quart casserole dish. Combine topping ingredients. Sprinkle over carrot mixture. Bake for 20 minutes.

Serves 6.

Betsy Smith

Chiles Rellenos Casserole

3	4-ounce cans whole green chiles	¾	cup milk
		1	egg
12	ounces mild cheddar cheese, grated	2	tablespoons flour
			Salt

Preheat oven to 350 degrees.

Gently open chiles and remove seeds. Overstuff each chile with grated cheddar, placing the bundles closely together in bottom of casserole dish, forming a single layer. Beat together milk, egg, flour and salt. Pour over chiles. Can be covered and refrigerated until ready to bake. Bake, uncovered, 45 minutes.

Easily doubled.

Serves 4.

Sandra Humphrey

Creamed Corn

1	pound frozen corn	1	teaspoon salt
1	cup whipping cream	6	teaspoons sugar
1	cup milk		
2	tablespoons melted butter	1	teaspoon vanilla
2	tablespoons flour		

Combine first five ingredients in a saucepan. Bring to boil, reduce heat and simmer for 5 minutes. Add butter, flour and vanilla. Cook until thickened, about 1-2 minutes more.

Serves 6 to 8.

This must be made at the last minute and served immediately.

Jane Alpert

Corn Soufflé With Green Chiles

¼	pound bacon, chopped	3	egg yolks
¼	cup flour	½	teaspoon salt
⅔	cup milk	¼	cup grated Gruyère cheese
1	package frozen cream style white corn, thawed (about 1 cup)	½	of 4-ounce can chopped green chiles
		3	egg whites, stiffly beaten

Preheat oven to 325 degrees.

Fry bacon until crisp and drain. Set aside. Save ¼ cup bacon grease (add butter if not enough grease to make ¼ cup). Over medium heat, add flour and blend well. Slowly add milk and blend. Add corn and cook until thickened. Remove from heat. Blend some of hot mixture into egg yolks; add salt and cheese. Add remaining corn and chiles to egg yolk mixture. Fold in beaten egg whites. Bake in greased 1½-quart baking dish for 45-60 minutes or until set. Sprinkle with reserved bacon.

Serves 4 generously.

Joan Capen

he art of dining well is not slight art, the pleasure not a slight pleasure.

Michael Eyquem De Montaigne

Eggplant Patrice

2	eggplants, sliced ¼-inch thick		Salt and pepper, to taste
4	medium tomatoes, sliced		Garlic salt, to taste
2	medium green bell peppers, chopped		Sugar, to taste
2	medium onions, chopped		MSG, optional
		¾	pound sharp cheddar cheese, sliced ⅛-inch thick

Preheat oven to 400 degrees.

Parboil eggplant until partially tender. Place layer of eggplant slices in 13x9x2-inch casserole dish. Add layer of sliced tomatoes. Fill spaces with mixture of chopped green peppers and onions. Sprinkle lightly with each of seasonings. Add layer of cheese. Repeat layers until casserole is filled, ending with cheese. Cover and bake until steaming, about ½ hour. Remove cover; reduce heat to 350 degrees. Cook until sauce is thick and golden, about ½ hour.

Serves 8.

Marby Varley

Italian Soufflé

2	packages frozen chopped spinach	2	tablespoons melted butter
1	clove chopped garlic, divided	1	tablespoon olive oil or canola oil
6	small zucchini squash		
	Salt, to taste	2	eggs, separated
½	cup sour cream	¼	cup or more Parmesan cheese

Preheat oven to 350 degrees.

Microwave spinach according to package directions with some of the garlic. Steam zucchini with a little salt and more garlic. Drain both vegetables well. Mix vegetables together and add sour cream, butter, oil, egg yolks and Parmesan cheese. Beat egg whites until stiff and fold into mixture. Put in buttered loaf pan or soufflé dish. Top with additional Parmesan cheese. Bake about 30 minutes.

Serves 6.

Loretta Greer

233

Corn & Spinach Fritters

1	10-ounce package frozen chopped spinach, thawed and drained	¼	cup mozzarella cheese, shredded
1	cup corn	2	egg whites, unbeaten
¼	cup carrot, finely chopped	1	tablespoon cornstarch
		¼	teaspoon garlic, minced
			Salt and pepper

Mix all ingredients together. Mixture will be loose. (You can add a small amount of bread crumbs to bind it some if you like.) Shape into patties. Heat 1 teaspoon olive oil in skillet. Place patties into skillet and brown on both sides.

Yield: 4 patties

Elayne Blecker

Mushrooms Florentine

2	10-ounce packages frozen chopped spinach	½	cup grated cheddar cheese
½	teaspoon salt	1	pound mushrooms
¼	cup chopped onion	4	tablespoons butter
2	tablespoons butter or margarine, melted	¼	teaspoon garlic powder
		½	cup grated cheddar cheese

Preheat oven to 350 degrees.

Cook spinach according to package directions. Drain well and squeeze out excess liquid. Spoon spinach evenly into bottom of shallow 2-quart casserole dish. Sprinkle with salt, onion, melted butter and cheddar cheese. Quickly rinse and dry the mushrooms. Sauté in 4 tablespoons butter. Spoon mushrooms over cheese layer in casserole and sprinkle lightly with garlic powder and ½ cup cheddar cheese. Bake for 20-25 minutes or until bubbly.

Serves 6.

Joyce Blanke

When a man talks to you about his mother's cooking, pay no attention, for between the ages of 12 and 21, a boy can eat large quantities of anything and never feel it.

Sarah Tyson Rorer

234

Onion Casserole

¼	cup unsalted butter	1	cup grated Swiss cheese
7-8	large sweet onions	⅔	cup light cream
½	cup uncooked rice		Salt, to taste
5	cups boiling salted water		

Preheat oven to 325 degrees.

Melt butter in large skillet. Cut onions into chunks and sauté in butter until transparent. Cook rice in boiling, salted water 5 minutes. Drain. Blend all ingredients and season to taste. Place in a shallow 2-quart dish and bake for 1 hour.

Serves 8.

This dish may also be served cold with a vinaigrette of:

6	tablespoons oil	2	tablespoons chopped herbs
2	tablespoons white vinegar		(parsley, tarragon, chives)
	Salt and pepper, to taste		

Joyce Blanke

Vidalia Tomato Bake

2	cups seasoned bread crumbs, divided	1	tablespoon chopped fresh basil
5	fresh tomatoes, sliced	2	tablespoons chopped fresh parsley
2	medium Vidalia onions, sliced	2-3	tablespoons minced fresh chives
½	cup butter, divided		Salt and pepper, to taste
1½	cups sour cream		

Preheat oven to 350 degrees.

Line a well-oiled 9x13-inch casserole dish with 1 cup of bread crumbs. Layer tomatoes and onions over top. Dot with ¼ cup butter. In small bowl combine sour cream, basil, parsley and chives. Spread over vegetables. Sprinkle with remaining bread crumbs. Dot with remaining ¼ cup butter. Bake, uncovered, for 50 minutes until lightly browned.

Serves 8.

Dried herbs may be substituted.

Bobbie Gerner

Vidalia Onion Rice Casserole

¼	cup butter	1	teaspoon salt
7	medium or 4 large Vidalia onions, sliced	1	cup grated Swiss cheese
		⅔	cup evaporated milk
½	cup raw rice		

Preheat oven to 350 degrees.

Sauté onions in butter until golden. Cook ½ cup rice in 5 cups of boiling water for 10 minutes. Drain rice. Mix onions, rice and remaining ingredients and pour into shallow pan. Bake for 1 hour.

Serves 8.

Note: You may substitute lowfat mozzarella cheese and top with Parmesan cheese for the Swiss cheese.

Betsy Smith

Vidalia Onion Casserole

3	large Vidalia onions, sliced, and then halve slices	1	teaspoon soy sauce
		2	cups shredded Swiss cheese
2	tablespoons margarine	8	slices French bread, buttered on both sides
1	can cream of chicken soup		
⅔	cup milk		Pepper to taste (optional)

Preheat oven to 350 degrees.

Sauté onions in margarine. Mix soup, milk and soy sauce together. Stir in Swiss cheese. Layer onions and cheese mixture in 9x12-inch casserole dish. Top with bread slices. Place in oven for 15 minutes. Push down bread and bake for 15 minutes more. Serve hot from oven.

Serves 6 to 8.

Ann McClure
Mary Hardy

east and your halls are crowded; Fast, and the world goes by.

Ellen Wheeler Wilcox

Les Onions en Vin

2-3 pounds of white pearl
onions, peeled
2 tablespoons margarine or
butter

3 ounces Marsala or port wine
Salt and pepper, to taste

Heat margarine or butter in skillet and when melted add onions in one layer. Brown gently on both sides. When brown, add Marsala or port wine and simmer gently to soften onions and blend flavors. Add salt and pepper, cover, turn off heat. Can be prepared ahead and reheated just before serving. Serves 6 to 8.

Anne A. Fleming

Vidalia Onion Pie

5 medium Vidalia onions,
sliced thin
1 stick margarine
¾-1 cup grated Parmesan cheese,
divided

1 sleeve (36) Ritz crackers,
crushed, divided
2-3 tablespoons milk (optional)

Preheat oven to 325 degrees.

Sauté onions in margarine until limp but not browned. Place half the onions in a glass casserole, sprinkle with half of the cheese and half of the crackers. Repeat layers. Bake in casserole dish, uncovered, for about 20 minutes until light brown. Milk may be added during baking period if too much liquid has been absorbed by cracker crumbs. Serves 6.

Ed Duffie

No man can worship God or love his neighbor on an empty stomach.

Woodrow Wilson

237

Sautéed Peas With Prosciutto

4	cloves garlic, peeled	2	10-ounce packages frozen
4	tablespoons olive oil		tiny peas, thawed
4	tablespoons prosciutto or	4	tablespoons finely chopped
	pancetta, diced into ¼-inch		parsley
	cubes		Salt and pepper, to taste

Sauté garlic in oil until lightly colored. Remove garlic and add prosciutto. Sauté for 1 minute. Add peas, parsley, salt and pepper. Turn heat to medium and cook until done, about 5 minutes. May be prepared ahead and reheated in microwave before serving.

Margaret McCulloch

Spinach Casserole

2	packages frozen chopped	1	8-ounce can water chestnuts,
	spinach, cooked and well-		sliced or chopped, drained
	drained	1	package dry onion soup mix
½	pint sour cream		Garlic powder to taste, optional

Preheat oven to 350 degrees.
Combine all ingredients in small greased casserole dish. Cover and bake for thirty minutes.
Serves 4 to 6.

Ginger Heussler

Aunt Buelah's Green Tomato Pie

2	unbaked pie crusts	¼	teaspoon nutmeg
2	cups diced green tomatoes	½	teaspoon cinnamon
1	cup sugar	3	tablespoons flour
1	tablespoon apple cider vinegar		

Preheat oven to 350 degrees.
Mix ingredients together and place in unbaked pie shell. Top with second pie crust. Bake 45 minutes or until crust is brown. Freezes well.
Serves 6.

Roberta Fields

Spaghetti Squash With Tomatoes, Basil & Parmesan

1½	pounds spaghetti squash, halved lengthwise	3	tablespoons Parmesan cheese
2	tablespoons olive oil	1	cup cherry tomatoes, thinly sliced
½	cup fresh basil, shredded		
¼	teaspoon dried oregano		

Place one squash half, cut side down, in glass baking dish; pour ¼ cup water around and cover with plastic wrap. Microwave on high 12 minutes or until soft when pressed. Let stand covered 3 minutes. In large bowl, whisk oil, basil, oregano and 2 tablespoons Parmesan. Stir in tomatoes and season mixture with salt and pepper. Scrape squash, add strands to tomato mixture and toss until combined. Sprinkle with remaining Parmesan.

Serves 2.

Bev Brucher

Summer Squash Casserole

2	pounds summer squash, sliced	1	can cream of mushroom soup, undiluted
1	small onion, chopped	1	cup cheddar cheese, shredded
2	tablespoons margarine or butter		Salt and pepper, to taste
2	beaten eggs		Buttered bread crumbs

Preheat oven to 350 degrees.

Cook sliced squash with chopped onion in water until just tender. Drain and mash squash. Add margarine or butter and toss. Stir in other ingredients and pour into buttered 1½-quart dish. Top with bread crumbs. Bake for 30-40 minutes.

Serves 6.

Carol Browning

Ɉf I had to choose just one plant for the whole herb garden, I should be content with basil.

Elizabeth David

239

Vegetables

Cherry Tomatoes Provençal

2	pints cherry tomatoes	½-1 cup fresh bread crumbs
¼	cup finely minced onion	½ teaspoon salt
¼	cup chopped parsley	Ground pepper
¼	teaspoon thyme	¼ cup butter, melted

Preheat oven to 350 degrees.
Place tomatoes in a single layer in a shallow baking dish. Combine all remaining ingredients. Sprinkle mixture over tomatoes and bake for 30 minutes.
Serves 8 to 10.

Eileen Stuhlreyer

Tomato Pudding

1	28-ounce can tomatoes	Salt and pepper, to taste
6	slices bread in large crumbs	¼ stick butter or margarine,
½	cup sugar	more if you like

Preheat oven to 375 degrees.
Stir first four ingredients together in buttered baking dish, dot with butter and bake until brown on top, about 45 minutes.

Gail Andrus

Aunt Fanny's Squash

3	zucchini	2 eggs, lightly beaten
1	medium onion, minced	½ cup butter, divided
¾	cup bread crumbs, divided	Salt and pepper, to taste

Preheat oven to 375 degrees.
Cut zucchini into 1-inch pieces and steam until tender. Drain and coarsely mash. In a bowl combine zucchini with ½ cup bread crumbs, onion, eggs and ¼ cup of melted butter. Season with salt and pepper. Transfer to 8x8-inch buttered dish. Pour remaining ¼ cup of melted butter over mixture and sprinkle with ¼ cup bread crumbs. Bake 1 hour.

Carol Toth

240

Baked Zucchini

2	cups sliced zucchini, divided	1½	cups milk
½	cup sliced onions	1	cup all-purpose baking mix
2	medium tomatoes, sliced		such as Bisquick
Salt and pepper		½	cup grated Romano cheese
3	eggs, beaten		

Preheat oven to 375 degrees.

In a greased 8-inch square baking dish, layer 1 cup zucchini, onions, tomatoes and remaining zucchini. Sprinkle lightly with salt and pepper. Combine eggs and milk, beating lightly; add Bisquick and cheese. Pour mixture over vegetables. Bake for 40 minutes.

Serves 6.

Irene Washenko

Roasted Summer Vegetables

1	red bell pepper, seeded and cut into strips	4	cloves of garlic, peeled and thinly sliced
1	yellow bell pepper, seeded and cut into strips	1	tablespoon olive oil
2	red onions, peeled and cut into wedges	1	tablespoon chopped fresh oregano or 1 teaspoon dried
2	small summer squash, ends trimmed and cut into ½-inch thick strips	Salt and pepper, to taste	
		2	tablespoons chopped fresh parsley
2	small zucchini, ends trimmed and cut into ½-inch thick strips	1	tablespoon balsamic vinegar

Preheat oven to 425 degrees.

In large bowl toss vegetables and garlic, olive oil, oregano, salt and pepper. Spread vegetables in metal roasting pan and roast for 20 minutes or until done, turning several times. Cool slightly; add parsley and vinegar and toss.

Adjust seasoning if necessary.

Margaret McCulloch

Zucchini & Carrot Julienne

½ pound carrots, trimmed and   2   tablespoons unsalted butter
   peeled   1½ teaspoons fresh lemon juice,
½ pound zucchini, scrubbed   or to taste
   and trimmed

With a mandoline or very sharp knife, cut the carrots and the zucchini, separately, into ⅛-inch julienne strips, about 2 inches long. In a steamer set over boiling water, steam the carrots, covered, for 2-3 minutes, or until they are crisp-tender, and transfer them to a bowl. In the steamer set over boiling water, steam the zucchini, covered for 30 seconds to 1 minute, or until crisp-tender, and transfer to the bowl of carrots. (The vegetables may be prepared up to this point 8 hours in advance and kept covered and chilled.) In a skillet, melt the butter over moderate heat, add the vegetables, drained if necessary, the lemon juice and salt and pepper to taste, and cook the mixture, stirring gently for 1-2 minutes or until the vegetables are heated through.
Serves 4.

Mary Lou Deeney

Fried Green Tomatoes

½ cup cornmeal   Bacon fat from 8 slices of bacon
½ teaspoon sugar   4   tablespoons peanut oil
1 teaspoon salt   Coarse salt
2 firm green tomatoes, cut into
   ½-inch slices

Combine cornmeal, sugar and salt. Dip each tomato slice into cornmeal mixture. Fry in hot bacon fat and oil until brown, turning once during cooking. Drain on paper towels. Sprinkle with coarse salt and serve hot.
Serves 2 to 4.

For a wonderful Southern-style sandwich, layer slices of fried green tomatoes, basil, bacon and mozzarella cheese between two slices of toasted white bread.

Janet Kuhn

Tomato Pie

1	9-inch frozen, unbaked, piecrust	Chives, to taste
3	medium tomatoes	Salt and pepper, to taste
½	cup finely chopped onion	1 cup mayonnaise
	Basil, to taste	1 cup sharp cheddar cheese, shredded

Preheat oven to 350 degrees.

Peel tomatoes and cover bottom of piecrust with thick slices. Sprinkle with onion, basil, chives, salt and pepper. Mix mayonnaise and cheese and spread over tomatoes. Bake 35 minutes.

Serves 6.

Gail Andrus

Zucchini Pesto

8	medium zucchini, sliced	Chopped garlic, if desired
7	ounces prepared pesto	1 cup Gruyère cheese

Preheat oven to 350 degrees.

Toss zucchini and pesto together, adding garlic if desired. Place in buttered 13x9-inch baking dish. Cover top with grated Gruyère cheese. Bake 20-30 minutes.

A combination of Swiss and Monterey Jack cheese can be substituted for the Gruyère.

Sandra Edgar Davis

Squash & Peach Casserole

2½	cups zucchini or yellow summer squash	2	tablespoons brown sugar
1	cup sliced peaches	2½	tablespoons butter or margarine

Preheat oven to 350 degrees.

Layer zucchini and peaches in 2-quart casserole dish. Sprinkle brown sugar on top. Dot with butter or margarine. Bake covered for 45-55 minutes.

Gail Andrus

243

Pineapple Casserole

1	1-pound can crushed pineapple, drained	1	stick butter, melted
½	cup sugar	4	eggs (3 if large), slightly beaten
4	heaping teaspoons cornstarch		

Preheat oven to 350 degrees.

Mix all ingredients; beat well. Pour into ungreased casserole dish. Bake 45 minutes or until set in center. Serve hot or cold. Especially good with ham.

Diane Paul

Pineapple Au Gratin

2	20-ounce cans pineapple chunks, drained	½	cup sugar
		¼	cup flour
2	cups sharp cheddar cheese, shredded	1	cup Ritz crackers, crumbled
		1	stick margarine, melted

Preheat oven to 350 degrees.

Mix first four ingredients and place in 11x17-inch casserole dish. Spread cracker crumbs over top and pour melted margarine over the crumbs. Bake 20-30 minutes.

Serves 8 to 12.

Bobbye Hildebrand

Brandied Peaches

2	16-ounce cans peach halves	⅓	cup brandy
4-6	whole cloves		

Drain peaches, reserving liquid. Boil syrup with cloves until reduced to 2/3 cup. Add peaches to syrup, heat thoroughly. Drain hot peaches, reserving syrup. Place peaches in a jar or crock. Pour brandy over peaches. Add syrup. Cover and store in refrigerator twenty-four hours before serving. Keeps well. Good with turkey or ham.

Carol Bocard

Barbie's Baked Pineapple

1	tablespoon flour	1	20-ounce can crushed
½	cup sugar		pineapple, undrained
Dash of salt		¼	pound butter or margarine
4	eggs	5	slices of bread, broken in
			pieces

Preheat oven to 350 degrees.

Mix flour, sugar and salt together. Add slightly beaten eggs. Pour in pineapple and syrup and mix well. Pour in casserole dish. Melt butter in skillet; add bread and stir, coating all bread with butter. Spoon buttered bread over pineapple mixture. Bake until brown, about 45 minutes.

Serves 6 to 8.

Wonderful with baked ham.

Gail Andrus

Hot Curried Fruit

½	cup butter	1	15-ounce can apricots
1	cup brown sugar	1	6-ounce jar maraschino
2	tablespoons curry powder		cherries
1	15-ounce can pears	1	15-ounce can peaches
1	20-ounce can pineapple		

Preheat oven to 325 degrees.

Drain fruit well. Melt butter in saucepan. Dissolve sugar in butter. Add curry. Cut fruit in bite size pieces. Place fruit in large casserole dish. Pour sauce over. Bake 1 hour, uncovered. May be made ahead to blend flavors.

Serves 8 to 10.

Betty Childs

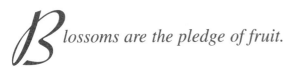

lossoms are the pledge of fruit.

Japanese Proverb

Cranberry Thing

1	cup water	2	cups fresh cranberries
1	cup sugar		

2	tablespoons apple cider vinegar	1	teaspoon cayenne pepper, or to taste
½	cup slivered almonds	½	cup seedless raisins
¼	teaspoon ginger	1	tablespoon brown sugar
		½	teaspoon garlic

Combine water, sugar and cranberries in saucepan and bring to a boil. Add remaining ingredients and continue to boil slowly, stirring until fairly thick. Remove from heat and cool 10 minutes.

A nice accompaniment to turkey or chicken.

Julie Barrett

Apricot Barley Casserole

⅓	cup slivered almonds	½	cup green onions, chopped
2	tablespoons margarine or butter	1	14-ounce can chicken broth
		⅓	cup dried, diced apricots
1	cup instant barley	¼	cup golden raisins

Sauté almonds in margarine or butter until golden. Remove from heat. Add barley, onions and broth. Cover and simmer 10-12 minutes. Stir in apricots and raisins. Let stand 5 minutes before serving.

Serves 4.

Nice substitute for rice. Good with chicken or pork.

Lois Flanagan

Hot Mustard Sauce

⅔	cup dry mustard	3	eggs
⅔	cup white vinegar	1	cup sugar

Combine all ingredients and mix in blender. Cook over low heat until thick, stirring constantly, about 10-15 minutes. Refrigerate when cool. Keeps about one month.

Barbara Hampton

Sausage Bread Stuffing

1	medium onion, chopped	4	cups ¼-inch cubes lightly
12	ounces breakfast pork		toasted sourdough bread or
	sausage		seasoned bread stuffing
2	teaspoons dried thyme		cubes
½	teaspoon salt	¾	cup chicken broth
	Freshly ground pepper to taste	4	teaspoons chopped fresh
½	cup toasted walnut or pecan		Italian parsley
	halves	1½	cups grated zucchini

Preheat oven to 350 degrees.

Cook onion and sausage until no pink remains, about 8 minutes. Drain off fat. Transfer into a bowl. Stir in thyme, salt, pepper, nuts, bread cubes, broth parsley and zucchini until well-mixed. Bake for 45 minutes or until hot.

This stuffing is good as a side dish and also for filling bell peppers or acorn squash.

Linda Torpie

Spicy Cranberry Chutney

1	12-ounce bag cranberries,	1	tablespoon ground cinnamon
	wash and pick over	1½	teaspoons ground ginger
1	cup seedless raisins	¼	teaspoon ground cloves
1⅔	cups sugar	1	cup water

Combine all ingredients and cook, uncovered, until thickened, about 15 minutes.

1	medium apple, pared,	½	cup thinly sliced celery
	cored and chopped		
1	medium onion, chopped		
	(½ cup)		

Stir apple, onion and celery into cranberry mixture. Simmer 15 minutes longer until mixture is thick. Cool and refrigerate. Before serving warm to room temperature.

Betty Baer
Char Hylbert

Mother's Sauerkraut Relish

2	pounds sauerkraut	1	cup sugar
1	cup chopped onion	½	cup vegetable oil
1	cup chopped green bell	½	cup cider vinegar
	pepper	1	grated carrot
1	cup chopped celery		

Wash and drain sauerkraut to remove the salt. Mix all ingredients thoroughly. Keep in refrigerator for 24 hours before using. Keep stored in refrigerator after serving.

Yield: 2 quarts

Martha Ernske
Harriet Lefkoff

Candied Dills

1	quart dill pickles	2	tablespoons mixed pickling
½	cup tarragon vinegar		spices
2¾	cups sugar		

Drain pickles; cut in ¼-inch pieces. Combine pickles, vinegar and sugar. Tie spices in small piece of cheesecloth and add to pickles. Let mixture stand at room temperature, stirring occasionally until sugar dissolves, about 4 hours. Return half of pickles to the jar; add spice bag; add remaining pickles, then fill jar with syrup. Cover and refrigerate at least 4 days.

Remove spice bag in one week, if desired.

Anne Armel

Piquante Sauce

½	cup mayonnaise	1	tablespoon cider vinegar
1-2	tablespoons Dijon mustard	1	tablespoon Worcestershire
1-2	tablespoons horseradish		sauce

Combine all ingredients, adjusting the amount of any "to taste."

Good served over asparagus or other vegetables.

Margaret McCulloch

Desserts

- cakes & frostings
- pies
- cookies
- other delights

WORD

Chocolate Raspberry Mousse Cheesecake

CRUST

2½ cups chocolate wafer crumbs (approximately 1½ boxes)
⅓ cup butter, melted
½ cup sugar

Mix together and press on bottom and 1½-inches up sides of 9-inch springform pan. Refrigerate.

FILLING

1 8-ounce package semisweet chocolate squares, cut into ½-inch cubes
¼ cup hot, strong coffee
3 8-ounce packages cream cheese, cut into 1-inch cubes

2 tablespoons whipping cream
1 8-ounce carton sour cream
1 cup sugar
2 eggs
1 teaspoon vanilla
¼ cup Chambord

Preheat oven to 350 degrees.

Position knife blade in food processor bowl; add chocolate cubes and process until finely ground. With processor running, pour hot coffee through food chute. Process until chocolate is melted and smooth. Add cream cheese and next 6 ingredients, scraping down sides of bowl. Pour mixture into prepared crust and bake for 55 minutes. (Center will still be soft.) Let cool to room temperature on wire rack. Cover and chill at least 8 hours or overnight. Remove from pan. Serve each piece on a pool of raspberry sauce and garnish with fresh raspberries and a dollop of whipped cream.

Serves 10 to 12.

RASPBERRY SAUCE

Defrost 2 10-ounce packages frozen raspberries with juice and purée in blender; strain.

Jane Heiser

ining is and always was a great artistic opportunity.

Frank Lloyd Wright

Company Lemon Cheesecake

2	cups cinnamon graham cracker crumbs	3	eggs
½	cup finely chopped walnuts	2	teaspoons grated lemon peel
6	tablespoons butter or margarine, melted	¼	cup lemon juice
1	cup sugar, divided	1	tablespoon vanilla, divided
24	ounces cream cheese, softened	2	cups dairy sour cream
			Lemon Glaze

Preheat oven to 350 degrees. Lightly butter a 9-inch springform pan.

In a medium bowl, stir together cracker crumbs, walnuts, melted butter and 2 tablespoons of the sugar. Press mixture evenly onto bottom and sides of prepared pan. Bake for 5 minutes. Cool.

In a large bowl, beat together cream cheese and ¾ cup of the sugar with an electric mixer. Add eggs one at a time, beating well after each addition. Mix in lemon peel, lemon juice, and 1 teaspoon of the vanilla until well blended. Pour into cooled crust. Bake for 35 minutes.

Meanwhile, for topping, in a small bowl stir together sour cream, remaining 2 tablespoons sugar, and remaining 2 teaspoons vanilla. Remove cheesecake from oven. Gently spread topping over cheesecake. Bake 12 minutes more. Cool on rack for 30 minutes. Spread Lemon Glaze on cheesecake. Chill several hours before removing sides of pan. If desired, garnish with flower petals, orange peel, mint leaves, etc.

Neufchatel cheese can be used in place of cream cheese for lower fat content; cake will be less firm.

LEMON GLAZE

½	cup sugar	⅓	cup lemon juice
4	teaspoons cornstarch	1	slightly beaten egg yolk
¼	teaspoon salt	1	tablespoon butter or margarine
¾	cup water		
1	teaspoon grated lemon peel (set aside)		

In heavy 1 quart saucepan, combine sugar, cornstarch and salt. In a small bowl, combine water, lemon juice and egg yolk. Add to sugar mixture. Cook over low heat, stirring constantly, until mixture is thickened and bubbly. Stir in butter or margarine and grated lemon peel. Cool slightly, but do not allow glaze to become set. Makes about 1⅓ cups.

Mike Crawley

251

Joan Keever's Cheesecake

1½ cups graham cracker crumbs (⅓ of box)
¼ cup sugar

⅓ cup unsalted butter, cut in pieces

Preheat oven to 350 degrees.
Finely crush graham crackers in food processor. Process sugar with crackers. Add butter and process until blended. Press crumb mixture firmly into a 9-inch springform pan. Bake for 7 to 10 minutes.

FILLING

30 ounces cream cheese, cut in small pieces
1 egg
½ cup whipping cream

7 ounces sugar
1 ounce cornstarch
1 teaspoon vanilla

Preheat oven to 350 degrees.
Blend cheese in small quantities in food processor. As softened cheese becomes heavier, slowing processor action, add egg and cream. Process in short bursts until smooth. Mix sugar and cornstarch together and add, processing until well mixed. Add vanilla and process until blended. Pour into baked crust in springform pan. Bake 50 to 60 minutes. It will be a golden brown when done. Cool and refrigerate. Can be frozen.

Joan Keever

Real Applesauce Cake

¼ teaspoon salt
2 cups brown sugar
½ cup vegetable shortening
2 eggs
2 cups applesauce
1 teaspoon nutmeg
1 teaspoon cinnamon

1 teaspoon allspice
2½-3 cups all-purpose flour
2 teaspoons baking powder
½ teaspoon baking soda
1 cup raisins
1 cup nuts

Preheat oven to 325 degrees.
Cream salt, sugar and shortening; then add eggs and beat. Add applesauce and spices; beat. Sift together flour, baking powder and soda; add to batter and mix. Add raisins and nuts; mix well. Bake in 9x13-inch greased and floured pan for 55-60 minutes.

252

Anita Madigan

Jane's Chocolate Cheesecake

CRUST

1¼ cups graham cracker crumbs   ¼   cup sugar
¼   cup butter

Preheat oven to 375 degrees.
Blend ingredients and press into a 10-inch springform pan. Bake for 8 minutes.

FILLING

1   package regular chocolate   3   8-ounce packages cream
    pudding   cheese
¾   cup sugar   3   eggs, separated
1   cup milk   2   teaspoons vanilla
1   1-ounce square unsweetened   ¼   teaspoon salt
    chocolate

Preheat oven to 425 degrees.
Combine pudding, sugar, milk and chocolate in a saucepan and cook until chocolate melts and mixture comes to a full boil. Remove from heat, cover with wax paper.
Beat softened cream cheese and egg yolks. Add vanilla, salt and cooked pudding. Blend. Beat egg whites until stiff and fold into cream cheese mixture. Pour into crust and bake for 30 minutes.

TOPPING

1 cup sour cream   ¼   cup confectioners' sugar

Combine sour cream and sugar and put on hot cake. Return to oven for 1 minute.

Nancy Neuman

Unquiet meals make ill digestions.

Shakespeare

253

Cheesecake Brûlée

16	ounces cream cheese, softened	¼	cup heavy cream
½	cup sugar (plus 4 tablespoons for caramelizing top)	1	teaspoon vanilla
		1	cup graham cracker crumbs
2	tablespoons sour cream	4	tablespoons unsalted butter, melted and cooled
2	eggs	2	tablespoons brown sugar

Preheat oven to 325 degrees. Have a pot of boiling water ready.

In the bowl of an electric mixer, combine cream cheese, ½ cup of sugar and sour cream; beat on medium speed until smooth. Add eggs, heavy cream and vanilla; beat until smooth.

In a separate bowl, combine graham cracker crumbs, butter and brown sugar; stir until blended and divide mixture among four mini springform pans. Pour cream cheese mixture into pans. Line outside of pans with heavy foil, shiny side out; arrange them in a baking pan. Add boiling water to fill baking pan half way up sides of springform pans.

Bake until filling is set, 35-40 minutes. Refrigerate at least 3 hours. Just before serving, unmold cheesecakes and sprinkle 1 tablespoon sugar over each surface. With a kitchen torch, move flame continuously in small circles around surface until sugar melts, bubbles and lightly browns.

Yield: 4 mini cheesecakes. Recipe doubled can be used in one large springform pan.

Norma Shaw

Apple Cake (No Fat)

2	cups sugar	3	cups flour
1½	cups applesauce	1¼	teaspoon baking soda
2	teaspoons vanilla	1	teaspoon salt
	Juice of ½ lemon	3	cups peeled and chopped apples
	Egg substitute to equal 3 large eggs		Chopped nuts, optional

Preheat oven to 325 degrees. Combine first 5 ingredients in bowl and beat well. Add flour, baking soda, salt and mix well. Stir in apples and nuts. Grease Bundt pan with cooking spray, pour in batter and bake 1½ hours. Freezes well.

Serves 12 to 15.

Nancy Sheets

Nutty Apple Spice Cake With Butterscotch Sauce

CAKE

2	cups sugar	¼	teaspoon ground nutmeg
½	cup vegetable oil	3	cups Granny Smith apples,
3	large eggs		about ¾ pound, diced
2	cups flour	½	cup walnut or pecans,
2	teaspoons cinnamon		chopped and roasted
1	teaspoon baking soda		Cooking spray
¼	teaspoon salt		

Preheat oven to 350 degrees.

Beat sugar, oil and eggs at medium speed of mixer until well-blended. Lightly spoon flour into dry measuring cup and level with a knife. Combine flour and next 4 ingredients in a small bowl. Add flour mixture to sugar mixture, beating until blended. Fold in apples and nuts. Pour batter into greased 13x9-inch baking pan. Bake for 55 minutes or until tester comes out clean. Cool. Serves 12.

BUTTERSCOTCH SAUCE

⅓	cup golden raisins	1	12.25-ounce container fat
¼	cup rum or apple juice		free butterscotch topping.

Combine raisins and rum in a microwave safe bowl. Let stand 5 minutes. Stir in butterscotch topping. Microwave on High 45 seconds or until hot. Serve in bowl with cake.

You do not need to peel apples. Cake will keep for several days in an airtight container but crunchy top will soften. Best if eaten day it is made.

Lois Flanagan

The right food always comes at the right time. Reliance on out-of-season foods makes the gastronomic year an endlessly boring repetition.

Roy Andries De Groot

Harriet's Chocolate Chip Apple Cake

2	large eggs	2	teaspoons vanilla
1	cup sugar	3	cups coarsely diced pared
¾	cup vegetable oil		apples
2	cups flour	⅔	cup chocolate morsels
1	teaspoon baking soda		

Preheat oven to 325 degrees. Beat eggs. Add sugar, oil and dry ingredients. Mix well. Stir in vanilla, apples and morsels. Pour batter into a greased 10-inch tube pan. Sprinkle with topping. Bake 45-55 minutes until cake tests done. Let sit 5 minutes on wire rack before removing from pan. Turn out on wire rack to cool completely.

TOPPING

1	tablespoon sugar	¼	cup chopped nuts
½	teaspoon cinnamon		

Combine all ingredients until well-blended.

Beth Roth

Guilt Free Sour Cream Pound Cake

3	cups sugar	4½	cups sifted cake flour
¾	cup margarine, softened	¼	teaspoon salt
1⅓	cups egg substitute	2	teaspoons vanilla
1½	cups lowfat sour cream		Vegetable cooking spray
1	teaspoon baking soda		

Preheat oven to 325 degrees. Cream sugar and margarine until combined. Add egg substitute, beating well. Combine sour cream and baking soda; stir well and set aside.

Combine flour and salt. Add to creamed mixture alternately with sour cream mixture, beginning and ending with flour mixture. Stir in vanilla. Spray a 10-inch tube pan with cooking spray. Bake for 1 hour and 35 minutes or until wooden pick comes out clean. Cool 10 minutes and remove from pan.

Serves 24.

Marie R. Cappuccio

Georgia Pecan Cream Cheese Pound Cake

1½ cups unsalted butter, cut in pieces
2 tablespoons all-purpose flour
8 ounces cream cheese, cut in pieces
3 cups sugar
6 eggs
1½ teaspoons vanilla
½ teaspoon almond extract
3 cups cake flour
1½ cups pecans, finely chopped

Preheat oven to 325 degrees. Using a little of the butter, grease a 10-inch tube pan. Dust with flour and shake out the excess.

Place remaining butter and cream cheese in an electric mixer and beat briefly to combine. Add sugar and beat at medium/low speed until light and fluffy, about 5 minutes. Beat in eggs, one at a time. Stir in vanilla and almond extract. Mix ¼ cup of cake flour with pecans and set aside. Add remaining flour ½ cup at a time to the egg mixture beating at the lowest speed to blend in. Fold pecans into batter by hand. Spoon batter into prepared pan, smooth top and rap the pan once or twice on countertop to even batter. Place in oven and bake 1 hour and 45 minutes. Top should be golden brown and beginning to shrink from sides of pan. A cake tester inserted in the middle should come out clean. Allow to cool on a rack for 30 minutes and then remove from pan to finish cooling.
Serves 18.

Elayne Blecker

Coconut Cream Cheese Pound Cake

1 cup margarine, softened
1 8-ounce package cream cheese
3 cups sugar
6 eggs
3 cups sifted cake flour
1 small can coconut
2 teaspoons vanilla extract

Preheat oven to 325 degrees. Combine margarine and cream cheese until well-blended. Gradually add sugar. Add eggs one at a time, beating well after each addition. Add flour to creamed mixture stirring until well-combined. Stir in coconut and vanilla. Pour batter into a well-greased 10-inch tube pan. Bake 1 hour and 45 minutes or until cake tests done. Cool in pan 10 minutes; remove from pan and cool completely.
Serves 12 to 14.

Hank Vaughn

Blueberry Pound Cake

2   cups granulated sugar
½   cup light butter
4   ounces lowfat cream cheese, softened
3   large eggs
1   large egg white
3   cups all-purpose flour, (reserve 2 tablespoons flour for blueberries)
2   cups fresh or frozen blueberries

1   teaspoon baking powder
½   teaspoon baking soda
½   teaspoon salt
1   8-ounce carton lowfat lemon yogurt
2   teaspoons vanilla
Cooking spray
½   cup confectioner's sugar
4   teaspoons lemon juice

Preheat oven to 350 degrees. Beat first 3 ingredients at medium speed of mixer until well blended (about 5 minutes). Add eggs and egg white, one at a time, beating well after each addition. Lightly spoon flour into dry measuring cup; level with a knife. Combine 2 tablespoons flour and blueberries in a small bowl, and toss well. Combine remaining flour, baking powder, baking soda, and salt. Add flour mixture to sugar mixture alternately with yogurt, beginning and ending with flour mixture. Fold in blueberry mixture and vanilla; pour cake batter into a 10-inch tube pan coated with cooking spray. Bake for 1 hour and 10 minutes or until a wooden pick inserted in center comes out clean. Cool cake in pan 10 minutes; remove from pan. Combine confectioners' sugar and lemon juice in a small bowl; drizzle over warm cake. Cut with a serrated knife.

Serves 16.

Donna Pfeifer

Flourless Chocolate Cake

16   ounces semisweet chocolate
1¼   cups clarified butter
1   cup sugar
1   cup heavy cream

1   tablespoon vanilla
½   teaspoon salt
8   eggs

Preheat oven to 350 degrees. In double boiler, melt chocolate with butter. In separate bowl mix remaining ingredients. Add chocolate and mix well. Pour into greased and floured 9-inch cake pan and bake for approximately 45 minutes or until sides are risen and center is sunken.

Serves 12.

Charles D'Ablaing
Chef, The Landings Club

French Pastry Cake

½	cup boiling water	1	stick unsalted butter
½	cup Dutch style cocoa	2	cups sugar
½	teaspoon baking powder	2	cups cake flour, sifted
1	cup sour cream	3	egg whites, stiffly beaten

Preheat oven to 300 degrees.

Make a paste of water and cocoa and cool. Mix baking powder with sour cream and set aside. Cream butter and sugar well. Add sour cream, blending well and then add cocoa paste. Add flour slowly and fold in egg whites. Pour into two greased and floured 8- or 9-inch cake pans and bake for 50 minutes.

FROSTING

6	tablespoons boiling water	3¾	cups sifted confectioners'
6	tablespoons Dutch style cocoa		sugar (10x)
6	tablespoons unsalted butter, melted		

Combine first three ingredients and add confectioners' sugar. Beat vigorously until smooth and thick. Frost cake.

Joan Keever

Chocolate-Chocolate Chip Cake

1	package devil's food cake mix	½	cup oil
		½	cup water
1	3-ounce package instant chocolate pudding mix	1	12-ounce package chocolate chips
4	eggs		

Preheat oven to 350 degrees. Grease Bundt pan. Blend all ingredients together, except for chocolate chips, and beat with mixer for 2 minutes. Fold in chocolate chips. Pour batter into Bundt pan. Bake 45-50 minutes. Cool and sprinkle with confectioners' sugar.

Hara Leavy

259

Wow-Zer Cake

1	cup chopped pecans	1	box German chocolate cake
1	cup coconut		mix
1	8-ounce package cream	1	stick margarine
	cheese	1	box confectioners' sugar

Preheat oven to 350 degrees.
Spread nuts on bottom of greased 9x13-inch pan. Spread coconut on top of nuts. Mix cake following package directions and pour over coconut. Bake cake for 45 minutes. Cool. Melt cream cheese and margarine in saucepan over medium heat blending in confectioners' sugar. Spoon over cake. Freezes well. Serves 12.

Bobbye Hildebrand

Fruit Cake With Zabaglione

1	pineapple, sliced	1	egg
1	kiwi, diced	1	egg yolk
1	banana, diced	¼	cup sweet Marsala wine
4	large strawberries, diced	⅔	cup sugar
	Juice of 1 lemon	1	cup heavy cream, whipped
½	cup maraschino cherry juice		(optional, only if you want to
½	cup cool water		make the zabaglione ahead)
1	8-inch round pound cake	¼	cup confectioners' sugar

Dice 2 slices of the pineapple and combine them with the kiwi, banana and strawberries in a bowl. Add the lemon juice. Set aside.

Combine the maraschino cherry juice with water; place the cake on a serving dish and brush the mixture over it.

Whisk the egg, egg yolk, Marsala and sugar in a bowl set over simmering water. Beat with a wire whisk until fluffy, light and tripled in volume; it will take about 5 minutes. This is the zabaglione. At this point, cool the zabaglione and fold in the whipped cream if you wish to hold the zabaglione cream for up to 4 hours in the refrigerator.

Sprinkle the cake with the confectioners' sugar, top it with the macerated fruit and garnish it with the reserved pineapple slices. Serve with zabaglione. Serves 8.

Dorothy Pero

Burnt Sugar Cake

½	cup shortening	¼	teaspoon salt
1½	cups sugar	2½	teaspoons baking powder
2	egg yolks	1	cup water or milk
1	teaspoon vanilla	3	tablespoons Burnt Sugar
2½	cups cake flour	2	egg whites, stiffly beaten

Preheat oven to 350 degrees.

Thoroughly cream shortening and sugar. Add egg yolks and vanilla and beat until fluffy. Add sifted dry ingredients alternately with water or milk, beating well after each addition. Add Burnt Sugar and fold in egg whites. Bake in 2 waxed paper lined 8-inch layer cake pans about 30 minutes. Put layers together with Caramel-Nut Frosting.

BURNT SUGAR

Melt ½ cup white sugar in heavy skillet over low heat until dark brown and smooth. Remove from heat; add ½ cup boiling water. Return to heat and stir rapidly until mixture resembles molasses.

CARAMEL NUT FROSTING

2	cups brown sugar		Pinch of salt
½	cup butter or margarine	1	teaspoon vanilla
½	cup light cream	1	cup walnuts, chopped

Combine ingredients in saucepan. Stir over low heat until dissolved. Heat to boiling and cook to softball stage (234 degrees). Remove from heat and beat until cool. Add vanilla. Spread between layers and on top and side of cake. Sprinkle with walnuts. (Use 1½ times frosting recipe for a layer cake.)

Judy Pelok

The ornament of the house is the friends who frequent it.

Ralph Waldo Emerson

Temptation Cake

1	package golden cake mix	1	3.9-ounce package instant
1	20-ounce can crushed		vanilla pudding
	pineapple with juice	2	cups milk
2	cups granulated sugar	1	8-ounce carton whipped
1	8-ounce package cream		topping
	cheese, softened	¼-½	cup finely chopped English
			walnuts

Bake cake mix as directed using milk instead of water and a greased 9x13-inch pan. While cake is baking, place pineapple and sugar in pan and boil for 2-5 minutes. As soon as cake comes from the oven, place on cooling rack. Immediately poke holes in cake with fork and pour hot pineapple/sugar mixture over hot cake. Let cool.

Mix cream cheese, vanilla pudding and milk together until thickened. Spread over cooled cake. "Frost" with whipped topping. Sprinkle nuts over top. Refrigerate overnight. Freezes well.

Serves 18 to 24.

Sliced bananas, maraschino cherries and/or coconut can also be used to top cake in place of, or in addition to, walnuts.

Winnie Hermann

Sour Cream Cherry Chocolate Chip Nut Cake

1	cup margarine	1	cup sour cream
2	cups sugar	1	10-ounce jar maraschino
4	eggs		cherries, drained and cut up
2	cups flour	1	cup chocolate chips
1	teaspoon baking powder	1	cup walnuts, chopped
1	teaspoon almond or vanilla		
	extract		

Preheat oven to 350 degrees. Grease baking pans with cooking spray.

Cream margarine and sugar. Add eggs and then flour, baking powder and extract. Fold in sour cream. Add small amount of flour to cherries, chocolate chips and nuts to hold them together and fold into sugar and egg mixture. Bake in greased Bundt pan for 55 minutes or in 3 7x3½-inch loaf pans for 30 to 40 minutes. Can also be baked in muffin tins for 20 minutes.

Nancy Gates

Marvelous Double-Rich Cake

1	box yellow butter flavor cake mix	½	cup (1 stick) butter
1	3¾-ounce package French vanilla instant pudding	4	eggs
		1	6-ounce package chocolate morsels
1	cup sour cream	2	ounces grated German chocolate
½	cup milk		
½	cup vegetable oil	1	cup chopped pecans

Preheat oven to 350 degrees. Place cake mix, pudding mix, sour cream, milk, oil, butter and eggs in large mixer bowl. Beat for 2 minutes. Stir in chocolate morsels, grated chocolate and nuts. Place in greased and floured 10-inch Bundt pan. Bake for 1 hour. Let cool and frost. Freezes well. Serves 10.

FROSTING

1	8-ounce package cream cheese, softened	1	teaspoon vanilla
		1	cup coarsely chopped nuts
1	1-pound box confectioners' sugar	1	3½-ounce can sweetened flaked coconut

Beat cream cheese, confectioners' sugar and vanilla until well-blended. Stir in nuts and coconut.

Anne Faxon

Italian Love Cake

1	box fudge marble cake mix	1	3¾-ounce box instant chocolate pudding
2	pounds ricotta cheese		
¾	cup sugar	1	cup milk
4	eggs	1	8-ounce carton whipped topping
1	teaspoon vanilla		

Preheat oven to 350 degrees.

Mix cake as directed on box. Pour into greased and floured 9x13-inch pan. In separate bowl, combine ricotta, sugar, eggs and vanilla; mix well. Spoon over top of unbaked cake batter. Bake for 1 hour. Cool. Mix pudding with milk; fold in whipped topping. Spread over cake; refrigerate.

Pat Dickinson

Gigi's Peppermint Cake & Chocolate Frosting

CAKE

3	cups all-purpose flour	2	cups sugar
2	teaspoons baking powder	3	extra large eggs
½	teaspoon salt	1	cup milk
1	cup butter, softened	1½	teaspoons vanilla

Preheat oven to 350 degrees.

Grease the bottom of a 10-inch tube pan. Sift together flour, baking powder and salt. Set aside. In large bowl, cream butter thoroughly. Gradually add sugar, mixing until light and fluffy. Blend in eggs one at a time, beating well after each addition. Measure milk and add vanilla to it. Add flour mix and milk alternately to butter mixture, beginning and ending with flour. Blend thoroughly after each addition. Use low speed with electric mixer. Pour two-thirds of the batter into the tube pan.

To the remaining batter add:

¾	cup chocolate syrup	1	teaspoon peppermint extract
¼	teaspoon baking soda		

Blend these ingredients together and pour over white batter. DO NOT MIX. Bake for 45 minutes. Place a sheet of aluminum foil on top of the pan. Bake another 20-25 minutes until cake tester comes out clean. Cool completely before removing from pan.

FROSTING

2¼	cups confectioners' sugar	1	egg white, unbeaten
¼	cup hot water	5	tablespoons butter, softened
4	envelopes of liquid unsweetened chocolate		

Mix sugar and water. Add chocolate and mix well. Beat in egg white. Add butter one tablespoon at a time, beating well after each addition.

Gail Vergoz

I awoke this morning with devout thanksgiving for my friends, the old and new.

Ralph Waldo Emerson

Whiskey Cake

1	package Pineapple Supreme cake mix	½	cup oil
1	3-ounce package instant coconut or vanilla pudding	1	cup milk
		½	cup chopped nuts
4	eggs	12	maraschino cherries, cut in half

Preheat oven to 375 degrees.
Grease and flour Bundt or tube pan. Mix all cake ingredients together except cherries. Put halved cherries, cut side up, in each groove of Bundt pan or evenly spaced in tube pan. Pour batter over and bake for 40-45 minutes. Let cake stand in pan 15 minutes then turn onto plate.

GLAZE

1	stick margarine	⅓	cup bourbon
½	cup sugar		

Over medium heat, heat margarine and sugar until blended and melted together. Remove pan from heat and add bourbon. Return to heat, bring to boil and simmer a few minutes. Pour ½ glaze over cake and let stand a few minutes then turn cake over and cover with remainder of glaze. Refrigerate before serving.

Martha Ernske

Snowball Cake

1½	envelopes unflavored gelatin		Zest of 1 orange
4	tablespoons cold water	1	pint whipping cream, whipped
1	cup hot water		
1	cup sugar	1	large angel food cake, cubed
1	lemon, juice and zest		Coconut
1	cup orange juice		

Dissolve gelatin in cold water. Mix hot water, sugar, lemon juice and lemon zest and orange juice and orange zest. Add dissolved gelatin and chill mixture until it is the thickness of egg white. Whip 1 cup of cream and add to gelatin mixture. Fold in cake. Pour into mixing bowl that will give shape of a snowball. Chill overnight. Invert onto serving dish and cover with remaining whipped cream. Sprinkle with coconut.

Mary Giacchini

Rum Cake

1	butter cake mix, white or yellow	½	cup oil
1	5-ounce package vanilla pudding, not instant	½	cup rum
		½	cup water
4	eggs	½	cup nuts, chopped

Preheat oven to 325 degrees.

Add all ingredients, except nuts, to cake mix and beat well. Grease tube pan. Sprinkle nuts in bottom of pan. Pour in batter. Bake for 1 hour. Toward the end of the hour, mix and heat glaze ingredients. For the last five minutes of baking time, pour glaze over cake.

GLAZE

1	stick margarine	¼	cup rum
1	cup sugar	¼	cup water

Very popular at Landlovers bake sale.

Katie Wood

Karen's Banana Cake

2	teaspoons lemon juice	1	teaspoon salt
⅔	cup milk	⅔	cup vegetable shortening
2⅓	cups flour, sifted	⅔	cup ripe bananas, mashed
1⅔	cups sugar	2	eggs
1¼	teaspoons baking powder	⅔	cup chopped walnuts
1	teaspoon baking soda		

Preheat oven to 350 degrees.

Place lemon juice in measuring cup and add enough milk to make ⅔ cup total. Sift the flour, sugar, baking powder, baking soda and salt in a large bowl. Add the shortening, bananas and milk. Mix. Beat 2 minutes. Add eggs. Beat 2 minutes. Stir in the walnuts. Bake in 2 greased and floured 9-inch round pans for 35 minutes. Cool 10 minutes in pans. Remove to a rack and cool completely. Frost with your favorite frosting or dust with confectioners' sugar and serve with ice cream.

Serves 10.

Karen Lantz

Cake Delight

1	butter recipe cake mix	½	cup vegetable oil
1	6-ounce can mandarin oranges, undrained		

Preheat oven to 350 degrees. Mix cake ingredients according to package directions using ½ cup of vegetable oil. Fold in mandarin oranges. Pour batter into a greased and floured 11x13-inch pan or 3 round cake pans. Bake for approximately 30 minutes. When cake is cool, frost and refrigerate until serving.

Serves 12 to 15.

ICING

1	5-ounce box instant vanilla pudding	1	9-ounce carton whipped topping
1	20-ounce can crushed pineapple, undrained		

Mix pudding and pineapple together. Fold in whipped topping. Refrigerate if not icing cake immediately.

Pat Sterenberg

Chocolate Ice Box Cake

3	packages ladyfingers	4	egg yolks
6	ounces chocolate morsels	1	teaspoon vanilla
2	tablespoons water	4	egg whites, stiffly beaten
1	stick (½ cup) butter		Whipped topping
1	cup confectioners' sugar		

Line a loaf pan with plastic wrap and then line bottom and sides with ladyfingers. Melt chocolate morsels in water and set aside to cool. Cream butter with confectioners' sugar. Beat in egg yolks and vanilla. Add cooled chocolate and fold in egg whites. Pour ⅓ of chocolate mixture over ladyfingers. Put down another layer of ladyfingers and top with chocolate mixture twice more. Top with whipped topping and refrigerate 8 hours or overnight. Can be frozen.

The saran wrap lining the loaf pan will make unmolding the dessert easier.

Marjorie Kahan

267

Mother Deek's Cherry Cake

⅓ cup shortening
1½ cups sugar
2 eggs
2¼ cups flour, sifted
1½ teaspoons baking powder
½ teaspoon baking soda

½ teaspoon salt
1 cup milk
2¼ cups sour pitted cherries, well-drained but save juice
½ cups pecans, chopped

Preheat oven to 350 degrees.
Cream shortening, add sugar gradually and cream until fluffy. Blend in well-beaten eggs. Sift flour, baking powder, salt and soda together and stir into creamed mixture alternately with milk. Blend in well-drained cherries and nuts. Pour into greased and floured 8x12 pan. Bake about 50 minutes. Cut in 3-inch squares and serve warm with Hot Cherry Sauce
Serves 12.

HOT CHERRY SAUCE

½ cup sugar
Dash salt
2 tablespoons cornstarch

¾ cup cherry juice
1 cup water
¼ teaspoon almond flavoring

Mix sugar, salt and cornstarch together in saucepan. Blend in cherry juice and water. Boil until mixture thickens and starchy taste disappears (about 10 minutes), stirring constantly until mixture boils, but only occasionally after that. Remove from heat and blend in almond flavoring.
Serves 6.

Bev Brucher

ust because you have four chairs, six plates, and three cups is no reason why you can't invite twelve people to dinner.

Alice May Brock
American cook & restaurateur

Apricot Nectar Cake

1	box lemon cake mix	⅔	cup vegetable oil
½	cup sugar	4	eggs
1	cup apricot nectar		

Preheat oven to 325 degrees.
Combine cake mix, sugar, nectar and oil in large bowl. Beat for 2 minutes. Add 1 egg at a time, beating after each addition. Pour batter into greased and floured tube pan. Bake for 1 hour or until done. Cool right side up for 15 minutes, then remove cake from pan. Pour Glaze over cake while it is still warm.

GLAZE

1 cup confectioners' sugar   Juice of 1 lemon

Mix together until well-blended.

Ruth Thorne

7-Up Cake

1	box yellow cake mix	¾	cup vegetable oil
4	eggs	1	10-ounce bottle 7-Up
1	3-ounce box vanilla instant pudding		

Preheat oven to 350 degrees. Beat all ingredients together except 7-Up. Add it last and beat well. Bake in 13x9-inch pan for 40-50 minutes.
Serves 16 to 20.

ICING

2	beaten eggs	1	cup crushed pineapple, undrained
1	tablespoon flour	1	can coconut
1½	cups sugar		
1	stick butter		

Combine first 5 ingredients in saucepan. Cook over medium-low heat until thick. Add coconut and pour over hot cake.

Barbara Hampton

Jackie's Special Lemon Cake

3	tablespoons fine dry bread crumbs	2	cups sugar
		4	large eggs
3	cups all-purpose flour	1	cup milk
2	teaspoons baking powder	1	tablespoon finely grated
½	teaspoon salt		lemon peel
2	sticks (1 cup) unsalted butter or margarine, softened		Glaze
			Garnish

Preheat oven to 350 degrees. Place one oven rack one-third up from bottom of oven. Grease a 12-cup Bundt or tube pan. Coat with bread crumbs, shaking out excess.

Mix flour, baking powder and salt in a medium bowl. In a large bowl, with mixer on medium speed, beat butter and sugar until creamy. Add eggs, one at a time, beating after each addition and scraping down the side of the bowl as necessary. Mixture may look curdled. On low speed, add flour mixture in 3 additions, alternating with the milk in 2 additions, beating only until blended after each addition. Stir in lemon peel. Scrape batter into prepared pan. Level batter by rotating pan briskly from left to right and right to left. Bake 1 hour and 5 to 10 minutes, until toothpick inserted in center comes out clean. Cool cake in pan 5 minutes, then cover with a rack and invert. Remove pan leaving cake upside down on rack. Place over a large piece of foil or waxed paper and prepare glaze. Let cake cool completely after glazing before transferring to serving plate. Garnish with candied lemon slices. Freezes well.

Serves 12.

LEMON GLAZE

⅓	cup fresh lemon juice	⅔	cup sugar

Mix lemon juice and sugar. Brush over warm cake until all is used.

CANDIED LEMON SLICES

2	thin-skinned lemons	1	cup water
1	cup sugar		

Cut lemons in thin rounds, removing seeds. Mix sugar and water together and bring to a boil in a wide skillet. Add slices, reduce heat and simmer 25 minutes or until slices are translucent. Let cool in syrup. When ready to garnish cake, remove slices from syrup and arrange on cake.

Jackie Buggy

Pat's Peach Cobbler

1	cup flour	4	tablespoons butter
1	cup sugar	6	fresh peaches, sliced
¾	cup milk	1	cup blueberries
1½	teaspoons baking powder		

Preheat oven to 350 degrees.

Mix flour, sugar, milk and baking powder. Put butter in 9x13-inch baking dish and melt in oven. Pour batter over melted butter. Place peaches and blueberries on the batter. Mix topping ingredients and sprinkle over the fruit. Bake 1 hour. Best served warm with ice cream or whipped cream. Serves 10.

TOPPING

¾	cup dark brown sugar	1	teaspoon cinnamon
1	teaspoon nutmeg		

Pat Palmer

Peach Cobbler

2	cups fresh peaches, peeled and sliced	2	teaspoons baking powder
			Pinch of salt
2	cups sugar, divided	¾	cup milk
½	cup butter		Whipping cream or ice cream,
¾	cup all-purpose flour		optional

Preheat oven to 350 degrees.

Mix peaches with 1 cup sugar. Melt butter in 2-quart casserole dish in oven. In medium bowl mix remaining 1 cup sugar, flour, baking powder, salt and milk. Pour over melted butter. Do Not Stir. Place sugared peaches on top of batter. Do Not Stir. Bake 1 hour. Batter will rise to top and will be brown and crisp when cobbler is done. Serve warm with whipped cream or ice cream.

Rene Lehrberger

Fudge Pie

⅓ cup butter
3 ounces unsweetened
chocolate
2 cups sugar

4 eggs beaten light and thick
with rotary beater or whisk
¼ teaspoon salt
1 teaspoon vanilla
⅔ cup chopped walnuts

Preheat oven to 300 degrees.
Melt butter and chocolate together in microwave or over low heat on stove. Stir in sugar. Blend in beaten eggs; add salt, vanilla and nuts. Pour into well-greased 9-inch pie plate. Bake 45 minutes, no longer. Serve with ice cream. Serves 6 to 8.

Charlene Soderstrom

Black Bottom Pie

2 cups milk
4 eggs, separated
1 cup sugar, divided
2 tablespoons flour
1 envelope unflavored gelatin
4 tablespoons water

1½ ounces unsweetened
chocolate
1 graham cracker pie crust
½ pint whipping cream
Chocolate for garnish

Scald milk. Add ½ cup sugar and flour to egg yolks. Pour into milk. Cook over medium heat until custard is thick enough to coat a spoon. Melt chocolate in saucepan. Add ½ of the custard to the chocolate. Pour into graham cracker crust. Dissolve gelatin in 4 tablespoons of water. Add to plain custard and cool. Beat the 4 egg whites until frothy and then add ½ cup sugar gradually until stiff peaks form. When custard mixture starts to congeal, fold in egg whites. Pour over chocolate layer. Top with whipped cream and grate chocolate over top. Serves 8.

Frances Blankenship

We should look for someone to eat and drink with before looking for something to eat and drink, for dining alone is leading the life of a lion or wolf.

Epicurus

Fresh Peach Cobbler

5	cups fresh peaches, peeled, pitted, sliced	1¼	cups sugar
		1	teaspoon cinnamon
3	tablespoons flour	4-6	tablespoons butter

Slice peaches into a heavy, greased baking dish measuring approximately 9-inches across by 3-inches deep. Mix together flour, sugar, cinnamon and sprinkle over peaches. Dot with butter.

CRUST

1	cup flour	2	tablespoons sugar
½	teaspoon salt	⅓	cup shortening
2	teaspoons baking powder	⅓	cup milk

Preheat oven to 425 degrees.

Sift together dry ingredients. Cut in shortening until mixture resembles coarse cornmeal. Pour milk in all at once and stir with a fork. Roll dough out on a floured board until it is the size of the baking dish and ¼- to ½-inch thick. Place crust on top of peaches. Sprinkle with sugar if desired. Bake 30 minutes.

Serves 6 to 8.

Paige Word

Blueberry Cobbler

1½	cups flour	½	cup butter
⅓	cup sugar	½	cup whipping cream
1	tablespoon baking powder	3	cups blueberries
½	teaspoon salt	1	tablespoon grated lemon zest

Preheat oven to 400 degrees.

Combine first 4 dry ingredients in medium bowl. Cut in butter until mixture resembles coarse crumbs. Add cream; stir gently with fork. Set aside. Stir lemon zest into blueberries; pour into ovenproof deep dish. Crumble or dollop batter over fruit. Bake 25-30 minutes until light brown. May be served with vanilla ice cream or whipped cream.

Serves 6.

June Hutchinson

Chocolate Mint Cookie Pie

14	Girl Scout chocolate mint cookies	½	teaspoon vanilla
3	egg whites	½	cup chopped nuts
	Dash of salt	1	cup whipping cream
¾	cup sugar		Curls of shaved, unsweetened chocolate

Preheat oven to 325 degrees.
Chill cookies in refrigerator several hours and then crumble in food processor.
Beat egg whites and salt until soft peaks form. Very gradually beat in sugar until stiff peaks form. Add vanilla. Fold in crumbled cookies and chopped nuts. Spread evenly in buttered 9-inch pie plate. Bake for 35 minutes. Cool thoroughly. Cover with cream which has been whipped and sweetened. Chill 3 to 4 hours. Garnish with chocolate curls.

Dottie Strickler

Banana Coconut Cream Pie

	Prebaked 9-inch pie shell	1	teaspoon vanilla
¾	cup sugar	1	cup flaked coconut
¼	cup cornstarch	2-3	firm bananas
¼	teaspoon salt		Lemon juice to coat bananas
2	cups milk (whole or 2%)	8	ounces whipping cream
3	egg yolks, beaten	¼	cup confectioners' sugar
2	tablespoons butter		

Mix sugar, cornstarch and salt in heavy saucepan. Slowly whisk in milk, blending well. Cook over medium heat, stirring constantly, until mixture bubbles; cook 1 minute or until mixture thickens. Slowly add ¼ cup of hot liquid to beaten yolks and then return yolk/milk mixture to remaining liquid in saucepan. Return to heat and bring to a slow boil (bubbly) and cook 3 minutes. Remove from heat and stir in butter, vanilla and coconut. Pour into the pie shell and cool completely. Chill 2-3 hours before serving. Slice bananas and toss gently with lemon juice to coat. Arrange on top of pie. Beat cream; add confectioners' sugar. Decorate pie with whipped cream or serve slices with dollops of cream.
Serves 6 generously or 8 smaller pieces.

Sally Robyn

274

Sixty Second Yogurt Pie

2	8-ounce containers of yogurt, any flavor	1	pie crust, baked pastry, graham cracker or chocolate crumb
1	8-ounce container of frozen whipped topping		

Fold yogurt into thawed, whipped topping. Pour into pie shell. Freeze until set. Remove from freezer 20 to 30 minutes before serving. Serves 6 to 8.

Lois Flanagan

Grandmother's Cream Pear Pie

⅔	cup sugar	1	cup heavy cream
4-5	tablespoons flour	4-5	ripe pears
	Pinch of salt	1	9-inch pie crust, uncooked

Mix the sugar, flour and salt together. Add the cream and mix well. Pour this mixture over the pears which have been peeled, sliced and placed in the pie crust. Preheat oven to 425 degrees and bake 10 minutes then reduce oven temperature to 375 degrees and continue baking until the pears are "forkable" and the pie is nicely browned and bubbling. Prepare and bake the day the pie is to be served. Refrigerate leftovers.

Aletha Dunlavy
Rhea Myers

Pecan Pie

3	whole eggs, beaten	¼	teaspoon cinnamon
1	cup dark corn syrup	1	cup pecans
1	cup sugar	1	9-inch pie crust, unbaked
1	teaspoon vanilla extract		

Preheat oven to 325 degrees.
Combine all ingredients and pour into unbaked pie shell. Bake for 1 hour.
Serves 6.

Charles D'Ablaing
Chef, The Landings Club

Light Peaches & Cream Pie

3	cups fresh peaches, chopped	½	cup nonfat sour cream
1	9-inch deep-dish pastry	⅓	cup sugar
	shell, unbaked	⅓	cup all-purpose flour
¾	cup sugar	2	tablespoons low calorie
⅓	cup all-purpose flour		margarine
⅛	teaspoon salt	1	fresh peach, sliced for
1	egg, beaten		garnishing
2	egg whites, beaten		

Preheat oven to 350 degrees.

Place the 3 cups peaches in the pie shell. Combine the next three ingredients. Add the whole egg and egg whites and the sour cream. Stir until well-blended. Spoon over peaches. Combine the remaining sugar and flour and using a pastry blender, cut in the margarine until the mixture resembles coarse meal. Sprinkle evenly over the pie. Bake for 1 hour or until golden brown. Use sliced peach for garnish.

Lynda Ibach

Derby Pie

1	cup sugar	1	cup semisweet chocolate
½	cup flour		pieces
1	stick butter or margarine	1	jigger (1 to 1½-ounce)
2	eggs, slightly beaten		bourbon
1	teaspoon vanilla	1	9-inch pie crust, unbaked
1	cup walnuts, chopped		

Preheat oven to 325 degrees.

Sift together sugar and flour. Blend in butter or margarine until creamy. Add eggs and mix until smooth. Add vanilla, nuts, chocolate pieces and bourbon. Pour into pie shell and bake for 1 hour.

Serves 8.

Suzie Busch

 good laugh is sunshine in the house.

William Makepeace Thackeray

Incredible Cheesy Pecan Pie

1	9-inch pie crust, unbaked	1	teaspoon vanilla
1	8-ounce package cream	1	cup coarsely chopped pecans
	cheese	1	cup corn syrup
¼	cup granulated sugar	¼	cup packed brown sugar
4	eggs, divided		

Beat cream cheese, sugar, 1 egg and vanilla until smooth. Spread evenly in unbaked pie shell. Sprinkle pecans over cheese layer. Beat well the remaining 3 eggs, corn syrup and brown sugar. Pour evenly over pecans. Bake at 425 degrees for 10 minutes and then reduce heat to 375 degrees and bake 25-30 minutes longer or until set and golden. Cool before serving.

Marjorie Mouat

Beautiful Berry Blast

1	can blackberry pie filling	1	can whole cranberry sauce
1	can cherry pie filling	2	unbaked pie crusts

Preheat oven to 400 degrees.

In large mixing bowl, empty pie fillings and cranberry sauce and mix well. Pour into pie crust. Roll out additional pie crust and cut into strips of about 1-inch. Lay over pie filling to form lattice work. Bake 30 minutes or until crust is browned. Serves 6.

Roberta Fields

Strawberry Meringue Pie

3	egg whites	1	quart fresh strawberries,
½	teaspoon baking powder		sliced and sweetened
1	cup sugar	¾	cup heavy cream, whipped,
15	saltine crackers, rolled fine		sweetened
½	cup chopped pecans		

Beat egg whites with baking powder until stiff. Gradually beat in sugar. Fold in saltines. Add in pecans. Spread in well-buttered 9-inch pie plate. Bake 30 minutes. (Meringue will come out white and fairly high but will drop some when cooling.) After meringue has cooled, fill with strawberries. Top with whipped cream. Save a few strawberries for garnishing top of pie just before serving.

Jean M. Grace

277

Miracle Raspberry Pie

Pastry for one crust pie:

1½ cups flour	½ cup vegetable shortening
½ teaspoon salt	3-6 tablespoons ice water

Preheat oven to 450 degrees.

Blend above ingredients together and line an 8-inch pie pan. Prick pastry with a fork and bake for 12 minutes or until golden brown.

Mix together:

1 can condensed milk	5 tablespoons lemon juice

1 12-ounce package frozen raspberries, thawed and drained

Fold raspberries into milk and lemon juice and put into baked pie shell. Set in refrigerator. When cool, top with whipped cream sweetened with confectioners' sugar and vanilla.

Sandy Trice

Old Calendar Key Lime Pie

1 9-inch prepared pie crust, prebaked	1 14-ounce can sweetened condensed milk
4 egg yolks	½ cup lime juice

Preheat oven to 350 degrees.

Combine the egg yolks and milk and beat well. Add the lime juice stirring only a few times or the mixture will begin to break down. Pour filling into pie crust and cover with meringue. Bake for 12 to 15 minutes.

MERINGUE

3 egg whites	¼ teaspoon cream of tartar
½ teaspoon vanilla	6 tablespoons sugar

Combine egg whites, vanilla and cream of tartar. Beat until peaks form; gradually add sugar and continue beating until whites are very stiff.

Carol McClelland

278

Sweet Potato Pie With Macadamia Praline

¾   cup sugar
1   teaspoon cinnamon
½   teaspoon ground ginger
½   teaspoon ground nutmeg
¼   teaspoon salt
1   teaspoon vanilla

1   21-ounce can sweet potatoes, in syrup, drained and mashed
1   12-ounce can evaporated milk
2   eggs, beaten
1   10-inch pie crust, unbaked

3   tablespoons light brown sugar
3   tablespoons light corn syrup
1   tablespoon butter or margarine

1   3-ounce package macadamia nuts, coarsely chopped
1   cup whipped cream or frozen whipped topping
½   teaspoon vanilla

Place foil or a cookie sheet on lowest rack in oven to prevent spillage. Heat oven to 425 degrees. In a large bowl, combine all filling ingredients and blend well. Pour into pie crust. Bake for 15 minutes. Reduce oven temperature to 350 degrees and bake 25 more minutes.

During last 10 minutes of baking, combine brown sugar, corn syrup and butter or margarine. Bring to a boil over low heat, simmer 2 minutes and remove from heat. Add vanilla. Sprinkle nuts over pie and drizzle with topping mixture. Bake an additional 20-30 minutes or until a knife inserted in the center comes out clean. Cover edge of crust with strips of foil during the last 10 minutes of baking to prevent excessive browning. Cool. Garnish with whipped cream or topping and serve. Store in refrigerator.

Serves 8.

A 23- to 25-ounce can of sweet potatoes may also be used in this recipe. ¾ cup chopped pecans can be used in place of macadamia nuts.

Jan Washenko

he best of all physicians is apple pie and cheese.

Eugene Field

French Peach Pie

5-6	fresh peaches	3	tablespoons flour
½	cup heavy cream	¼	cup sliced almonds
1	cup sugar	1	9-inch pie shell, unbaked

Peel and slice peaches. Set aside. Mix well the cream, sugar and flour. Place a layer of peaches in pie shell and pour some of cream mixture over them. Alternate peaches and cream twice, ending with cream. Sprinkle almonds over top. Bake at 425 degrees for 15 minutes; reduce heat to 350 degrees and bake for 30 minutes more.

Janet Hietbrink

Fresh Peach Pie

1	unbaked pie crust	1	tablespoon flour
8	fresh peaches, peeled and cut in half	1	cup sugar
		1	tablespoon butter
2	scant tablespoons tapioca	1	egg, slightly beaten

Mix together the tapioca, flour, sugar, butter and egg. Add peach halves and mix gently. Put in pie crust and bake at 400 degrees for 10 minutes. Reduce heat to 350 degrees and bake 50-60 minutes. Cover the edge of crust if it begins to get too brown before end of baking time. Serve with ice cream. Serves 6.

Charlene Soderstrom

Aunt Sandy's Rhubarb Cream Pie

2	tablespoons sugar	2	eggs, beaten
2	tablespoons flour, divided	1	cup milk
1½	cups diced rhubarb	2	unbaked 9-inch pie crusts
1½	cups sugar		

Preheat oven to 375 degrees.

Mix 2 tablespoons sugar and 1 tablespoon flour with rhubarb and place in pie shell. Combine remaining sugar with remaining flour, eggs and milk. Pour over pie filling and cover with second crust. Bake for 55 minutes. It may be necessary to place aluminum foil over edges of crust to prevent overcooking. Serves 6.

Jessica Scholten

Nectarine Blueberry Pie

3	pounds nectarines, peeled, pitted and sliced	2½	tablespoons quick-cooking tapioca
1	pint fresh blueberries	1½	teaspoons grated lemon peel
¾	cup plus 3 tablespoons sugar		Basic Pie Crust
		1	egg, beaten to blend (glaze)

Mix nectarines and blueberries in large bowl. Mix ¾ cup sugar, tapioca and lemon peel in small bowl. Add to fruit. Toss to coat. Let stand until tapioca is moistened, about 15 minutes.

Preheat oven to 425 degrees. Divide dough into 2 pieces, 1 slightly larger than the other. Roll larger dough piece out on lightly floured surface to ⅛-inch thick round. Transfer to 10-inch pie dish with 2-inch high sides. Roll remaining dough piece out on floured surface to 14-inch round.

Spoon fruit filling into pie shell. Top with 14-inch dough round. Press edges to seal; trim off excess dough. Crimp edges decoratively. Brush top with glaze. Sprinkle remaining 3 tablespoons sugar over. Cut 5 slits through top crust, spacing evenly. Bake 15 minutes. Reduce oven temperature to 350 degrees and bake until top is golden brown and juices bubble, covering edges with foil if browning too quickly, about 50 minutes. Cool at least 1 hour. Serve warm or at room temperature.

BASIC PIE CRUST DOUGH

Makes one bottom and one top crust for one 9- or 10-inch diameter pie.

2	cups all-purpose flour	¼	cup ice water
½	teaspoon salt	1	tablespoon sugar
10	tablespoons (1¼ sticks) chilled unsalted butter, cut into small pieces	1	large egg yolk

Sift flour and salt into large bowl. Add butter and rub with fingertips until mixture is size of large peas. Stir water, sugar and yolk in small cup until sugar dissolves. Add to flour mixture and toss with fingertips until dough begins to come together. Gather dough into ball, wrap in plastic and refrigerate at least 1 hour. Pie crust dough can be prepared 1 day ahead.

Mary Lou Deeney

Coconut Chocolate Chip Cookies
With Macadamia Nuts

⅔	cup butter or margarine, room temperature	6	ounces white chocolate morsels
⅔	cup granulated sugar	6	ounces semi-sweet chocolate morsels
½	cup packed light brown sugar	1½	cups sweetened flaked coconut
1	large egg	1	3½-ounce jar macadamia
1	teaspoon vanilla		nuts (about ¾ cup), chopped
1½	cups all-purpose flour		coarsely

Preheat oven to 325 degrees.

Lightly grease two 17x14-inch cookie sheets. In large bowl of electric mixer, beat butter, sugars, egg and vanilla at medium-high speed until fluffy. Reduce mixer speed to low, add flour, increase mixer speed gradually and beat just until blended. Stir in white and chocolate morsels, coconut and nuts. Drop heaping tablespoonfuls of dough 2½-inches apart onto prepared cookie sheets. Bake 1 sheet at a time 16 to 17 minutes or until edges of cookies are lightly browned and tops look dry. Cool on sheet on wire rack 5 minutes. Remove to rack to cool completely.

Yield: 3 dozen

Karen Sellick

Savannah Pralines

3	tablespoons butter	1	tablespoon light corn syrup
1½	cups light brown sugar	1	cup pecans
½	cup whipping cream	1	teaspoon vanilla extract

Melt butter in heavy saucepan. Stir in brown sugar, whipping cream and corn syrup. Bring to a boil, then lower heat to medium low. Slow bubbles should continue. Cook 10 minutes, stirring constantly, making sure not to let mixture burn. Add pecans. Stir and cook 5 minutes more at same temperature. Temperature will reach about 200 degrees on candy thermometer. Remove pan from heat. Add vanilla to mixture. Stir vigorously to blend. Drop mixture by tablespoons onto wax paper lined cookie tins sprayed with Pam. Allow to cool, then store immediately in tins.

Makes 8 large pralines – about 1 pound.

Betty Graham

Peanut Butter Chocolate Chip Cookies

1	cup margarine	3	cups flour
1	cup chunky peanut butter	2	teaspoons baking soda
1	cup granulated sugar	¼	teaspoon salt
1	cup packed brown sugar	12	ounces chocolate chips
3	eggs		

Preheat oven to 375 degrees.

Cream together margarine, peanut butter and sugars. Beat in eggs one at a time. Mix in dry ingredients. Stir in chocolate chips. Roll into balls and place on ungreased cookie sheet. Flatten with fork tines. Bake for 12-15 minutes, just until edges brown.

Donna Elwell

Butterscotch-Pecan Tiles

½	cup butter (no substitutes)	1⅓	cups all-purpose flour
⅔	cup brown sugar, packed	¼	teaspoon salt
1	large egg	⅔	cup chopped pecans
1	teaspoon vanilla		Dulce De Leche or vanilla ice
¾	teaspoon baking powder		cream, optional

Preheat oven to 375 degrees.

Microwave butter and sugar in a microwaveable bowl on High 1 minute 45 seconds; stir until smooth. Stir in egg and vanilla. Sprinkle baking powder over top; stir in with flour and salt until blended. Grease a 15½x10½-inch jelly-roll pan. Spread dough evenly to cover bottom of pan. Sprinkle top with pecans. Bake 11 to 12 minutes, until golden. Cool 5 minutes on a rack. Cut into 16 triangles. Serve with ice cream, if desired.

Serves 16.

For perfect triangles, cut cookies before they cool.

Helen Lantz

on't let love interfere with your appetite. It never does with mine.

Anthony Trollope

283

Apricot Coconut Balls

1½ cups dried apricots, chopped   1   can condensed milk
2   cups shredded coconut   Confectioners' sugar
1   cup chopped pecans

Blend apricots, coconut and pecans. Stir in condensed milk. Shape into small balls and roll in confectioners' sugar. Let stand in air 2 hours or until firm. Freezes well.

Yield: about 4 dozen

Charlene Soderstrom

Drop Brownies

1   12-ounce bag semisweet   1   stick butter or margarine
     chocolate chips (2 cups)   1   cup flour
1   14-ounce can sweetened
     condensed milk

Preheat oven to 350 degrees.

Melt chocolate chips, condensed milk and butter in saucepan over low heat, stirring occasionally. When chocolate is melted, remove saucepan from heat and stir in flour. Drop by rounded teaspoon on ungreased cookie sheet. Bake 7 minutes. Do not overbake. Cookies should be soft.

Yield: 36 cookies

Diane Paul

Brownie Peanut Butter Bites

1   15-ounce package brownie   1   egg
     mix   48 miniature chocolate covered
⅓   cup hot water   peanut butter cups
¼   cup oil

Preheat oven to 350 degrees.

Combine brownie mix, water, oil and egg. Beat well with a spoon. Fill paper lined mini-muffin cups about ½ full. Press one unwrapped peanut butter cup into batter in each cup. Bake for 15 to 20 minutes or until brownie is set. Cool completely.

Suzie Busch

Czechoslovakian Squares

½ pound butter	1 cup chopped walnuts
1 cup granulated sugar	½ cup strawberry jam
3 egg yolks	Confectioners' sugar
2 cups all-purpose flour	

Preheat oven to 325 degrees.
Cream butter until soft. Gradually add sugar, creaming until light and fluffy. Add egg yolks and blend well. Gradually add flour and mix thoroughly. Fold in chopped nuts. Spoon ½ of batter evenly into 8-inch square pan. Top with jam. Cover with remaining dough. Bake for 1 hour. Cool in pan ½ hour. Sprinkle with confectioners' sugar. Cut in small squares. Freezes well.
Yield: 20 squares

Judy Roth

Banana Nut Bars

1½ cups flour	1 medium size, very ripe banana, sliced
1 cup sugar	
½ teaspoon soda	⅓ cup milk
½ teaspoon salt	1 teaspoon lemon juice
½ cup shortening	½ cup chopped nuts, optional
2 eggs	

Preheat oven to 350 degrees.
Combine and beat all ingredients at medium speed of electric mixer. Spread in greased 13x9-inch pan. Bake 25 to 30 minutes or until dough springs back when touched lightly in center. Cool and frost. Sprinkle with nuts if desired. Freezes well.
Serves 12 to 20.

BANANA FROSTING

2 tablespoons butter, softened	1 teaspoon vanilla
2 cups confectioners' sugar	½ medium size banana
¼ teaspoon salt	

Combine all ingredients and beat until smooth and creamy. If necessary, thin with a few drops of milk.

Sheila Kautz

285

Wheat Germ Cookies

2	teaspoons baking soda	1½	cups brown sugar
½	cup boiling water	1	teaspoon salt
3	cups Quick Quaker Oats	2	cups vegetable oil, melted
2¾	cups Rice Krispies		shortening or melted butter
¼	cup unsalted soybeans	1	beaten egg
1½	cups wheat germ	½	cup honey
1¼	cups flour		

Preheat oven to 375 degrees.

Dissolve baking soda in boiling water. Set aside. Mix dry ingredients. Stir in wet ingredients. Form into "meatballs". Widely space the "meatballs" on ungreased cookie sheet. Bake 12 minutes. Let the cookies rest on cookie sheet a few minutes before removing with a wide spatula.

Yield: 72 large, flat cookies

Karen Blado

Mixed Nut Bars

1½	cups all-purpose flour	½	cup light corn syrup
¾	cup sugar	2	tablespoons butter or
½	teaspoon salt		margarine
½	cup butter or margarine	1	teaspoon water
1	6-ounce package (1 cup)	1	12-ounce can mixed nuts
	butterscotch morsels		

Preheat oven to 350 degrees. Grease a 13x9-inch pan.

Combine flour, sugar and salt; cut in butter or margarine. Press mixture into prepared pan. Bake for 10 minutes. Combine butterscotch morsels, corn syrup, 2 tablespoons butter or margarine and water in medium saucepan; heat and stir over medium heat until mixture is smooth. Spread mixture over crust and top with nuts. Continue to bake for 10 minutes more or until surface is bubbling. Cool slightly; cut into bars. Cool completely.

Yield: 24 bars

Carol Foster

Audrey's Cookies

½	cup butter	1	tablespoon vanilla
¾	cup confectioners' sugar, sifted	1½	cups flour, sifted
		⅛	teaspoon salt

Preheat oven to 350 degrees.

Mix butter, sugar and vanilla. Measure flour. Blend flour and salt thoroughly with butter mixture either by hand or dough hook. If dough is dry, add 1 to 2 tablespoons cream. For each cookie wrap 1 level tablespoon of dough around filling. Place 1-inch apart on ungreased cookie sheet. Bake 12 to 15 minutes, until set but not brown, cool; dip tops of cookies in Icing.

Yield: 20 to 25 cookies

For chocolate cookies, blend in 1 square melted unsweetened chocolate to above mixture.

Suggested fillings: candied or maraschino cherries, nuts, chocolate pieces.

WHITE ICING

Mix 1 cup sifted confectioners' sugar, 2 tablespoons cream and 1 teaspoon vanilla. To make Chocolate Icing add 1 square of melted unsweetened chocolate and increase cream to ¼ cup.

Gail Vergoz

Raisin Peanut Butter Bonbons

1	cup chunky peanut butter	1½	cups seedless raisins
2	tablespoons butter or margarine, softened	1	6-ounce package semisweet chocolate pieces
1	cup confectioners' sugar, sifted	2	tablespoons vegetable shortening

Combine peanut butter, butter or margarine and confectioners' sugar, mixing until smooth. Stir in raisins. Shape into small balls. Melt chocolate with shortening over warm water. With a teaspoon, dip balls, one at a time, into melted chocolate. Place on waxed paper until set.

Yield: 3 dozen

Marie R. Cappuccio

Lemon Velvet

2½	cups graham cracker crumbs	2	tablespoons, or more, grated lemon rind
⅔	cup margarine or butter, melted	1	cup chopped nuts
2	8-ounce packages cream cheese, softened	2	cups heavy cream
1	cup sugar		Thinly sliced lemons for garnish, optional
1	tablespoon milk		Graham cracker crumbs for garnish, optional
1	teaspoon almond extract		

Mix graham cracker crumbs with melted margarine or butter and press into an 8x8-inch or 9x13-inch pan making a smooth crust. Using an electric mixer, combine the cream cheese, sugar, milk, almond extract and lemon rind. Mix until smooth. Add nuts. Whip cream and fold into cheese mixture. Spread on graham cracker crust. Put in freezer for at least 2 hours. Cut into squares and serve. Keep leftovers in freezer.

Chris Persons

Princess Pat's Bars

Cream together:

1	cup sugar	6	tablespoons vegetable shortening
½	cup butter or margarine		

Add to above mixture cutting in as for pie dough:

1	egg, beaten	½	cup coconut
1½	cups flour, sifted	½	cup chopped walnuts

Apricot or raspberry jam

Preheat oven to 350 degrees.
Press ⅔ of the mixture into an ungreased 12½x7½-inch pan or 9x9-inch pan. Spread top with apricot or raspberry jam. Dot with remaining mixture making sure the edges are covered. Bake until brown and bubbly for 25 to 35 minutes. If edge is too crusty, cut off while warm. Cut into bars.

Nancy Gates

Rocky Road Fudge Bars

½ cup butter	1 cup chopped nuts of your
1 square unsweetened baking	choice
chocolate (1 ounce)	1 teaspoon baking powder
1 cup sugar	1 teaspoon vanilla
1 cup flour	2 eggs
6 ounces cream cheese,	½ teaspoon vanilla
softened	¼ cup chopped nuts
½ cup sugar	1 cup (6 ounces) chocolate
2 tablespoons flour	morsels
¼ cup soft butter	2 cups miniature
1 egg	marshmallows

Preheat oven to 350 degrees. Melt butter and chocolate together in saucepan. Add mixture to sugar, flour, nuts, baking powder, vanilla and eggs and mix well. Spread into greased and floured 9x13-inch pan.

In small mixer bowl, blend cream cheese, ½ cup sugar, 2 tablespoons flour, butter, 1 egg and ½ teaspoon vanilla. Beat until fluffy. Spread over chocolate layer. Sprinkle nuts and chocolate morsels over top and bake until toothpick in center comes out clean, about 25 to 35 minutes. Sprinkle marshmallows over top and bake 2 minutes longer. Remove from oven and immediately pour frosting over marshmallows, swirling the chocolate and marshmallows together. Cut when cool. Store in refrigerator.

FROSTING

¼ cup butter	¼ cup milk
1 square unsweetened baking	3 cups confectioners' sugar
chocolate	1 teaspoon vanilla
2 ounces cream cheese	

Melt butter, chocolate, cream cheese and milk over low heat in large saucepan. Add confectioners' sugar and vanilla beating until smooth.

Louise Walker

When love and skill work together, expect a masterpiece.

John Ruskin

Mint Surprise Cookies

½	cup butter	1½	cups flour
½	cup granulated sugar	½	teaspoon baking soda
¼	cup brown sugar, firmly	½	teaspoon salt
	packed	24	thin chocolate covered mints
1	egg		(approximately)
1½	teaspoons water	24	walnut halves
1½	teaspoons vanilla		(approximately)

Preheat oven to 375 degrees. Lightly grease cookie sheet or line with parchment paper. All ingredients should be at room temperature.

Cream the butter and gradually add the granulated sugar, then brown sugar. Beat in the egg, water and vanilla. Sift together the flour, baking soda and salt. Blend into the butter mixture. Wrap in wax paper and chill for at least 2 hours.

Enclose each thin mint with about one tablespoon of the dough. The mints may be cut in half for a smaller cookie. Place on cookie sheet and top each with a walnut half. Bake for 10 to 12 minutes, or until lightly browned. Let stand a minute or so, then remove and cool on a cake rack.

Yield: 2 dozen cookies

Donna Pfeifer

Savannah Date Chewies

1	cup butter	½	teaspoon vanilla
1	cup sugar	1	cup chopped walnuts
2	eggs	1	8-ounce package dates,
1	cup flour		chopped and sugared
¼	teaspoon salt		

Preheat oven to 350 degrees.

Cream butter, sugar and eggs. Add flour and salt. Beat and add vanilla, dates and nuts. Spread in a well-greased jelly-roll pan. Bake for 20-25 minutes. Cut in squares while hot. When cool, sprinkle with confectioners' sugar.

Yield: 35-40 cookies

Linda Powers

Pecan Chews

1	cup dates, cut into eighths	1	cup confectioners' sugar
1	cup pecans, chopped	1	egg white, unbeaten

Preheat oven to 375 degrees.

Mix first 3 ingredients until well-blended; add egg white. Mix well. Drop by teaspoonful onto well-oiled cookie sheet. Bake 8-9 minutes. Allow to cool on cookie sheet.

Claire English

Peanut Butter Chocolate Chip Cookies

2	eggs	1	cup peanut butter, smooth or
⅓	cup water		chunky
¼	cup butter or margarine,	1	package yellow cake mix
	softened	1	12-ounce package semisweet
			chocolate pieces

Preheat oven to 375 degrees.

Beat eggs, water, butter or margarine, peanut butter and half of cake mix (dry) until smooth. Stir in remaining cake mix and chocolate pieces. Drop by rounded teaspoonful on ungreased cookie sheet. Bake 10 to 12 minutes. Can be frozen.

Yield: about 4 dozen

Debbie Leecock

Layered Peanut Butter Brownies

2	cups peanut butter	1	large family-size package
1	cup sugar		brownie mix
2	eggs		

Preheat oven to 350 degrees.

Combine peanut butter, sugar and eggs. Spread in 13x9-inch pan. Prepare the brownie mix according to package instructions and spread evenly over the peanut butter layer. Bake for 40 minutes. When cool, frost with your favorite chocolate frosting.

Betty Brian

Nancy's Best Oatmeal Cookies

1¼	cups margarine	2	teaspoons cinnamon
¾	cup packed brown sugar	½	teaspoon nutmeg
½	cup granulated sugar	2¾	cups old fashioned Quaker
1	egg		oats
2	teaspoons vanilla	⅓	cup wheat germ
1½	cups flour, scant	2	cups crushed Total cereal
1	teaspoon baking soda	1	cup raisins
1	teaspoon salt	1	cup broken walnut pieces

Preheat oven to 375 degrees.

Beat margarine and sugars. Add egg and vanilla. Combine flour, baking soda, salt and spices. Add to sugar mixture and mix well. Stir in oats, wheat germ and cereal. Combine well. Add raisins and nuts. Drop by rounded teaspoons onto ungreased cookie sheet. Bake 9-11 minutes. Cool 1 minute on cookie sheet. Remove to wire cooling rack. Freezes well.

Yield: 8 dozen

Nancy Craig

Lemon Bars

1	cup butter	½	cup confectioners' sugar
Dash of salt		2	cups flour
4	eggs, beaten	6	tablespoons lemon juice
2	cups sugar	1	teaspoon baking powder
¼	cup flour	Dash of salt	

Preheat oven to 350 degrees.

Combine first four ingredients and press into 9x13-inch pan. Bake until brown, about 15 minutes. Mix remaining ingredients and pour over slightly cooled crust; continue to bake 20-30 minutes more. When done and cool, sprinkle with confectioners' sugar.

Louise Walker

Meringue Cookies

2	egg whites	½	of a 6-ounce bag of chocolate
¾	cup sugar		morsels
4	drops mint or almond extract		

Preheat oven to 350 degrees.

In the evening, beat egg whites until stiff. Add sugar gradually; fold in chocolate morsels and flavoring extract. Drop by teaspoon on ungreased cookie sheets which have been lined with brown paper. Use upward twist of spoon to make peaks on meringues. Place in oven and turn off heat immediately. Leave in oven overnight with door closed.

Yield: approximately 2 dozen

Fewer chocolate morsels may be used and chopped nuts can be added. Do not make meringues on a humid day.

Joy Borden

Frozen Oatmeal Cookies

1	cup shortening	1½	cups sifted flour
1	cup brown sugar	1	teaspoon salt
1	cup granulated sugar	1	teaspoon baking soda
2	beaten eggs	3	cups quick cooking oatmeal
1	teaspoon vanilla	½	cup chopped nuts

Preheat oven to 375 degrees.

Cream shortening and sugars. Add eggs and vanilla; mix thoroughly. Add dry ingredients mixing well. Add oatmeal and nuts. Form into two rolls. Wrap in waxed paper. Chill overnight. Cut in ⅛-inch slices. Place on ungreased cookie sheets and bake for 10-12 minutes.

Joyce Blanke

O ne cannot think well, love well, sleep well, if one has not dined well.

Virginia Woolf

Ozark Pudding

1	egg	⅛	teaspoon salt
¾	cup sugar	½	cup chopped apples
⅓	cup flour	½	cup chopped pecans
2	teaspoons baking powder	1	teaspoon vanilla

Preheat oven to 325 degrees.

Beat egg well. Add sugar and beat until creamy. Sift flour, baking powder and salt and add to egg mixture. Add remaining ingredients and pour into a greased 8- or 9-inch pie plate. Bake for 30 minutes. Serve with vanilla ice cream or whipped cream.

Serves 6.

Barbara Coakley

Mousse Au Chocolat

8	ounces bittersweet chocolate	8	eggs, separated
	Pinch of salt	1	teaspoon vanilla

Melt the chocolate in a double boiler. Add salt and cool slightly. Add the beaten egg yolks and vanilla to the chocolate. Fold the stiffly beaten egg whites into the chocolate mixture. Place in a soufflé dish or crystal bowl. Refrigerate 24 hours before serving.

Serves 4 to 5.

This recipe can be increased keeping the ratio of 1 egg to 1 ounce of chocolate.

Joan Keever

Custard Rice Pudding

½	cup uncooked rice (1½ cups cooked)	1	teaspoon vanilla
		1½	teaspoons lemon rind
3	eggs, beaten	½	cup raisins
½	cup sugar	3½	cups milk
¼	teaspoon salt		Nutmeg

Preheat oven to 300 degrees.

Mix all ingredients except nutmeg. Pour into shallow baking pan. Sprinkle nutmeg on top. Set pan in larger pan of water. Bake 1½ hours.

294

Barbara Burney

Lemon-Curd Pastry With Mixed Berries

½   of a 17¼-ounce package
     (1 sheet) frozen puff pastry
1   slightly beaten egg white
1   teaspoon water
Coarse sugar or granulated
     sugar
⅔   cup lemon curd (at room
     temperature)
⅔   cup dairy sour cream
¼   teaspoon ground ginger

1-2 drops almond extract
3   cups desired fresh berries,
     such as raspberries,
     blackberries, blueberries,
     and/or quartered
     strawberries
¼   cup toasted sliced almonds
2   tablespoons honey
Confectioners' sugar (optional)

Preheat oven to 375 degrees.

Let folded pastry thaw at room temperature for 20 minutes. On a lightly floured surface unfold pastry and roll into a 15x10-inch rectangle. Cut from edges of rectangle, 2 lengthwise ¼-inch wide strips and 2 crosswise ¼-inch wide strips. Set aside the 4 pastry strips.

Place the pastry rectangle on an ungreased baking sheet. Combine egg white and water; brush onto the rectangle. Place the 4 pastry strips atop edges of rectangle trimming to fit. Brush strips with egg white mixture; sprinkle with coarse sugar. Prick the bottom of the pastry several times with the tines of a fork. Bake for 20-25 minutes or till light brown. Remove from oven. Cool on a wire rack.

For filling, in a medium bowl stir curd till smooth. Stir together sour cream, ginger and almond extract; fold into lemon curd. Spread filling atop cooled pastry. Cover and chill till serving time up to 4 hours. Before serving, top with desired berries and sliced almonds. Drizzle with honey. Sprinkle with confectioners' sugar.

Serves 8.

Jan Hazel

*S*how me another pleasure like dinner which comes every day and lasts an hour.

Tallyrand

Bread Pudding

6	slices white bread, cubed	2	cups milk
4	eggs, divided	1	8-ounce package cream
1	cup sugar, divided		cheese
1	teaspoon vanilla	2	teaspoons pumpkin pie spice
Dash of salt		1	cup raisins

Preheat oven to 350 degrees.

Place bread cubes in buttered 11x7-inch baking pan. Beat 3 eggs and ½ cup sugar, vanilla, salt and milk; pour over bread cubes. Mix cream cheese and ½ cup sugar with remaining egg. Add pumpkin pie spice and raisins. Spread over bread and milk mixture. Bake for 45 minutes. To serve, drizzle with maple syrup and top with whipped cream. Serve warm or cold.

Serves 6 to 8.

Sally Clark

Lemon Sponge Pudding

3	tablespoons flour	6	tablespoons lemon juice
¾	cup sugar	2	tablespoons grated lemon
¼	teaspoon salt		zest
1	cup milk	1	tablespoon melted butter
3	egg yolks	2	egg whites

Preheat oven to 350 degrees.

In a small bowl, stir together flour, sugar and salt. In a large bowl, blend milk, egg yolks, lemon juice and lemon zest. Add dry ingredients to wet ingredients and stir to a smooth, liquid batter. Stir in melted butter. Beat egg whites until stiff but not dry. Add egg whites to batter, gently and thoroughly folding together. Pour batter into buttered 3-4 cup ovenproof mold. Place large baking dish in oven and place filled mold in dish. Add hot water to large dish to come up 1-inch on the side of the mold. Bake 40 minutes until brown on top. Best served warm but can be served cold as well.

Serves 6.

Ann Quinn

Overnight Eggnog Bread Pudding
With Apricot-Whiskey Sauce

28	slices day-old French bread, $\frac{1}{2}$-ounce each, $\frac{1}{2}$-inch thick, crusts removed	$\frac{1}{2}$	teaspoon ground nutmeg
		$\frac{1}{4}$	teaspoon salt
Butter flavored cooking spray		4	cups 2% milk
1	cup sugar, divided	1	cup evaporated skim milk
$\frac{1}{2}$	cup golden raisins	$\frac{1}{3}$	cup whiskey
3	large eggs	2	teaspoons vanilla
4	large egg whites	$\frac{1}{2}$	teaspoon ground cinnamon

Arrange $\frac{1}{3}$ of bread slices in a single layer in a 13x9-inch baking dish coated with cooking spray. Coat bread lightly with cooking spray; sprinkle with 2 tablespoons sugar and $\frac{1}{4}$ cup raisins. Repeat procedure; top with remaining bread slices. Sprinkle top layer with 2 tablespoons sugar; coat with cooking spray.

Combine $\frac{1}{2}$ cup sugar, eggs, and next 7 ingredients (egg whites through vanilla); stir with a whisk until well-blended. Pour milk mixture over bread. Cover; refrigerate overnight. Combine remaining 2 tablespoons sugar and cinnamon; sprinkle over pudding. Bake for 1 hour and 10 minutes or until set. Serve warm. Drizzle with Apricot-Whiskey Sauce.

Serves 16 ($\frac{1}{2}$ cup servings with 2 tablespoons sauce)

APRICOT-WHISKEY SAUCE

2	cups apricot preserves (about 2 12-ounce jars)	$\frac{1}{2}$	cup water
		$\frac{1}{3}$	cup whiskey

Combine preserves and water in a medium-heavy saucepan. Bring to a boil; cook 1 minute. Strain mixture through a sieve into a medium bowl, stir in whiskey.

Betsy Smith

W *hat calls back the past, like the rich pumpkin pie?*

John Greenleaf Whittier

297

Light Fruit Dessert

2½ cups washed, sliced strawberries	1 cup reduced fat sour cream
1 cup washed blueberries	Cinnamon to taste
1 tablespoon Grand Marnier liqueur	¼ cup packed light brown sugar

Mix berries with liqueur. Chill 20 minutes. Spoon berries into 4 ovenproof dessert dishes. Mix sour cream with cinnamon and spread over berries. Sprinkle with brown sugar. Broil 4 inches from heat for 15-20 seconds or until brown sugar melts slightly. Let stand 3 minutes.

Serves 4.

Nonfat sour cream may be substituted for reduced fat sour cream. A 15-ounce can of Queen Anne cherries can be used instead of the berries. Replace the liqueur with 1 teaspoon vanilla, mixing vanilla into sour cream before spreading on fruit.

Karen G. Hickman

Deluxe Dessert

Graham cracker crumbs	1 cup whipped topping
1 cup confectioners' sugar	2 packages chocolate pudding
1 8-ounce package cream cheese	3 cups milk
	Extra whipped topping

Spray bottom of 9x13-inch pan with cooking spray. Pat graham cracker crumbs down on bottom of pan. Beat confectioners' sugar and cream cheese until fluffy. Add whipped topping. Pour cream cheese mixture over graham cracker crust. Beat pudding with 3 cups of milk and pour over cream cheese mixture. Top with additional whipped topping and chill overnight. Cut in squares when ready to serve.

Serves 8 to 10.

In place of two packages of chocolate pudding you can use one chocolate with one of vanilla or banana.

Hank Vaughn

*C**ome to me all of you whose stomachs cry out and I will restore you.*

Latin motto

Frozen Chocolate Dessert

¼	cup sugar	3	egg yolks
½	cup water	1½	cups heavy cream
1	6-ounce package semisweet chocolate morsels		Whipped cream

Combine sugar and water in small saucepan; boil 3 minutes. Place chocolate morsels in blender. Pour hot syrup over chocolate and blend at high speed, covered, for 6 seconds. Add egg yolks; blend at high speed for 5 seconds or until smooth. Add cream; blend at high speed for 10 seconds. Pour into six 6-ounce soufflé dishes or small parfait glasses, set on tray and cover with foil. Freeze 2-3 hours until firm. Remove from freezer 20-30 minutes before serving and place in refrigerator to soften slightly. Garnish with whipped cream and, if desired, a maraschino cherry.

Serves 6.

Sandy Andrews

Frozen Caramel Dessert

½	cup (1 stick) butter, melted	½	cup firmly packed brown sugar
2	cups vanilla wafer crumbs		
1	cup chopped pecans	½	gallon vanilla ice cream, softened
1½-2	cups caramel ice cream topping, warmed		Chocolate ice cream topping, optional

Preheat oven to 350 degrees.

Combine butter, vanilla wafer crumbs and brown sugar; mix well. Spread onto baking sheet and bake for 15 minutes or until browned; stir occasionally. Remove crumb mixture from oven; cool.

Sprinkle ¼ of the crumb mixture in bottom of 9x13-inch pan. Sprinkle pecans over crumb mixture. Drizzle caramel sauce over pecans. Spread ice cream on top of sauce; top with remaining crumb mixture. Chocolate ice cream topping can be drizzled over all at this point if you choose. Freeze until solid. Remove from freezer a few minutes prior to serving to ease cutting. Cut in squares and serve.

Serves 12 to 15.

Ellie Crawley

Lowfat Chocolate Sauce

2	tablespoons margarine	2	tablespoons white corn
2	tablespoons cocoa		syrup
½	cup sugar	¼	cup evaporated skim milk
Dash salt		1	teaspoon vanilla

In a saucepan, melt the margarine and add the cocoa, sugar, salt and syrup. Add the milk, bring to a boil and stir until smooth. Remove from the heat and stir in the vanilla. Serve warm or cold over ice cream.

Yield: 1 cup

Jean Morris

Fresh Lemon Ice Cream

2	cups half-and-half	⅓	cup freshly squeezed lemon
1	cup sugar		juice

In large bowl, stir together half-and-half and sugar until sugar is thoroughly dissolved. Mix in lemon juice. Pour into ice cube tray, 8-inch square pan or directly into sherbet dishes. Freeze several hours until firm.

Yield: about 1½ pints

Serves 6.

Julie Powell

Plum Tart Tatin

4	plums, each sliced ¼-inch thick	1½	ounces dried cherries, plumped in plum wine
1	9-inch puff pastry round		Butter, softened
¼	cup sugar		

Cover bottom of 9-inch springform pan with parchment paper. Brush generously with butter. Dust with sugar; dot with cherries; layer in the plums. Place puff dough on top. Bake until golden. Let stand for 5 minutes then flip out onto serving plate.

Serves 10.

Charles D'Ablaing
Chef, The Landings Club

Danish Summer Dessert

2	cups cranberry juice	⅓	cup finely ground blanched
2½	tablespoons cornstarch		almonds
½	cup sugar	1	cup heavy cream
1	10-ounce package frozen		
	raspberries, thawed		

Put cranberry juice, cornstarch and sugar into blender. Process until well-blended and pour into saucepan. Process raspberries in blender until liquefied. Pour raspberries into cranberry mixture. Cook over low heat stirring constantly until thickened. Pour into serving dishes. Sprinkle with almonds and pour unsweetened cream over top.

Serves 4 to 6.

Can be made two days ahead of serving.

Helle Lee

Apple Crisp

8	medium apples, peeled and	1	cup rolled oats
	sliced	1	teaspoon cinnamon
1	tablespoon fresh lemon juice	¼	teaspoon nutmeg
½	cup all-purpose flour	½	cup butter
1	cup brown sugar		

Place apple slices in 2-quart baking dish. Sprinkle with lemon juice. Combine flour, sugar, oats, cinnamon and nutmeg. Cut butter into 1-inch chunks. Blend into dry ingredients, using a pastry blender or 2 forks. When crumbly, sprinkle over apples. Bake at 375 degrees for 15 minutes. Turn oven down to 350 degrees and bake for 30 minutes more. Serve warm with vanilla ice cream or whipped cream.

Serves 8.

Charles D'Ablaing
Chef, The Landings Club

The only way to get rid of a temptation is to yield to it.

Oscar Wilde

301

Lemon Butter

2	lemons	2	eggs
1¾	cup sugar	¼	pound butter

Grate rind from one lemon. Squeeze juice from both lemons. Beat eggs, add sugar and beat well. Add lemon rind, lemon juice and butter. Mix well. Cook in double boiler until thick, stirring frequently, about 20 minutes.

A delicious spread for toast or biscuits.

Gail Andrus

Lowfat Hot Fudge Sauce

2½-3	tablespoons cocoa	1	tablespoon canola oil
½	cup sugar	1	teaspoon vanilla
⅓	cup 1% lowfat milk		

Combine all ingredients in a small saucepan; mix well and cook over low heat. Cook, uncovered, until mixture reaches a boil; reduce heat and cook for 5-7 minutes or until mixture begins to thicken.

Yield: about 1 cup

Joy Borden

Crimson Raspberry Sauce

1	10-ounce package frozen red raspberries	2	teaspoons cornstarch
		1	cup currant jelly

Thaw and crush raspberries. Combine with cornstarch and jelly. Bring to boiling. Cook and stir until clear and slightly thick. Strain and cool. Use over sherbet or ice cream.

Suzie Busch

*O*ne might stop the flowing water, but the things that never return are the days and months.

Japanese Proverb

302

Chocolate Eclair Icebox Dessert

22½ sheets (about 1 14-ounce box) lowfat honey graham crackers, divided
Cooking spray
3 cups fat free milk
2 3.4-ounce packages fat free vanilla instant pudding mix
1 8-ounce tub fat free cream cheese

1 8-ounce frozen whipped topping, thawed
¼ cup fat free milk
2 tablespoons margarine or butter, softened
2 tablespoons honey
2 ounces unsweetened chocolate, melted
1½ cups sifted confectioners' sugar

Arrange 7½ graham cracker sheets in bottom of greased 13x9-inch baking dish. Combine milk, pudding mix and cream cheese in a bowl and beat at low speed of mixer 1 minute or until thick. Fold in whipped topping. Spread half of the mixture over graham crackers and top with 7½ graham cracker rectangles. Repeat with the remaining half of pudding and 7½ graham cracker rectangles. Combine ¼ cup milk, softened margarine, honey and unsweetened chocolate in a medium bowl. Beat well with a mixer. Gradually add confectioners' sugar to mixture and beat well. Spread chocolate glaze over graham crackers. Cover and chill 4 hours.
Serves 16 to 18.

Lois Flanagan

Mocha Toffee Torte

2 3-ounce packages ladyfingers
6 1¼-ounce toffee candy bars
½ gallon coffee ice cream, softened

3 tablespoons coffee liqueur
1 8-ounce carton frozen whipped topping, thawed

Line bottom and sides of a 9-inch springform pan with ladyfingers. Crush 5 candy bars into small pieces. Stir candy into ice cream and spoon mixture into pan of ladyfingers. Stir liqueur into whipped topping and spread over top of ice cream. Crush remaining candy bar and sprinkle over top of dessert. Place toothpicks around edges, cover with plastic wrap and freeze 8 hours. Let stand 20 minutes before serving.
Serves 12.

Marby Varley

Cold Lemon Soufflé

1	envelope unflavored gelatin	1	tablespoon grated lemon
¼	cup cold water		rind
5	eggs, separated	1¼	cups sugar
¾	cup fresh lemon juice (about	1	cup whipping cream
	4 large lemons)		

Mix gelatin in cold water to soften. Combine egg yolks, lemon juice, rind and 1¼ cups sugar in saucepan. Cook over low heat, stirring constantly, until mixture is slightly thickened, about 8 minutes. Remove from heat and stir in gelatin mixture until completely dissolved. Chill about 20 minutes. Beat egg whites; fold into lemon mixture. Whip cream; fold into lemon mixture. Pour into 2-quart soufflé dish and chill at least four hours. Serve with Lemon Sauce.

LEMON SAUCE

½	cup sugar	2	teaspoons grated lemon rind
1	tablespoon cornstarch	2	tablespoons butter
½	cup water	¼	cup dry white wine
3	tablespoons fresh lemon		(optional)
	juice		

In small saucepan, mix sugar and cornstarch; add water, lemon juice and rind. Stir until smooth. Add butter. Bring to a boil, lower heat and cook until thickened (happens very quickly). Remove from heat. Stir in wine if using. Chill. Allow to come to room temperature before serving.

Carol Diver

Frozen Chocolate Frango

1	cup butter	2	cups confectioners' sugar
4	squares unsweetened	4	eggs
	chocolate, melted in double	2	teaspoons vanilla
	boiler	⅛	teaspoon oil of peppermint

Combine butter with chocolate. Add remaining ingredients to chocolate mixture and blend well. Pour into paper-lined muffin tins filling each half-full. Freeze. Remove paper liners and top with whipped cream or frozen whipped topping before serving.

Serves 12.

Mary Ellen Fox

Irish Mist Valhalla

1	3-ounce package ladyfingers	1	cup heavy cream, divided
1	3½-3¾-ounce package instant vanilla pudding mix	1	tablespoon confectioners' sugar
1¼	cups milk	1	tablespoon finely minced
¼	cup Irish Mist liqueur		crystallized ginger

Split the ladyfingers Line a 1-quart serving dish with ladyfingers. Set aside. In large mixing bowl, blend together pudding mix, milk, Irish Mist and ½ cup heavy cream. Beat 2-3 minutes or until thickened. Pour into lined serving dish. Beat remaining cream and sugar until stiff. Fold in ginger. Spread over pudding mixture. Chill several hours or overnight.
Serves 6.

Helen Lantz

Flan

1	cup sugar	2	cups water
6	eggs, well-beaten	1	teaspoon almond extract
1	can sweetened condensed milk		Whipped cream, optional

Preheat oven to 325 degrees.

Place sugar in large heavy skillet; caramelize by cooking over medium heat, stirring constantly with wooden spoon, until sugar melts and turns golden brown. Pour and spread quickly on bottom and sides of ungreased 10x6-inch baking dish. Cool.

In large bowl, combine eggs, condensed milk, water and extract. Pour into caramel-coated dish. Place dish in large shallow baking pan which is filled with water. Bake 1 hour or until knife inserted in center comes out clean. Cool 2 hours. Loosen around sides and turn onto serving platter. Refrigerate until ready to serve. Top with whipped cream, if desired.

Marjorie Kahan

C ooking is like love. It should be entered into with abandon or not at all.

Harriet Van Horne

Lemon Trifle

1	14½-ounce package angel food cake mix or 1 16-ounce angel food cake	1	8-ounce container reduced fat, frozen whipped topping, thawed
1	14-ounce can lowfat sweetened condensed milk	1	cup sliced fresh strawberries
2	teaspoons grated lemon rind	1	cup fresh blueberries
⅓	cup fresh lemon juice	1	cup fresh raspberries
1	8-ounce carton lemon nonfat yogurt	½	cup flaked coconut, lightly toasted

Prepare cake. Cut into bite-size pieces and set aside. Combine milk and next 3 ingredients. Fold into 2 cups whipped topping and set aside. Place ⅓ of cake pieces in bottom of a 4-quart trifle bowl; top with ⅓ of lemon mixture. Top with strawberries. Repeat layers twice, using remaining cake pieces, lemon mixture, blueberries and raspberries, ending with raspberries. Spread remaining whipped topping over raspberries and sprinkle with toasted coconut. Cover and chill 8 hours or more.

Serves 16 to 18.

Bobbie Gerner

Chocolate Trifle

1	large-size chocolate pudding mix, not instant	1	package chocolate cake mix
1	pint whipping cream, whipped	½	cup Kahlúa or chocolate-flavored liqueur
			Fresh strawberries

Prepare pudding as directed. Cool to room temperature. Whip cream to soft peaks. Sweeten lightly. Prepare and bake chocolate cake mix according to package directions. Cool cake and break into 1-inch pieces and place half in a serving bowl. Sprinkle ½ of the liqueur over cake. Cover with half of the cooled pudding and top the pudding with a scant half of the whipped cream. Repeat layers and refrigerate 12-24 hours. When ready to serve, decorate top with whole ripe strawberries.

Serves 12.

Sandra Williams

Irish Trifle

1½ prepared pound cakes (about 10¾-ounces per cake, thawed if frozen)
3 tablespoons sugar
1½ tablespoons cornstarch
3 egg yolks
2½ cups milk
2 teaspoons vanilla, divided
1½ cups heavy cream

5 tablespoons confectioners' sugar, divided
½ cup seedless raspberry jam
2 10-ounce packages frozen raspberries, thawed and drained
½ cup rum (or more!)
¼ cup sliced almonds, toasted

Cut the cakes into slices ¼-inch thick; spread out flat for several hours to dry. Whisk the granulated sugar, cornstarch and egg yolks in a saucepan. Slowly whisk in the milk. Cook, stirring constantly, over medium heat until thickened to the consistency of custard, about 12-15 minutes. Whisk in 1 teaspoon of the vanilla; set aside to cool completely. Whip the cream until soft peaks form. Beat in 3 tablespoons of the confectioners' sugar and the remaining vanilla; continue beating until stiff. Chill until ready to use.

Assembling the trifle:
Spread a very thin layer of custard on bottom of a large glass bowl (2½ quarts, or 10 cups). Cut cake slices into 1-inch squares. Spread raspberry jam on ⅓ of the cake squares; layer on top of custard. Pour ⅓ of the remaining custard evenly over the cake. Toss the raspberries with remaining confectioners' sugar; spoon ⅓ of the mixture over the custard. Follow with ½ of the remaining cake squares; pat down to make an even layer; sprinkle ½ of the rum onto cake. Add ½ of the remaining custard. Spoon ½ of remaining raspberries on top of custard. Cover raspberries with remaining cake squares; sprinkle with last of the rum. Pour rest of custard on top of cake; then add remaining raspberry mixture. Spoon reserved whipped cream over top; sprinkle with almonds. Chill until ready to serve.

Serves 10.

Ann Robertson

*A*mericans are just beginning to regard food the way the French always have. Dinner is not what you do in the evening before something else. Dinner is the evening.

Art Buchwald

Lemon Biscuits With Strawberry Maple Compote

1½	cups all-purpose flour	6	tablespoons chilled unsalted
5	tablespoons sugar		butter, cut in pieces
1½	teaspoons grated lemon peel	9	tablespoons chilled whipping
1½	teaspoons baking powder		cream
¼	teaspoon baking soda	2	tablespoons fresh lemon
¼	teaspoon salt		juice

Preheat oven to 350 degrees. Mix flour, 3 tablespoons sugar, lemon peel, baking powder, baking soda and salt in food processor. Add butter, cut in using on/off turns until mixture resembles coarse meal. Add 8 tablespoons whipping cream and lemon juice and blend until soft moist dough forms. Drop dough by generous ¼ cupfuls onto heavy, large baking sheet, spacing apart and forming a total of 6 biscuits. Brush tops with 1 tablespoon whipping cream. Sprinkle with 2 tablespoons sugar. Bake until golden, about 25 minutes. Cool.

Serves 6.

COMPOTE

2	1-pint baskets strawberries, hulled	½	cup pure maple syrup

Mash half of berries in bowl. Slice remaining berries. Add sliced berries and syrup to mashed berries. Chill.

To Serve:
Reheat biscuits in 350 degree oven for 5 minutes. Place biscuits in bowls. Spoon compote over and top with ice cream. Biscuits and compote can be made 4 hours ahead.

Bev Brucher

French Fruit Tart

1	precooked pie crust	8	ounces sour cream
1	3-ounce package vanilla	¼	teaspoon almond extract
	instant pudding mix		Fresh fruit of your choice
8	ounces milk		Apricot jam

Beat together pudding mix, milk, sour cream and almond extract. Pour into crust. Top with fresh fruit. Glaze with melted jam. Chill.

308

Carol S. Toth

The dining room is a theater . . .
the table is the stage.

Chatallon-Plessis

WORD

My Favorite Recipes

A

B

Index

313

Index

Index

Index

Index